ESSENTIAL
PRACTICAL PSYCHOLOGY

Also in the HarperCollins Essential Series

Essential Psychology
G.C. Davenport

Essential Government and Politics
Jim Cordell

Essential Marketing
Tony Proctor

Essential Accountancy and Finance
Bijon Kar

Essential Business Studies
Stephen Barnes

Essential Mechanics
Owen Elbourn

Series Editor: Roger Gomm

ESSENTIAL
PRACTICAL PSYCHOLOGY

Keith B. Maglennon B.Sc., M.Sc., PGCE

Collins Educational
An imprint of HarperCollins *Publishers*

The author asserts the moral right to be
identified as the author of this work.

Published by
Collins Educational Ltd
77–85 Fulham Palace Road
Hammersmith
London W6 8JB

First published in 1993

British Library Cataloguing
in Publication Data
is available on request
from the British Library

ISBN 0-00-3222969

Typeset by CG Graphics, Aylesbury
Cover design by Ridgeway Associates
Printed in Great Britain by Cambridge University Press

Contents

Foreword

Every book in the Essential Series is designed carefully to put you in control of your own learning.

When you use this book, you will not only cover the core elements of your course but you will also benefit from the author's use of modern teaching and learning techniques, with the result that you will make the best possible use of your time.

This book has:

- an introductory section at the beginning of each chapter, which focuses your attention on its contents and which tells you exactly what you should have learned by the end of the chapter. These are your 'learning objectives'

- periodic summaries and reviews which regularly remind you of the content you are covering and so reinforce your learning

- notes in the margin of the text, where the author takes the role of a tutor: picking out key facts, highlighting and explaining difficult concepts and guiding you to a better understanding of the main text

- a guide to making notes as you work through the book

- past exam questions and other assignments which will give you exam practice and help you to develop your skills in presenting written work

- suggestions for further reading that you can fit in will help you to develop a broader understanding of your subject, and this is always worth extra marks in the exam, as well as being more satisfying

- a section on study skills which gives valuable advice and suggestions for making the best use of your study time and improving your learning. When you have developed these basic skills you will be much better equipped to direct and control your own learning.

Learning is not easy: nobody learns without effort. However, if you use this book effectively you will not only succeed in your course but you will also enjoy the experience of learning.

Author's preface

This book has developed out of work which I did for the National Extension College's (NEC) A level Psychology course in 1990. The original commission was to write a module to cover the coursework component of the AEB A level Psychology course. A number of people in the NEC's A level Psychology team read through and made valuable comments on the module. In particular I would like to thank: Dr Elizabeth Clark, Penny Henderson and Linda Deer Richardson. My thanks also go to Debbie Maglennon who read through and made many useful suggestions regarding the clarity of the original work.

To turn the original NEC module into this book has required a substantial amount of reorganization and new material. I have had invaluable help and support with this task from Roger Gomm and my thanks go to Pam Gallagher who checked the final manuscript. Although I have had a great deal of help with this book, as author I accept full responsibility for any defects or shortcomings in the final product.

Finally, I wrote this book in far from ideal circumstances and I would like to say a big **thank you** to Mum, Dad, Amy, Matt and Caroline for their love and support.

Acknowledgements

The author and the publisher would like to thank the following: the Associated Examining Board for permission to reproduce past examination questions, their Guidance Notes and Marking Scheme; The British Psychological Society for permission to reproduce their 'Ethical Principles for Conducting Research with Human Participants'; H.J. Eysenck and S.B.G. Eysenck authors of the *Manual for the Eysenck Personality Inventory*, published by Hodder & Stoughton Ltd, for permission to reproduce Figure 4.3 and Eysenck Personality Inventory (EPI) material; The Journal of the American Statistical Association for permission to reproduce Critical Values of Spearman's Rho from *Significance Testing of the Spearman Rank Correlation Coefficient* by J.H. Zar; The Longman Group UK Ltd, on behalf of the Literary Executor of the late Sir Ronald A. Fisher, FRS and Dr Frank Yates FRS for permission to reproduce Critical Values of T and Critical Tables of χ^2 from *Statistical Tables for Biological, Agricultural and Medical Research*, 6th ed. (1974); McGraw Hill for permission to reproduce Critical Values for the Mann-Whitney Test from *Fundamentals of Behavioral Statistics* by Runyan and Haber; W.W. Norton for permission to reproduce Stroop Effect materials from *Psychology* by Henry Gleitman; The Open University for permission to reproduce their Extract 'Imagery and Memory' from DS 262 Summer School Project Workbook and also 'Stimulus Sheets A and B' from DSE 202 Summer School Project Workbook 1991.

We have been unable to trace the copyright holder of the table for Critical Values of T in the Wilcoxon Signed Ranks Test but will be happy to include an acknowledgement in future reprints.

The material appearing in Chapters 2, 3, 4, 5, 7, 8, 9, 10 of this book is adapted from the Methodology Guide in the National Extension College's *A Level Psychology* open learning course. *A Level Psychology* is available as a resource pack for teachers or as a distance course with tutorial support for learners.

Further details about *A Level Psychology*, and other open learning courses, are available from Customer Services, National Extension College, 18 Brooklands Avenue, Cambridge CB2 2HN Tel: 0223 316644, Fax: 0223 313586.

How to use this book

INTRODUCTION

This book is written especially for students following the AEB A or A/S level Psychology courses which require candidates to complete practical Psychology projects, officially called 'Psychological Investigations', but usually just called 'practicals'.

The knowledge on which the Psychology syllabus is based has been derived from psychological research. Being a psychologist means being able to do research in the characteristic way that psychologists do research. Therefore it is appropriate that A level students should be given first-hand experience of researching, and should be examined on the results. In fact candidates are examined in two ways on their grasp of research methods: firstly through presenting a series of research project reports as examinable coursework, and secondly through a compulsory examination question on research methods and statistics. Much of what you need to know for the compulsory examination question can be learned through the experience of completing the practicals.

This book is built around the instructions for completing five Psychology practicals, and there are suggestions for three more in Chapter 10. Wrapped around this is more general guidance about research methods which you will need to put into practice when you tackle the practicals. Reading the more general guidance and completing the practicals will put you in a good position to answer the compulsory examination question on methodology and statistics. Chapter 11 gives you advice on this.

▶ The book contains detailed guidance for five Psychology practicals, with suggestions for three more.

Understanding the requirements for practicals

Don't dive into this book before you have a good grasp of what it means to do a Psychology practical. Whatever projects you attempt in life, you are likely to be more successful if you have a good idea

► You will see this sign where I
have suggested an activity for you
to carry out.

► For each practical this book
takes you step by step through
writing the report.

► Most marks are gained from
showing what you have learned
from doing a practical.

of what the finished product should look like. In order to help you
here I have included a specimen of a student practical report.

 Turn to appendix A where you will find a specimen of a
completed A level Psychology practical report. I would like
you to read this now, not in any detail but enough to notice
its length, its style and its structure. Although the topics will
be different, something like this is what you will need to
produce – five times – if you are going to be successful.

When writing examinable coursework for any subject it is always
important to know in advance how it is going to be marked. The
AEB provide very full guidance on this for Psychology.

 Turn to appendix B. This is the Guidance Notes from the
AEB to A level Psychology students followed by the
marking scheme. It tells you how a practical report should
be laid out, and just as importantly how many marks are
available for each section. Read through this quickly now,
but pay particular attention to the way the marks are
distributed. The marks are given in the form of what is
called a 'band-marking' scheme. Thus for each section the
marks against the first paragraph of comments are the
maximum available.

One of the things you will have noticed is that there are relatively
few marks given for conducting the investigation and doing the research ('Planning and implementation'). Far more marks are
awarded for interpreting the results. Although there is a section in
the mark scheme called 'Interpretation and discussion' – your interpretations and discussions will run though all the other sections.
This relates to something important about examining these practicals. You are not so much marked for your ability to carry out psychological research, as for your ability to learn from doing it.

Your first thoughts about doing practicals probably centred on
conducting the experiment, or carrying out the surveys or interviews. Think again. These are only a small part of the activity. Most
of your effort will be spent in planning in advance of conducting
the investigation, and particularly afterwards in reporting on it and
interpreting the results. This means that it is possible to make a
mess of conducting the investigation, and still produce a passable
practical report, so long as you can identify where you went wrong
and show that you have learned from this. I am certainly not rec-
ommending that you skimp on conducting the investigation, but I
am making the point that what you get most marks for is showing
what you have learned.

Your practical reports are not examined in terms of what they
have added to the sum of psychological knowledge. An A level
Psychology student with twenty hours to spend on an investigation is most unlikely to come up with any world-shattering psychological discoveries. You are being examined for what you know.

The practicals for which guidance is given in this book are all in well-worn areas of research. This has an advantage for you because one of the skills you will have to show is that of relating your investigation to the relevant psychological literature. If the investigation is into some aspect of personality, for example, then you will need to relate what you have done, why you have done it, and how you have interpreted the results, to what else has been written on this topic. As the marking scheme says, for full marks on 'Interpretation and discussion' the candidate needs to show that: 'The investigation was appropriately discussed in the light of relevant background research and/or theory.'

This makes the 'References' section of your report particularly important. I have chosen topics for practicals from areas where you will have no difficulty in finding relevant background research and theory to read and comment on.

▶ You get no marks for listing books. You get marks for showing that you have learned from reading them. Chapters in this book contain suggestions for further reading.

Research methods and substantive topics

When you conduct your investigations you will of course learn about research methods, but you will also learn about what are sometimes called the 'substantive topics' of Psychology: matters such as personality, or memory. Unfortunately the time-scales for conducting investigations, and the sequence of learning about substantive topics frequently do not marry up. Meaning that even with the best planning you will sometimes be doing a practical on a topic which you have not yet studied in depth in class. To help you (and your tutor) to plan as best you can, here are the substantive topics for the practicals in this book:

Chapter 4	Practical 1	**Personality**
Chapter 5	Practical 2	**Cognitive Dissonance**
Chapter 7	Practical 3	**Memory – Rehearsal and Imagery**
Chapter 8	Practical 4	**Selective Attention – the Stroop Effect**
Chapter 9	Practical 5	**Organization and Long-term Memory**
Chapter 10	Project 1	**Interpersonal Attraction**
	Project 2	**Cognitive Development – Conservation**
	Project 3	**Prosocial Behaviour**

There are no problems in carrying out a practical after you have studied the substantive topic: that makes for excellent revision. But it is worth trying to make sure that you have studied the substantive topic before, or concurrently with conducting the investigation.

Time for practicals

On an A level course preparing for, conducting, and especially, writing up the practicals is a very time-consuming matter. Five practicals are very unlikely to take you less than 150 hours' work, and it would be wise to plan for 200 hours. They carry twenty per cent of the final marks, and they will take between fifteen and twenty-five per cent of your study-time, depending on how much time you spend in class and in private study for the subject. It would be silly to spend much less than fifteen per cent of your time on the practicals when they carry twenty per cent of the marks, and equally it would be silly to spend much more than twenty-five per cent of your time on something that only gains twenty per cent of the marks – although remember that in conducting practicals you will always be learning things which you can use in the examination room.

Apart from being time-consuming in an absolute sense, practicals need to be phased over most of the period during which you are studying for the A level. If you leave them all until the second term of the second year, you will have no time at all for studying the remainder of the syllabus and revising for the examination.

► For more details on study skills turn to appendix F.

► Failing to plan is planning to fail.

(ACT) For this activity I suggest you draft out a calendar for your practical work. (The AEB recommends that practical work for assessment should not be done too early. On a two-year course avoid the first term and on a one-year course the first six weeks.) First draw up a chart of all the months of your course – or what remains of your course. Then write in the final date for submitting the five completed practicals. Your tutor will give you this. Block out any holidays you are going to take from study. Now work out how you are going to fit in the completion of six practicals: six because it often happens that one practical goes awry and has to be replaced with another. You need a contingency plan for this. Allow twenty hours for each practical (and hope that you can complete in fifteen). Try to arrange things to avoid peak-loading. Remember that the penultimate term of an A level course is usually peak-loaded anyway as people desperately try to finish the syllabus and revise what they have learned already. Take into account the demands of any other subjects you are studying.

Complete this task by writing down target start-dates and finish-dates for each practical. Make a neat copy of this and put it at the front of your Psychology file, and transfer the dates into your diary or study plan.

► Don't forget to check your progress against your plan as the year goes on.

The results of this activity are likely to look daunting. Don't panic. Thousands of Psychology students just like you have completed their courses successfully, and this book is precisely designed to make things as easy as possible for you.

The sequence of practicals

The practicals in this book are presented as a progressive sequence. The earlier ones are easier to conduct, and the statistical techniques used in the earlier practicals are less demanding. The earlier practicals are given with a great deal of guidance. This tails off in the later practicals because by then you will need less guidance. For these reasons I strongly recommend that you attempt the practicals in the order presented, unless there is some very good reason for not doing so. Such reasons might include your personal interest in a substantive topic and your desire to conduct an investigation in that area, instead of one of the practicals given. That's fine. But I suggest that you still read through the practical(s) you are not going to conduct, to learn what you might need to know about methodology and statistics for the compulsory question on the examination paper. Alternatively, your tutors may want to substitute practicals of their own design for those in this book.

▶ Think very carefully before you commit yourself to too many personally designed practicals: you may not have sufficient time to plan and conduct them successfully.

Pooled class data

Because time is of the essence on an A level course I have introduced an important time-saving device. Most practicals require a reasonably sized set of results. Once you have administered a questionnaire, or interviewed, or observed a few people you have probably learned as much as you are going to learn about interviewing or observation. Going on doing this just to gather enough data for analysis will not teach you a great deal more. Therefore for each practical I have asked you to collect a little data of your own, and have supplied you with more data collected in the same way, which you can add to your own for analysis. In this book this is called **pooled class data**.

However if you are working with a class of fellow students, then quite a lot of data can be collected quickly by each collecting a little. The examiners place no restrictions on cooperation between candidates to conduct investigations and collect data, although the reporting and interpreting has to be your own work. If you cooperate in this way, you can either use this pooled data instead of that provided in the book, or add it to that provided. Unless you want to change the way the practical is conducted, the latter is preferable, because you can be more confident about conclusions drawn from large sets of data than from small ones.

Taking notes from this book

In using this book you will be working on three fronts simultaneously. Firstly you will be following the guidelines for doing the practicals. This will produce notes on background reading, materials for conducting the practical, raw data, statistical analyses and then a series of drafts resulting in the final practical report. All this has the potential to get into a mess, so I recommend that you always store all this material in one place; in a separate file, or in a separate section of a file marked with a file-spacer. And that whatever you write you always head the paper with the name of the practical.

Secondly you will be learning more generally useful information about research methods. This will be important when it comes to revising for the methodology and statistics compulsory question. Here I suggest that the best way of taking notes is to use a card-index system. To make this easy for you, at the beginning of each of most chapters the last of the chapter objectives is a list of key terms, the meaning of which you should know. If you are making a card index of methodological terms then something like the following is what you could produce. This card relates to one of the terms given at the beginning of Chapter 3.

Mean

Measure of central tendency.

Arithmetic average. Add all scores together and divide by number of scores: $\dfrac{X}{N}$

Preferable to median or mode because can be used in advanced stats., but can give distorted impression if there are extreme scores (then use median instead).

See Maglennon Chapter 3.

Of course if you knew all about the mean, there would be no need to make up such a card. When you make up cards, don't forget to cross-reference them to your practicals, or to other notes where appropriate.

Thirdly you will be learning about some of the substantive topics of Psychology. For example in doing Practical 1, you will have to read about Eysenck's ideas on personality. Some of the notes on what you read will contribute to your practical report. But the same notes are equally relevant to your broader study of the topic of personality. When they have served their purpose for the practical, the proper place to file them is with your other notes on personality.

Knowing the contents and layout of the book

The last thing I want you to do before you move on is to familiarize yourself with the contents and layout of the book. Doing this now will make it easier to use later. Initially you may find the layout confusing. This is because each of the chapters containing advice for practicals has its own appendix usually containing:

- the materials you will need to conduct the practical
- instructions for calculating the appropriate statistical test
- pooled class data to add to your own.

In addition the book as a whole has a number of appendices – as you already know.

The reason for gathering materials into appendix sections in the book, is the same reason you will create appendices for your practical reports. The appendices include lengthy materials which would interrupt the flow of the text if they were put into it.

In addition the main text contains many boxed insets. Each of the insets contains material which, while it is relevant to the text around it, will also be relevant in a more general sense. I have boxed the material so that when you look for it again you will be able to find it easily.

 This activity is designed to help you familiarize yourself with the structure of the book. You should do something like this whenever you start to use a book which you will be using frequently.

1 Turn back to the contents pages. Review the contents to see what is in the book. To focus your mind look for things which come up again and again: for example 'choosing an appropriate statistical test', or 'analysing the data'. These common areas will show you that the book goes round the same circuit again and again, so once you get a feel for what the circuit is, you will coast through it.

2 In this book the contents pages are probably more useful for locating material than the index pages. But turn to the index pages and see what kind of index it is. Is it a topic index, or an author index, both together, or both separately?

3 Look again at the contents pages and at what is listed for the appendices. Look at the remainder of the contents and work out which appendices you are going to need to look at again and again. Then find them.

4 Turn to Chapter 5, which contains Practical 2. Look at its structure: chapter objectives at the beginning, general text on cognitive dissonance, instructions for conducting the practical and writing up the report; inset material, and appendices. Each of the chapters containing practicals has a layout something like this. Being familiar with the layout will mean that you will be able to use each chapter more effectively when you come to it.

That's enough of that. Proceed to Chapter 2 which is a general introduction to research methods in Psychology.

The aims of psychological research

The purpose of this part of the book is to give you a short introduction to some of the key concepts in research methods and statistics in Psychology.

RESEARCH METHODS IN PSYCHOLOGY

The aim of research in Psychology is to gather data to describe, and/or to test out ideas about, behaviour and experience. Psychologists carry out research using a wide variety of methods, such as:

● experiments
● surveys
● observation studies
● case studies.

Each research method has its own particular set of advantages and disadvantages: there is no single 'best' method of research.

  Descriptive research aims to gather accurate, objective data about the frequency and distribution of behaviour. Research with a descriptive goal often involves questions like: How often? How much? How many? or Who? Where? and When? For example, developmental psychologists have taken a great deal of interest in describing the development of play in children. They have observed children to find out the age at which they start to play, how play develops and changes, what situations encourage or hinder play.

Testing theories

Accurate description is an important first step in research but psychologists frequently wish to do more than describe. They also want to **explain** human behaviour and experience. To do this psychologists put forward **theories** – explanations about why people behave the way they do. We all have our own theories about why people behave the way they do; so is there anything different about the theories proposed by psychologists? Most psychologists consider themselves to be scientists and it is widely accepted among scientists that a scientific theory must be 'testable'. But how can a theory be tested? The usual method is to use the theory to make a **prediction**, and then set about gathering data to test the prediction. When undertaking research to test a theory the prediction of what is expected to occur is known as the **research hypothesis**. I will use an example from one of the practicals described later in the book, to illustrate the ideas of theory and hypothesis testing.

Leon Festinger (1957), a social psychologist, has proposed a theory called **cognitive dissonance** to explain what happens when people hold attitudes that are inconsistent, or behave in ways which are inconsistent with their attitudes. In such situations Festinger claims people are likely to experience 'dissonance'; a state of 'psychological discomfort or tension'. As dissonance is experienced as a negative drive state, a person is motivated to reduce or eliminate it.

Smokers are strong candidates for experiencing dissonance if they wish to remain healthy, given the publicity concerning the health risks of smoking. One way smokers have of reducing dissonance is to deny, or at least play down, the evidence that there are serious health risks attached to their habit. A research hypothesis which can be derived from Festinger's theory therefore, is that smokers are more likely than non-smokers to view smoking as having low health risks attached to it. Non-smokers, on the other hand, are more likely to accept the publicity and accept that the health risks of smoking are high.

▶ Scientific theories are testable. The usual test is to use the theory to make a prediction, and then see whether the prediction is true.

▶ A research hypothesis is a prediction about what should be observed if a theory is true.

One and two-tailed hypotheses

A research hypothesis can be stated as either a one or two-tailed hypothesis. I will use the example of cognitive dissonance and smoking to illustrate the difference. A researcher could predict simply that there will be a **difference** between the attitudes of smokers and non-smokers towards the health risks associated with smoking. This is known as a **two-tailed** research hypothesis because it allows for two possible outcomes:

1 Smokers might believe that the health risks associated with smoking are high compared to non-smokers.

OR

2 Smokers might believe the health risks associated with smoking are low compared to non-smokers.

(Logically there is a third possible outcome – the researcher could find no difference in the attitude of smokers and non-smokers concerning the health risks of smoking. This is the **null hypothesis**.)

A **one-tailed** research hypothesis predicts that the difference will be in a particular direction. As is indicated in the text, cognitive dissonance theory predicts that smokers are more likely to play down the health risks associated with smoking, as this is one way of reducing their dissonance. As only one of the two outcomes described above is likely, number two, a one-tailed hypothesis is appropriate.

In deciding whether to state a one or a two-tailed research hypothesis the researcher is guided by the theory being tested or previous research. If the theory under investigation, or previous research, suggests that the results will be in a particular direction then a one-tailed hypothesis should be stated. If a difference is expected but the direction of the difference is unclear then the research hypothesis should be two-tailed.

Here then, is an example of a clear and testable hypothesis derived from a theory. It is at this point that a psychologist would need to select an appropriate method of research to gather the data to test the hypothesis.

How would you set about testing this hypothesis? The most direct way would be to question a group of smokers and a group of non-smokers about what they consider are the health risks associated with smoking: then examine the results to see if, as dissonance theory predicts, there is a difference in the attitudes of smokers and non-smokers to the health risks of smoking. This is basically what you will be doing in Chapter 5!

Let us imagine that you have used a suitable method and collected data to test the hypothesis, and also that the data shows that more smokers than non-smokers believe there is a low health risk attached to smoking. What do you do next?

WHY DO I NEED TO KNOW ABOUT STATISTICS?

The data you collect directly from your subjects is referred to as the **raw data**. Once the raw data has been collected statistics can provide you with useful 'tools' for summarizing, presenting and analysing your results.

You may want to communicate the results of your research to others but it can be inconvenient for you, and your readers, if you use the raw data, particularly if there is a large amount of data. It may therefore be necessary to summarize or condense the raw data in some way.

Descriptive statistics

Statisticians have developed a number of useful **descriptive statistics** whose purpose is to provide a convenient description of the major features of a set of data. Two aspects of the data are of particular importance: the most typical score, and the extent to which the scores are close together or spread out.

There are statistics of **central tendency** which provide a measure of the most typical score, e.g. the average or arithmetic mean. There are also statistics which measure the amount of **dispersion** or **variation** in a set of scores, e.g. the range and the standard deviation.

You will learn more about descriptive statistics, how to calculate them and their advantages and disadvantages, in Chapter 3.

Describing and summarizing data is therefore one important reason why psychologists use statistics. Closely linked to this idea of describing data is the use of graphs and charts. I am sure you have heard the phrase, 'a picture is worth a thousand words'. Well, the same idea can be applied in reporting research findings. A well-constructed chart or graph can often make it easier for the reader to 'see' the results of a piece of research. I will explain how to construct graphs later in the book.

▶ Statistics of central tendency describe how the data clump around a central point: averages such as the mean, the median or the mode. See Chapter 3.

▶ Statistics of dispersion describe how the data are spread out between extremes: measures such as the range or the standard deviation. See Chapter 3.

Inferential statistics

To understand another reason why psychologists use statistics, let us return to the research hypothesis concerning the attitudes of smokers to the health risks of smoking. **Inferential statistics**, as the name implies, are statistics that enable inferences or conclusions to be drawn from research data. More specifically there is a range of statistical tests available that enable psychologists to test research hypotheses.

For example, we have assumed that the data collected to test Festinger's theory of cognitive dissonance showed that more smokers than non-smokers believe that there is a low health risk attached to smoking. These results are open to two interpretations:

1 That there is no real difference in the attitudes of smokers and non-smokers and thus the results are due to chance (this is known as the **null hypothesis**).
2 That the results represent real differences between the attitudes of smokers and non-smokers (the research hypothesis).

How does a psychologist decide which of these two competing explanations of the results to accept? Inferential statistics enable a psychologist to assess the **probability** of their results occurring by chance:

▶ The null hypothesis is always that any observed differences were merely due to chance.

- if the probability of the results occurring by chance is low, the null hypothesis can be rejected in favour of the research hypothesis

- if the probability of the results occurring by chance is high then the null hypothesis must be accepted.

At this point I am sure you are wondering just how low the probability needs to be before the null hypothesis can be rejected. The psychologist will normally set a **significance level** before starting research. More details on significance levels are shown in the inset below.

Many psychologists use a 0.05 (5 chances in 100) level as the cut-off for statistical significance. This means that the difference between two sets of scores is assumed to be due to chance unless it is sufficiently large that it would be expected to arise by chance only 5 times in 100, (this is often expressed more simply as 1 chance in 20) or less.

If the probability of the results occurring by chance is greater than the significance level set by the psychologist then he/she must accept the null hypothesis and reject the research hypothesis.

Significance levels: type 1 and type 2 errors

It is very important that you understand the concept of statistical significance as this is vital to interpreting the results of your practicals. It is also important for understanding and evaluating the results of much of the research published in scientific journals.

A key point to remember is that if a statistically significant difference is found between two sets of scores this does **not prove** that the results didn't occur by chance. Similarly, if a difference was found not to be statistically significant this does **not prove** the results **were** due to chance. What significance indicates is the likelihood or probability of the results occurring by chance. Thus there is always the possibility that a difference found to be statistically significant did occur by chance, or that a result found to be not significant didn't occur by chance. Mistakes or 'errors' such as these have special names – the first is called a type 1 error and the second a type 2 error. To state this more formally:

A type 1 error – this occurs when you find a difference statistically significant and reject the null hypothesis when it was actually due to chance and therefore the null hypothesis should have been accepted. You might be wondering how this could happen. Well, let us return to the meaning of statistical significance. A result that is significant at the 0.05 level indicates that the probability of the results occurring by chance is equal to or less than 1 chance in 20. We usually interpret this as meaning that the results are unlikely to have occurred by chance and therefore the null hypothesis is rejected and the research hypothesis is accepted. This is the most likely explanation of the results. But you must remember that with a 0.05 level of significance there is a 1 in 20 chance that you will make a mistake i.e. a type 1 error. This is because you do not know that your results are not that 1 time in 20 when a difference of the size you have found occurred by chance.

 Before reading on try to work out how you could reduce the possibility of making a type 1 error?

To reduce the possibility of making a type 1 error you could set a more stringent level of significance. If the significance level were set a 0.01 rather than 0.05 then the possibility of a type 1 error is reduced from 1 in 20 to 1 in 100. Thus the more stringent the level of significance the lower the probability of a type 1 error. So why not always set a very stringent level of significance? The problem is that when you decrease the chance a type 1 error, by having a stringent level of significance, you increase the chance of **a type 2 error**! The process operates the other way round: if you decrease the chance of a type 2 error by having a less stringent level of significance then you increase the chance of a type 1 error. There is no escape! What is required is a compromise. That is what the two most common levels of significance, 0.05 and the 0.01, are. There is no mathematical reason for using these levels of significance. There is simply general agreement among statisticians that they represent a reasonable compromise in the chances of making a type 1 error and a type 2 error.

How do I find the probability of my results occurring by chance?

The answer to this question is that you select a suitable inferential statistical test and apply it to your data. The statistical tests consist of mathematical formulae which enable you to convert your data into a test statistic, often referred to as an **observed value** of the test. This observed value can then be compared with a table of critical values for the test. If you turn to appendix D of this book you will find that it is made up of tables of critical values for different statistical tests. Don't be intimidated. Later in the book I will explain how to read these tables. These critical values have already been calculated by statisticians and show the probabilities that they could have occurred by chance. By comparing the observed value, obtained by applying a statistical test to your data, with an appropriate critical value, it is possible to establish the probability of your results occurring by chance (exactly how you do this will be explained fully as you carry out the practicals in subsequent chapters of the book). As discussed above, if the probability of the results occurring by chance is equal to, or less than, the significance level you have chosen, then you can reject the null hypothesis.

CORRELATION AND EXPERIMENTATION

The process of hypothesis testing outlined above applies to all hypotheses. However, as you will find in the practicals you are asked to carry out, there is an important distinction drawn between experimental and correlational hypotheses.

An **experiment** is a method of research, widely used by psychologists, to examine the effect of one variable upon another. In the ideal world this would involve the psychologist directly manipulating an **independent variable** (IV) and then observing the consequences on a **dependent variable** (DV), while holding all **extraneous variables** (EV) constant. EVs are any variables that could change the DV other than the IV. For an example of an IV, DV and EV see the boxed inset.

An example of an experiment

A psychologist is interested in testing the effects of two techniques for learning word-pairs. One technique involves creating mental images. The other is simply repeating or rehearsing the word-pairs. These techniques form the two **conditions** of the experiment; they are what the experimenter directly manipulates (the independent variable). To test the effectiveness of the two memory techniques the subjects are tested for their ability to recall the word-pairs. The number of word-pairs recalled (the dependent variable) is thought to be 'dependent' upon the memory techniques (the independent variable). Extraneous variables would be anything, other than the two memory techniques, which might affect the number of word-pairs correctly recalled e.g. the existing memory ability of the subjects, or any distractions (such as noise) in the room used for the test.

The experiment described above is the basis of one of the practicals you will be doing later in the book – Practical 3, Chapter 7.

► An experimental hypothesis – one kind of research hypothesis – is a prediction that values for dependent variables are the result of manipulations of independent variables.

► In a true experiment the researcher can directly manipulate the independent variables.

In a situation such as that outlined in the boxed inset above any change in the DV must be a consequence of the psychologist's manipulation of the IV. Hence an experimental hypothesis involves a prediction about the effect that one variable (the IV) has on another variable (the DV). This ability to test hypotheses about cause and effect is the major reason why the experiment has a special place among the methods used by psychologists.

In order to carry out a 'true experiment', a psychologist must be able to directly manipulate the IV involved. However, there are many variables that psychologists are interested in that cannot be directly manipulated. Some variables, like age and sex differences, simply cannot be manipulated directly. Other variables, such as deprivation experiences, cannot be manipulated for ethical reasons. So what do psychologists do in such situations?

One option open to them is to investigate whether there is a **correlation** between variables. An example of two variables that psychologists have investigated with the technique of correlation is intelligence and academic achievement. Neither of these variables can be directly manipulated, so psychologists have sought to measure both variables and then assess the direction and strength of the relationship between them. As you might have predicted psychologists have found a moderate positive correlation between IQ and academic achievement.

Correlation

Correlation is a collection of statistical techniques which can assess the direction and strength of association between any two measurable variables. The direction of a correlation can be either **positive** (where a high score on one variable is associated with a high score on the other variable) or **negative** (where a high score on one variable is associated with a low score on the other variable).

The strength of a correlation is usually measured on a scale – +1 to 0 to –1:

- the closer the correlation is to 1 (either + or –1) then the stronger the relationship
- the closer the correlation is to 0 the weaker the relationship. (You will be using the technique of correlation in your first practical, so I will leave a detailed discussion of the statistics involved until then.)

Correlation as a statistical technique, measures how one variable varies with another and may be used in all kinds of psychological research. However, correlational research is done as an alternative to experimental research, when the researcher does not manipulate independent variables.

Look back to the chapter objectives at the beginning of the chapter. These tell you what you should have learned by now. Look through the objectives, check back with the text in the chapter as necessary and make sure that you do understand what the objectives say you should understand. Pay particular attention to the key terms in the last objective. These are terms which will be used over and over again in the remainder of the book, and terms you will have to use in writing up practical reports, so the sooner you get used to them the better.

CHAPTER SUMMARY

What I have outlined in this chapter is a very brief introduction to research methods and the use of statistics in Psychology. At this point I just want you to get a 'feel' for some of the concepts and issues. If you have found it hard going please do not worry. All of the concepts and issues mentioned above are dealt with at a slower pace and in more detail as you work through the practicals in subsequent chapters of the book.

Measures of central tendency and measures of dispersion

INTRODUCTION

► Descriptive statistics use measures of central tendency and measures of dispersion.

In this chapter I want to introduce you to some basic techniques for organizing and presenting the results of your practicals. The basic aim of psychological research is to obtain data to describe and test hypotheses about human behaviour and experience. Once the raw data has been collected the psychologist needs to summarize the main features of it and present them in a clear and unambiguous way. To help with this task the psychologist has a range of descriptive statistics to choose from. Measures of central tendency and measures of dispersion are two important tools of descriptive statistics. I have given an outline of a small-scale experiment below and will use the data it generates to explain how to calculate the major descriptive statistics.

An experiment on the effects of listening to music on the ability to solve mathematical problems

A group of twenty college students, all of whom were studying mathematics, were asked to take part in an experiment in which they had to solve as many mathematical problems as possible in thirty minutes. Ten of the students, picked at random, wore headphones and listened to a tape of music of their own choice. The other ten students wore headphones but heard no music. The results of the study are shown overpage.

Group 1 – who listened to music	Group 2 – without music
10	22
23	25
17	19
45	23
30	31
14	27
15	21
40	24
12	30
14	18

The table shows the number of problems solved correctly by the two groups of students – the maximum score was sixty.

Measures of central tendency

Measures of central tendency tell you how much a set of scores cluster around a central point which can be regarded as the most typical or representative value. A number of statistics have been developed to do this.

The mean
The statistic known as the average, or more correctly the arithmetic **mean**, is the most frequently used measure of central tendency. It is calculated by adding up all the scores in a group and then dividing by the number of scores in the group. Let us see how this is done by using the data in the table above.

Calculation of the mean
The mean for Group 1 is found by:

● **step** 1 – adding the scores together:

$$10 + 23 + 17 + 45 + 30 + 14 + 15 + 40 + 12 + 14 = 220$$

● **step 2** – the total of the scores is then divided by the number of scores, which is 10.

$$\frac{220}{10} = 22$$

 Now it is your turn, calculate the mean for Group 2. The answer should be 24.

At this point it is necessary to introduce you to some statistical symbols and formulae. These can seem a little daunting at first but are really just a form of 'shorthand' by which mathematicians show what needs to be done to calculate statistics. I will not give you a full list of statistical symbols now, but will gradually introduce them as you need to use them. If you are making a card index then note down the meaning of the symbols on your cards.

▶ Measures of central tendency include the mean, the median and the mode.

Our first statistical formula shows how to calculate the mean:

$$\bar{x} = \frac{\Sigma x}{N}$$

There are four symbols used in the formula above:

- $\bar{x}$ – this is the symbol for the mean
- Σ – this is a Greek letter called sigma and it instructs you to 'add up' or 'sum'. But what do you add up? You add up all the values or scores which follow sigma. If sigma is followed by x, then you add up all the xs
- x – this stands for any score within a set or group of scores
- N – this is the number of scores. Some formulae use N to refer to the total number of scores or subjects in the study. In such cases n is used to refer to scores in a particular group or condition. By adding little numbers or letters below the n (known as subscripts) it is possible to show which group is being referred to. So n_1 refers to the scores in condition 1 of the study.

If we go back to the formula for the mean you will now see that it tells you to:

1 Σx, add up each score in the group.
2 Then divide Σx by N, the number of scores in the group.

There are two other measures of central tendency – the **median** and the **mode**.

The median

The median is defined as the score which has as many scores below it as above it. More technically it is the score below which are fifty per cent of the scores and above which are fifty per cent of the scores.

Calculation of the median score
- **step 1** – arrange the scores in ascending order – from the lowest score to the highest.

For group 1 this gives us:

10, 12, 14, 14, 15, 17, 23, 30, 40, 45

- **step 2** – there are ten scores so five must lie below the median, and five must lie above the median. The fifth score up is 15 and the fifth score counting down is 17. So the median must lie between 15 and 17.

10, 12, 14, 14, 15, | 17, 23, 30, 40, 45
          Median

The median then lies between the two middle scores; here they are 15 and 17 and the median is $\dfrac{15 + 17}{2} = 16$

▶ **Note**: If there is an odd number of scores then the median is literally the middle score. If there are several scores which are the same the median is still the middle score e. g.

5, 6, 8, 8, | 8, 9, 12
          Median.

However the formula for an exact calculation is:

$$\text{Median} = L + \left(\frac{N/2 - F}{FM} \right) \times w$$

Where L = the exact lower limit of the interval containing the median. In this case the median will lie between 7.5 and 8.5, so $L = 7.5$

F = the total number of values below L. In this case 2 (the values 5 and 6)

FM = the number of values in the interval containing the median; here there are 3 values of 8

N = the total number of values; here 6

W = the width of the size of the interval containing the median; here this is 1.

▶ The previous calculation is sufficient in most cases. This formula is a more advanced one than you are likely to need.

Hence:

$$7.5 + \left(\frac{6/2 - F}{3} \right) \times 1 =$$

$$7.5 \times 0.33 \times 1 = 7.83$$

 Now calculate the median for Group 2. The answer should be 25.3.

The mode
The mode is defined as the score that occurs most frequently in a set of scores.

Identifying the mode
With a small set of scores this can be found quite simply by a visual inspection of the scores. With a large amount of raw data it would be necessary systematically to count the frequency of each score.

For Group 1 the mode is 14 as there are two scores of 14; all the other scores only occur once.

If you look at the figures for Group 2, you will see that there is no mode at all, because each score only occurs once. This shows the limitation of the mode when dealing with small samples.

The advantages and disadvantages of the mean, median and mode
The aim in calculating a measure of central tendency is to have a single score which is typical of a set of scores. With this in mind let's consider the advantages and disadvantages of the measures of central tendency described.

Advantages of the mean
The mean is generally the most accurate and useful measure of

central tendency because it uses the amount of every score and thus makes maximum use of the data you have collected.

The mean is also used in many advanced statistical techniques such as the *t* test (this statistical test is used in Practical 4, Chapter 8) and analysis of variance.

Disadvantages of the mean

There are some circumstances where the mean may give an inaccurate or misleading impression of the typical value of a set of scores. One such situation is where there is an extreme score. Take the scores below:

Group A   5, 6, 8, 8, 9, 12, 92

        Mean = 20   Median = 8

Group B   5, 6, 8, 8, 9, 12, 15

        Mean = 9   Median = 8

▶ Only extreme scores in one direction have this effect on the mean. Extreme scores in both directions tend to cancel each other out.

The scores are the same for both groups except for the last score which for Group A is 92 and Group B is 15. The score of 92 is not typical in that it is considerably larger than any of the others in the set. Its effect is to substantially increase the value of the mean and the result is a mean of 20 which does not give an accurate picture of the majority of the scores. The median, however, is unaffected by the extreme score. This is because the amount of each score is not taken into account but rather the position of the scores from lowest to highest.

Advantages of the median

As demonstrated above the median can be a useful and more accurate measure of central tendency where extreme scores exist.

The median is relatively easy to calculate.

Disadvantages of the median

As the median does not use the amount of each score there is a sense in which an important feature of the data is being wasted. In the absence of extreme scores the mean would normally be used.

The median is rarely used in more advanced statistics.

Advantages of the mode

With a reasonable sized sample it can often give an accurate idea of the most typical score.

It is not subject to the influence of extreme scores.

Disadvantages of the mode

It does not use the amount of every score and therefore, like the median, wastes information.

It can be indeterminate with small samples, as you will have seen with regard to the mode for Group 2 in the experiment. There was in fact no mode.

Measures of dispersion

A second important feature of a set of scores is how spread out the scores are. Again I will use the scores from the experiment on page 17 to demonstrate how to calculate the major measures of dispersion.

The range

The **range** is simply the difference between the smallest and the highest score.

Calculation of the range

- **step** 1 – arrange the scores for Group 1 in ascending order:

  10, 12, 14, 14, 15, 17, 23, 30, 40, 45

- **step** 2 – take the smallest score away from the highest score:

  45 – 10 = 35

The range is 35.

The interquartile range

One problem with range, like the mean, is that it can be misleading if there are extreme scores. This is because the range only takes account of the smallest and highest scores. Look at the figures below:

Group A   5, 6, 8, 8, 9, 12, 92

          Range = 87

Group B   5, 6, 8, 8, 9, 12, 15

          Range = 10

You can see what a dramatic effect the extreme score of 92 has had on the range for Group A.

One way to avoid the effect of extreme scores is to have a measure of dispersion that does not use the smallest or highest scores. Such a measure exits and is called the **interquartile range**. This is the difference between the score that falls at the 25% and the score that falls at the 75%.

Calculation of the interquartile range

- **step 1** – arrange the scores in order from smallest to highest
- **step 2** – find the score that falls at the 25% point – this is called Q1
- **step 3** – find the score that occurs at the 75% point – this is called Q3
- **step 4** – subtract Q1 from Q3

► Measures of dispersion include: the range; the inter-quartile range; the mean deviation; the variance; the standard deviation.

► You will notice that we have only calculated Q1 and Q3 roughly. Since there are 7 scores, 6 is not quite the point below which 25% of scores fall. But this is good enough for most purposes.

The interquartile range (IQR) = Q3 – Q1

Group A   5, 6, 8, 8, 9, 12, 92

$$\begin{array}{cc} | & | \\ | & | \\ Q1 & Q3 \end{array}$$

IQR = 12 – 6 = 6

Group B   5, 6, 8, 8, 9, 12, 15

$$\begin{array}{cc} | & | \\ | & | \\ Q1 & Q3 \end{array}$$

IQR = 12 – 6 = 6

If you compare the IQR for Group A and Group B with their respective ranges you can see the effect of not including the extreme score of 92.

Semi-interquartile range
You can also calculate a statistic called the **semi-interquartile range**. This is simply the IQR divided by 2:

$$\text{semi-IQR} = \frac{Q3 - Q1}{2}$$

The mean deviation

One problem with both the range and the interquartile range is that they both make use of only two scores. If you have gone to the trouble of collecting a large amount of data it seems rather wasteful to use only two of the scores. This might lead you to ask whether there is a measure of dispersion which, like the mean, takes the amount of each score into account. There are in fact a number of such statistics. Let us start by looking at the **mean deviation** (MD). This is the average or mean of the amount that each score deviates from the mean.

Calculation of the mean deviation:
- **step 1** – find the mean of the set of scores ($\bar{x}$)
- **step 2** – find the amount that each score deviates from the mean by subtracting the mean from each score
- **step 3** – add up the deviations from the mean using their absolute values i.e. ignoring any minus signs, (see the note at the top of p. 23)
- **step 4** – divide the sum of the deviations by the number of scores (*N*)

► Straight brackets mean that all results are positive numbers.

This can be summarized in the formula:

$$MD = \frac{\Sigma \mid x - \bar{x} \mid}{N}$$

If we return to the data from our experiment the MD for Group 1 is calculated as follows overpage:

	step 1	**step 2**
Group 1 – who listened to music	Mean	Deviation $(\bar{x} - x)$
10	22	−12
23	22	1
17	22	−5
45	22	23
30	22	8
14	22	−8
15	22	−7
40	22	18
12	22	−10
14	22	− 8

step 3 – $\Sigma \mid x - \bar{x} \mid = 100$

step 4 – $\dfrac{\Sigma \mid x - \bar{x} \mid}{N} = 10.$

$$MD = 10$$

If you were to take the minus signs into account when adding up the deviations then the result would be 0. In fact the result would always be 0 no matter what data you used! This is because the mean by definition has an equal amount of positive deviations and negative deviations and these simply cancel each other out.

The variance

The mean deviation is a useful measure of the amount of dispersion in a set of scores. However I expect it has occurred to you that there is something not quite right about simply ignoring the minus signs. As explained above something has to be done with the minus signs or you simply end up with a value of 0. A mathematically more sophisticated way of dealing with the minus sign is to square the figures – a minus number multiplied by a minus number gives a positive number. This technique is used in the statistic known as the **variance**. The variance is the mean of the deviations squared.

► The variance is the mean of the deviations from the mean squared.

Calculation of the variance
- **step 1** – find the mean of the set of scores $(\bar{x})$
- **step 2** – find the amount that each score deviates from the mean (d) by subtracting the mean from each score
- **step 3** – square each of the deviations (d^2)
- **step 4** – add up the squared deviations (Σ)
- **step 5** – divide the sum of the squared deviations by the number of scores (N).

This can be summarized with the formula:

$$s^2 = \frac{\Sigma (\bar{x} - x)^2}{N}$$

If we return to the data from our experiment the variance for Group 1 is calculated as follows overpage:

► The symbol s^2 is used to indicate the variance of a sample of scores. The symbol is used when you are estimating the variance of a population of scores. (A population of scores is all the scores relevant to the hypothesis under investigation.)

	step 1	**step 2**	**step 3**
Group 1 – who listened to music	Mean $\bar{x}$	Deviations d	Deviations squared d^2
10	22	−12	144
23	22	1	1
17	22	−5	25
45	22	23	529
30	22	8	64
14	22	−8	64
15	22	−7	49
40	22	18	324
12	22	−10	100
14	22	−8	64

step 4 – the sum of the deviations squared is 1364
step 5 – the sum of the deviations squared divided by N is 136.4

The standard deviation

The variance gives us a mathematically more acceptable measure of dispersion and it plays an important role in more advanced statistics. However, if you compare the MD with the variance you will notice how much larger the latter is: 10 compared to 136.4. This is because with the variance the deviations have been squared. To bring the variance back down to its original level we can do the opposite of squaring which is to find the square root. If you find the square root of the variance you calculate another important measure of dispersion called the **standard deviation**.

Calculation of the standard deviation
You simply follow steps 1 to 5, as for the variance, and then find the square root of the variance. The formula is thus:

$$s = \sqrt{\frac{\Sigma(\bar{x} - x)^2}{N}}$$

If you are estimating the variance of a population then the formula is modified to:

$$s = \frac{\Sigma(\bar{x} - x)^2}{N-1}$$

▶ The square root of the variance is the standard deviation.

Now look back through the chapter. Is there anything you remain uncertain about? If so look at it again and if you remain uncertain ask your tutor or a numerate friend. Check the list of key terms in the chapter objectives. Have you taken any notes you need on these topics? If not, do so.

The advantages and disadvantages of different measures of dispersion

As with the mean, median and mode there are various advantages and disadvantages to the measures of dispersion.

The Range

Advantages
Quick and easy to calculate.

Disadvantages
Subject to the influence of extreme scores.

Wastes information because it is based on only two scores.

Interquartile range

Advantages
Avoids the problem of extreme scores by using the 25% and 75% points.

Quick and easy to calculate.

Disadvantages
Wastes information because it is based on only two scores.

Mean deviation

Advantages
Utilizes the value of every score.

Relatively easy to calculate.

Disadvantages
Lacks mathematical properties for use in more advanced statistical procedures.

Variance and standard deviation

Advantages
Make the maximum use of data collected by taking the value of each score into account.

Can and are used in more advanced statistical procedures.

Are the most sensitive measures of dispersion.

Disadvantages
Complicated to work out.

CHAPTER SUMMARY

This chapter has shown you how to calculate various measures of central tendency, and various measures of dispersion. From now on you can regard it as a reference section. You can refer back to it whenever you want to choose and use one of these statistics.

4 Investigating personality: the first practical

▶ Practical 1.

> **Chapter objectives**
>
> By end of this chapter you should:
>
> ▪ have completed your first practical report and will be familiar with the standard structure for reports
>
> ▪ have experienced the use of a psychometric test of personality
>
> ▪ understand the difference between quantitative and qualitative data
>
> ▪ know the different kinds of quantitative data used by psychologists
>
> ▪ understand the concepts of reliability and validity
>
> ▪ know how to choose an appropriate statistical test
>
> ▪ be able to draw a scattergram
>
> ▪ be able to calculate a Spearman's rank correlation coefficient
>
> ▪ know and be able to use the following key terms: correlation, correlation coefficient, scattergram, reliability, validity, quantitative and qualitative data; ratio level, interval level, ordinal level and nominal level data, parametric and non-parametric statistics.

THE PRACTICALS

In this and a further five chapters I will describe in detail how to carry out five Psychology practical projects, analyse the results and write them up as practical reports. The practicals have been written so that you have a great deal of help at the beginning, with the first two practicals. In the later practicals the amount of help is reduced slightly, to encourage you to use the skills and knowledge that you will, by then, have developed.

None of the practicals should take you more than one hour or so to carry out. However, analysing the data and writing up your reports will take quite a long time. I would suggest that you timetable yourself ten to fifteen hours to carry out, analyse and write up each practical report. You might find the first three reports take longer than the last two, as the former involve learning a substantial amount of new material. Do not be concerned if it seems to be taking you quite a lot of time to do this work – it should!

▶ This chapter includes materials for Practical 1. Turn to the end of the chapter to locate these materials which are:

- Table of pooled data for Practical 1
- the EPI form A: shortened version
- the EPI form B: shortened version
- scoring for form A
    E scores
    N scores
- scoring for form B
    E scores
    N scores
- calculation of Spearman's Rho.

Remember, if you are studying for the AEB A, or A/S, level in Psychology that the coursework is twenty per cent of your final A level grade.

Unfortunately, you cannot carry out and write up practical reports in easy stages; you have to carry out a practical and write a complete report right from the start!

PRACTICAL 1 – AN INVESTIGATION INTO THE RELIABILITY AND VALIDITY OF THE EYSENCK'S PERSONALITY INVENTORY

This practical has two major learning aims; the first is to give you experience of using a **psychometric test** and the second is to cover the very important statistical technique known as **correlation**.

Since you will be a subject in this practical yourself, I will not say exactly what the hypotheses to be tested are until later.

► For the meaning of the term 'hypothesis' see Chapter 2 page 9.

Carrying out the practical

You are to be a subject in this practical. Please carry out the following activities in the order given.

1 Write a description of your own personality. Try to be as detailed and honest as possible, but concentrate on broad issues rather than minor idiosyncracies. For example, if you write that you are sociable and outgoing, this says quite a lot about you. If, however, you write that you are a supporter of Liverpool Football Club, this is not very informative.

2 From the list of words below write down any which you think apply strongly to you.

Place a tick by any of the words below which you feel apply to you.

passive	a leader	reserved
active	reliable	sober
lively	restless	moody
thoughtful	easygoing	talkative
excitable	rigid	carefree
impulsive	optimistic	quiet
careful	calm	sociable
responsive	anxious	aggressive
changeable	outgoing	even-tempered
peaceful	pessimistic	touchy
controlled	unsociable	

3 Read the instructions for the EPI shortened version (form A) at the end of the chapter on page 48 and answer the questions.

4 Complete the questions for the EPI (form B) at the end of the chapter on page 50.

5 Score your responses to the EPI (forms A and B) using the scoring instructions given at the end of the chapter on page 52.

Having completed the above you should have:

- your description of your own personality
- a list of words you think apply strongly to you
- four scores:
- An E score for EPI shortened version (form A)
- An N score for EPI shortened version (form A)
- An E score for EPI shortened version (form B)
- An N score for EPI shortened version (form B)

The aims of this practical

This practical focuses on the topic of personality. A primary concern of psychologists interested in personality has been to develop ways of measuring or assessing it. A wide variety of techniques have been developed to do this, such as **interviews**, **rating scales**, psychometric tests and **projective tests**. When psychologists develop measures of such things as personality and intelligence they are expected to provide evidence as to how accurate and consistent their tests are. The accuracy of a test; that is the extent to which it measures what it is claiming to measure, is referred to as its **validity**. The ability of a test to measure something consistently is referred to as its **reliability**. There are a number of different ways of establishing whether or not a psychometric test is reliable and valid; look at the inset boxes for detailed discussion.

► Validity.

► Reliability.

Methods of assessing the reliability of a psychological test

Reliability refers to whether a psychometric test, or some other measuring device, measures consistently. There are a number of ways in which the consistency of a test can be assessed:

1 **Test/retest reliability** – this measures whether a test is reliable over time. The usual method of establishing whether a test has test/retest reliability is to administer the test to subjects at one point in time, and then some weeks/months later give the **same test** to the **same subjects**. If the two sets of scores are very similar then there is a high level of consistency. The degree of consistency can be measured by correlating the two sets of scores; a strong positive correlation indicates a high level of test/retest reliability.

2 **Parallel form reliability** – this measures whether two, or more, versions of the same test measure in the same way. To assess this type of reliability the two versions of the test are administered to subjects at the same time. As above, if subjects get the same, or very similar, scores for both then the tests can be said to have high parallel form reliability.

► Correlation – see page 00.

You might be wondering what, exactly, it means to have two versions of the same test: you might also be wondering why psychologists would want two shortened versions of the same test! The practical discussed in this chapter involves using two versions of Eysenck's personality inventory – forms A and B. If you examine these two forms you will see that they have the same number of questions and that the questions cover the same kind of issues. This is what is meant by two versions of the same test. It is perhaps easier to understand why psychologists might want two versions of a test if we consider the case of intelligence tests. If, as a researcher, you wanted to study whether intelligence changes over time then you could give subjects an intelligence test on a number of different occasions. Problems might arise if you gave the subjects exactly the same test on each occasion. They might, for example, remember some of the answers from the previous testing, and this could affect the results. The researcher could give a different IQ test but this would make any direct comparison of the scores difficult. It is in situations such as this that it is useful to have more than one version of the same test.

Methods of assessing the validity of a psychological test

Validity refers to whether a test measures what it is supposed to measure: does an intelligence test accurately measure intelligence?

There are a number of different types of validity:

1 **Face validity** – this refers to whether a test appears to be measuring what it is said to measure. This can be important in that a test which lacks face validity may not be taken seriously by subjects.

2 **Criterion-related validity** – this refers to the ability of a test to predict behaviour in specific situations. To establish this, performance on the test is compared with a criterion, i.e. an independent measure of the behaviour the test is designed to predict.

Scores on the E scale of the EPI might, for example, be compared with a friend's rating of the subject's behaviour in various situations.

Some books on psychometrics distinquish between two types of criterion-related validity:

● **Concurrent validity** – this refers to a test's ability to measure some existing state or level of functioning. Psychologists have developed tests that help in the diagnosis of brain damage. Such tests are designed to measure the current level of mental functioning: they may, or may not, say anything about a patient's future level of functioning.

- **Predictive validity** – this concerns a test's ability to predict future behaviour or performance. It is important where psychological tests are used for selection purposes. If a test is designed to select people to train as computer programmers, then scores on the test would need to be compared to subsequent job performance as a programmer.
- **Construct validity** – refers to the extent to which the test measures the trait or theoretical construct that it is designed to measure.

This is an important type of validity, but one which can be difficult to establish.

Analysing the results

Now that you have worked out your EPI scores, I expect that you are interested to know what they mean. You can get an idea of what your scores mean by reading your psychology textbook to find out what Eysenck means by the typical:

- **extrovert** (someone with a high E score)
- **introvert** (someone with a low E score)
- **neurotic** (someone with a high N score)
- emotionally **stable** individual (someone scoring low on N).

There has been considerable criticism of Eysenck's choice of the term 'neurotic' to describe individuals with a high N score; many psychologists feel 'worrier' would be more appropriate!

To analyse the data the first thing you should do is take your four scores and place them in the appropriate spaces in Table 4.1 on page 47 (you are subject 15). I have provided you with some pooled class data from students I have taught recently. They carried out the practical exactly as you have been asked to.

Now you need to calculate some descriptive statistics. Look back to Chapter 3 and read the section on measures of central tendency and then calculate the median for each column of results in Table 4.1. Also calculate the median for males and females. One aim of this practical is to examine the validity of the EPI. You can do this by comparing your personality description and the words you selected to your scores on the EPI. This comparison will be qualitative rather than quantitative (see boxed inset over page) and will form an important part of your discussion. I will therefore save further comment on this issue until later.

▶ Standardized Psychological Tests, such as the EPI, are restricted in their availability. This means that they should only be administered by a qualified psychologist or someone trained in the use of the test. This is to ensure that the test is administered, scored and interpreted accurately. The full version of the EPI has 24 E questions and 24 N questions. The shortened version you are using contains 12 of the E questions and 12 of the N questions, which are reproduced here by permission of Hodder & Stoughton. Note that the *Eysenck Personality Inventory* (first published in 1963) has been superseded by the *Eysenck Personality Questionnaire* (EPQ, 1975) and subsequently by the *Eysenck Personality Questionnaire – Revised* (EPQ-R, 1991), which incorporates additional Psychoticism (P) and Lie (L) scales.

Quantative and qualitative data

Quantative data – this involves the use of numbers which are usually obtained by counting or measuring some aspect of behaviour. The scores obtained from asking subjects to complete the EPI are a good example of quantative data. When the EPI is scored it gives two numbers, which can range from 0 to 12; a score for extroversion and a score for neuroticism. The researcher therefore has a numerical measure of personality along two dimensions. The advantage of this kind of data is that it can be subjected to the range of statistical techniques that I outlined in Chapter 2. This kind of data enables psychologists to test experimental and correlational hypotheses. There are some psychologists, however, who argue that there are many important aspects of human behaviour and experience that cannot be quantified.

Qualitative data – this is really the opposite of what has been described above; it is data that has not been, or cannot be, quantified. Examples of qualitative data that a psychologist might find useful are: diaries, informal or open-ended interviews, case studies and introspective reports. (In an introspective report a person tries to report as accurately as possble how they have experienced something). This kind of information can be very useful for helping to understand the **meaning** people give to their actions. Attempts are being made to develop methods of quantifing qualtitative data; content and discourse analysis are examples. These are specialized techniques and beyond the scope of this book but I have included some references at the end of this chapter should you wish to find out more about these methods.

Another aim of this practical is to assess the reliability of the EPI. We will do this by comparing the E scores for form A with the E scores for form B and the N scores for form A with the N scores for form B. This kind of analysis is called parallel form reliability (see boxed inset on page 29).

As the name implies, the question here is whether two (or more) forms of the same test measure something in the same way; whether they are equivalent or parallel measures. Common sense would suggest that if two tests are equivalent, then subjects should obtain the same score on each test. Therefore, in this practical we would expect a subject's E score on form A to be the same as their E score for form B. If this were the case for every subject there would be perfect parallel form reliability. In the real world you rarely find perfect reliability.

So how can we assess the consistency of forms A and B of the EPI? One way is simply to study the raw data and see how closely matched each subject's scores are. Examine the scores in the table of

▶ Some books use the term **alternate form reliability**.

pooled class results (Table 4.1). How closely matched are they?

The problem with this as a means of analysis is that it involves a subjective judgement, on the part of the person examining the data, as to what constitutes 'closely matched'. This is a particular problem when some subjects' scores are very similar but other subjects' scores are quite different. What is needed is an objective way of measuring the degree of association between two sets of numbers: correlation is the statistical technique developed to do this.

The first step in a correlation analysis is to draw graphs, known as **scattergrams**. These give you a visual representation of the data and can indicate the strength and direction of correlation between two sets of scores. (In correlation the measures or scores the researcher has collected are referred to as **variables**.)

Please read the inset on scattergrams.

► For a definition of correlation see page 15.

How to draw and interpret scattergrams

Now you are ready to draw two scattergrams: one for the E scores on form A and the E scores on form B; and the other for the N scores on form A and the N scores on form B. I will show you how to draw a scattergram using the data for the E scores on form A and the E scores on form B from the end of the chapter.

- **step 1** – decide on the scale for your two axes using inches or centimetres. The scale you choose will depend on the size of your graph paper, and remember that the E and N scores have a range of 0 to 12
- **step 2** – draw two axes of equal length, one vertical and the other horizontal, and mark on each the scale from 0 to 12. Label each axis clearly
- **step 3** – now you can add the scores to the scattergram. You do this by taking the pair of E scores for subject 1, which are EA = 10 and EB = 5. Locate 10 on the EA scale and 5 on the EB scale and mark a small cross at the point where straight lines drawn from these two points meet. See Figure 4.1 overleaf
- **step 4** – continue to mark a small cross at each point where the remaining pairs of scores meet.

If two or more pairs of scores fall in the same place simply write the relevant number by the side of the cross, e.g. if three pairs of scores fall in the same place use one cross but write three by the side of it.

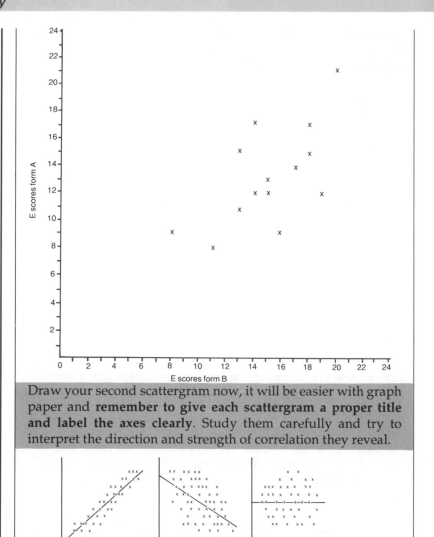

Figure 4.1
Scattergram of subjects' extroversion scores on forms A and B of Eysenck's personality inventory

Draw your second scattergram now, it will be easier with graph paper and **remember to give each scattergram a proper title and label the axes clearly**. Study them carefully and try to interpret the direction and strength of correlation they reveal.

Figure 4.1a

The limitations of scattergrams

While scattergrams are useful they have two important limitations. Firstly, a degree of subjective judgement is needed in order to interpret them. For example, on the basis of a scattergram, it might be possible to talk about a 'strong positive correlation' or a 'moderate negative correlation' but these are rather vague terms.

The second limitation is that they do not allow us to accept or reject our research hypothesis(es). To do this we need to establish the probability of our correlation occurring by chance. As referred to in Chapter 2, if the probability of our results occurring by chance is less than 5 in 100 (a significance level of 0.05), then we consider the results to be statistically significant and reject the null hypothesis. To be able to do this, a precise numerical measure of the degree of correlation between our two sets of scores (variables) is required.

Correlation coefficients

Statisticians have developed a number of different tests to measure correlation. If you subject your data to any one of these tests, the result is always known as a **correlation coefficient**: a number between +1 and –1. A correlation coefficient of +1 indicates a perfect positive relationship. A correlation coefficient of –1 indicates a perfect negative relationship (perfect correlations rarely occur in nature). A coefficient of 0 shows that there is no relationship (strictly speaking, one should say there is no linear or straight line relationship).

Having calculated a correlation coefficient to measure the precise degree of relationship between two variables, it is then possible to establish the probability that a correlation of that magnitude could have occurred by chance. This is done, (as explained in Chapter 2 in the section on 'inferential statistics') by comparing the calculated value (correlation coefficient) with a critical value obtained by consulting statistical tables. I will explain how this is done in the next section.

Applying an appropriate statistical test

As a psychologist you need to learn how to select the appropriate statistical test to analyse the data from your research. Choosing an appropriate test involves making a number of decisions which are summarized in the Figure 4.2 overleaf.

- **decision 1** – difference or correlation
- **decision 2** – how many samples? 1 **or** 2 **or** k (more than 2)
- **decision 3** – is the design – **related** or **unrelated**?
- **decision 4** – **parametric** or **non-parametric**?

I will explain how to work your way through Figure 4.2. In this practical, you are not predicting a difference, but attempting to measure the degree of relationship between two variables, therefore decision number 1 leads us to correlation. As this practical involves correlation, decisions 2 and 3 do not apply (they will be dealt with in subsequent practicals). This brings you to decision number 4 – can you use a **parametric test** or must you use a **non-parametric test**? Before you continue read the boxed material on parametric and non-parametric statistics, and on levels and scales of measurement.

> ### Parametric and non-parametric statistical tests
> Parametric statistical tests are powerful tools for analysing the results of research but their use is restricted. This is because a number of conditions need to be met before parametric tests can be applied. For example, because parametric tests operate on the raw data directly and involve calculating means and standard deviations the data needs to be of ratio or interval level (see the boxed material on levels of measurement on page

► Correlation coefficients.

37). There are two other assumptions which need to be considered before using a parametric test, these are discussed in Chapter 8.

Non-parametric statistical tests are very useful because although they are less powerful than parametric tests they can be used in situations where parametric tests cannot. For example, where the data is of a nominal or ordinal level (see boxed inset on levels of measurement on page 37).

Figure 4.2
*Chart for deciding on an
appropriate statistical test*

Note 1
There are tests for multiple correlation but not in this book.

Note 2
There are tests for multivariate analysis but not in this book.

Note 3
In this case you must be comparing the sample with the population from which it was drawn. For nominal level data use a Chi-square Goodness of fit test.

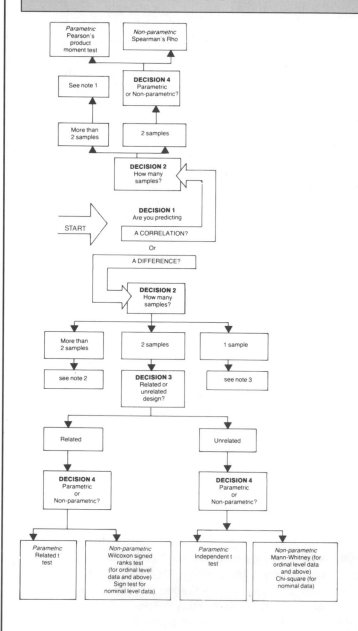

Levels or scales of measurement

When we use numbers we tend to make assumptions about what we can do with them. For example, we assume that we can add numbers together, divide or multiply them. However, when numbers are used as an aid to measure things then we need to be careful about what we do with them. This is because measurement operates on different levels. There are 4 levels or scales of measurement: **nominal, ordinal, interval and ratio.**

Ratio level – this is the highest level of measurement but one not often found in psychological research. An example of a ratio scale is time as measured in seconds. This level of measurement has 2 important properties.

1 It has a **true 0**. This means that 0 on the scale represents the absence of what you are measuring. Thus 0 seconds means: no time. This may be rather difficult to understand but I hope it will be clearer in a moment when we consider scales which lack a true 0.

2 It has **equal** or **standard units** of measurement. This means that one second is equal to any other second. With an accurate clock this would hopefully be true!

These 2 characteristics of a ratio scale have important consequences for what we can say about scores on the scale. Imagine a simple experiment in which a psychologist times how long it takes 2 rats to run a maze: one takes 10 seconds and the other takes 20 seconds. Now what can we conclude from these measurements. We can say the second rat took longer to run the maze, and we can say how much longer it took: 10 seconds. Further we can talk about the ratio between the two times: the second is twice as long as the first. It is this property that gives the scale its name: a ratio level.

Interval level – this is where a measurement scale has equal units but lacks a true 0. Take, as an example, temperature as measured in degrees centigrade. We have equal units here; one degree centigrade is the same as any other. But have we got a true 0? Consider for a moment what 0 degrees centigrade actually means. Does it mean the absence of temperature? Obviously not, because it is possible to have a temperature of – 10 degrees. If you can have minus on your scale then the scale does not have a true 0. But what are the consequences of this? If we have two liquids; one measures 10 degrees centigrade and the other 20 degrees. As with a ratio scale we can say confidently that the second liquid has more of what is being measured (heat) than the first. And we can quantify this: the second liquid is 10 degrees warmer than the first. But can we say that it is twice as hot! This is where it is easy to be misled by the numbers themselves. Yes, 20 is twice 10 **but** this assumes a true 0. In this case the scale goes below 0. In fact the centigrade scale goes down to –273 degrees (absolute or true 0)! So in a sense you are comparing two liquids, one of which has –273 + 10 units while the other has –273 + 20 units. Obviously the second is not twice as hot as the first. So this scale gets its name from the fact that we can talk about the interval or distance between two points on such a scale, but no more.

Ordinal level – quite a lot of measurement in Psychology lacks either a true 0 or equal units of measurement. Suppose you asked a subject to rate the physical attractiveness of 3 people on a scale from 0 to 10, and they gave one person a score of 5, one a score of 7 and one a score of 10 (with 10 being very attractive and 0 being unattractive). What level of measurement do you think this is?

I do not think it is reasonable to say the person rated 10 is twice as attractive as the person rated 5 (a ratio scale), nor that the person rated 10 has 5 more units of attractiveness (an interval scale). This is because our hypothetical attractiveness scale does not have a true 0 or equal units of measurement. So what can we conclude from the 3 scores? One simple conclusion is that the people have differing amounts of what is being measured (attractiveness). If we were to take these scores we could turn them into a **rank order** with the person who scored 10 being given a rank of 1, most attractive, and the person who scored 7 getting a rank of 2, and the person who scored 5 being given a rank of 3. It is the ability to place these numbers into a rank order that leads to the name ordinal level of measurement. Further discussion on this level of measurement is given below. However sometimes numbers are used in such a way that even ranking is not possible.

Nominal level – this is the lowest level of measurement and is most commonly found where named categories are used. If, for example, we are measuring smoking as a behaviour and we decide to simply count the number of people who smoke and the number who do not smoke then we are measuring at a nominal level; counting the frequency with which behaviour occurs in certain named categories. This is discussed at greater length in Chapter 5.

 Before continuing, consider what level of measurement you have in this practical. Remember you are measuring personality using two scales E and N.

I will now explain what level of measurement I think you have in this practical and why. You are measuring two variables, *E* and *N*, on a scale from 0–12. A score of 0 on the E scale can be interpreted to mean a person is very introverted, whereas a person scoring 12

on the E scale would be judged to be highly extroverted. The level of measurement here is therefore quite sophisticated because it is not simply a question of a subject being introvert or extrovert (named categories, a nominal level of measurement) but of **how** introverted or extroverted they are. Thus a subject who scored 12 on the E scale would be judged to be **more** extroverted than someone who scored 6. This means we can place subjects in a rank order i.e. the subject with the highest E score would be given a rank of 1, the subject with the next highest score would get a rank of 2 etc. This is what happens in a race when contestants are placed in rank order i.e. who came 1st, 2nd, 3rd and so on.

The ability to place scores in a rank order gives us an ordinal level and this is the level of measurement I would say you have in this practical. Some psychologists have argued that scores obtained from psychometric tests, like the EPI, can be treated as interval level. Do you think the EPI measures with equal units?

If one subject has an E score of 6 and another an E score of 12 it is tempting to say the second subject has 6 units more extroversion than the first subject. But can we assume that each E question on the EPI measures the same amount of extroversion?

The reason why it is important to know what level of data you have is because it determines what mathematical operations you can perform on the data, and this in turn influences what statistical tests can be used. Some statisticians have argued that even basic mathematical operations, like addition and subtraction, assume that you are dealing with interval or ratio level data.

As is often the case with difficult issues there are different opinions even among experts. I will take the purist view and regard EPI data as ordinal data, and not interval data. This seems to be the approach the AEB examiners adopt.

What does all of this mean for you? Firstly, it explains why I asked you to calculate medians and not the mean scores in the previous section. Calculating the median involves placing the scores in rank order, which is perfectly legitimate with ordinal data. Calculating the mean involves addition and division and if you take the purist view, these operations should only be used with interval or ratio level data.

The level of data not only determines what descriptive statistics you can use but also what kind of statistical test you can use for inferential statistics. Assuming the level of measurement in this practical is ordinal, this means the answer to question number four, in Figure 4. 2 is non-parametric.

And if you consult Figure 4. 2 you will see that the recommended non-parametric test of correlation is Spearman's Rho (r_s) correlation coefficient.

► Spearman's Rho – a non-parametric test of correlation.

Doing the calculations

You now need to apply Spearman's Rho, to the data set you created, by adding your own results to the pooled class data in Table 4.1. At the very end of this chapter there is a section on calculating

Spearman's Rho which takes you step by step through the necessary calculations. Remember you need to calculate two correlation coefficients:

1 The E scores for form A with the E scores for form B.
2 The N scores for form A with the N scores for form B.

Read the section on calculating Spearman's Rho and then do the calculations for your data set.

Calculating statistical significance

Having calculated the correlation coefficients it is time to see if they are statistically significant. To do this consult the table of critical values for Spearman's Rho (appendix D).

To use them you need to know: the number of pairs of scores, N (not to be confused with Eysenck's N scale), whether your hypothesis was one or two-tailed, and what level of significance you require. N is equal to 15, your hypotheses are one-tailed (see my comments on the research hypotheses in Chapter 2 on page 9) and let us start with the a 0.05 level of significance (the minimum needed for statistical significance).

Armed with this information you will see that the appropriate critical value, in the table of critical values, is 0.443; and the decision rule is that the calculated Rho value must be equal to, or greater than this to be statistically significant. If your results are significant at the 0.05 level, check to see whether they reach a higher level of significance (i.e. 0.025).

Levels of significance for a one-tailed test

	0.05	0.025	0.01	0.005
N = 14	0.464	0.538	0.622	0.675
N = 15	0.443	0.521	0.604	0.654

► A correlation coefficient of 0.56 indicates a moderately strong positive correlation. A statistically significant result means that it is unlikley to have occurred by chance.

For example, using the pooled class results (without your scores) I calculated a correlation coefficient of 0.56 for the E scores on form A and the E scores on form B, using Spearman's Rho. This value of Rho is significant at the 0.025 (1 in 40) level. This is because the calculated value of Rho (0.56) is greater than the critical value of 0.538 (remember N in this case is only 14).

However, it is not significant at the 0.01 (1 in a 100) level, as the calculated value is **less** than the critical value of 0.622.

It is possible to have a strong correlation which is **not** statistically significant, and a weak correlation which **is** statistically significant. This is because whether a correlation coefficient is significant or not depends on the size of the sample. Look at the critical values for Rho in appendix D. You will see that with an N of 5 (5 pairs of scores) with a one-tailed hypothesis, the value of Rho needed for significance at the 0.05 level is 0.9 or above. However, if N is 30, then Rho only has to equal 0.306 to be significant at the 0. 05 level.

Let us turn our attention to the issue of the validity of the EPI. You can explore this issue by looking at the words that you selected to describe yourself. If you look at Figure 4. 3 you will see the thirty-two words you were asked to choose from at the beginning of the practical organized in terms of Eysenck's model of personality types.

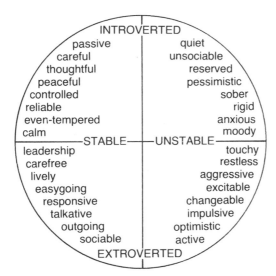

Figure 4.3

From your E and N scores you should be able to place yourself in one of the four quarters of Figure 4. 3 (unless you scored twelve for both E and N). How many of the eight words shown in your quarter did you select? A match between the words you choose to describe yourself and the words shown in your quarter would support the claim that the EPI is a valid measure of personality. More detail on the question of validity is provided on page 45 where I explain how to write the discussion section of your practical report.

WRITING UP THE EPI PRACTICAL

Now that you have completed the analysis of your results, all that remains is for you to write your first practical report! However, before you start please re-read appendix B carefully. This gives you the official guidelines for writing reports. I now want to show you what these would look like when applied to this practical.

Title

The title of your report needs to be concise, yet it should convey clearly to the reader what it is you have done. I think that it is useful to include the name of the research method used in the title, for example, 'An experiment into' . . . or . . . 'A survey on' . . . . In the case of this practical 'An investigation into the reliability and

► One thing you certainly must not do is to copy text word for word from this book into your practical report. If you do so you will fail.

validity if the Eysenck Personality Inventory' would be an appropriate title.

Summary or abstract

The summary should be relatively short, approximately 100 words, and contain:

- a brief summary of your aims and hypothesis
- the method and sample of subjects used
- what statistical test(s) were applied to the data and whether they were found to be statistically significant or not
- conclusions which can be drawn from the research.

Writing a good abstract is a skill all of its own, so if you find it difficult at first do not despair! It is a good idea to put the title and abstract on the first page of your report – leaving a couple of lines empty so that later you can add your examination candidate number and centre number.

Introduction

Start the introduction on a new page.
 Here are a list of points which the introduction could focus on:

- what do psychologists mean by the term personality?
- how have psychologists approached the question of personality differences? You could give a brief outline of the **type** and **trait** approaches and go on to describe Eysenck's type theory of personality
- how has Eysenck attempted to measure what he believes to be the major dimensions of personality? Briefly outline the development and structure of the EPI
- introduce the concepts of reliability and validity and the different ways these can be tested.

 This leads on to the aim of this practical which is to investigate the reliability and validity of the EPI.
 You will find many of the above issues discussed in Psychology textbooks in the chapter on personality. I have included some relevant sources of information in the reference section (page 46).

Research hypotheses
Your research hypotheses should state there will be a significant positive correlation between the E scores on form A and the E scores on form B.

 Write your own research hypothesis for the N scale scores.

Null hypotheses
Your null hypotheses should state 'any correlation between the E

> ► You will need to read something on personality in a Psychology textbook in order to complete the introduction.

scores for form A and the E scores for form B is due to chance'; **or** 'There will not be a significant positive correlation between the E scores for form A and the E scores for form B.'

 Write your own null hypothesis for the N scores.

The research hypotheses are one tailed because they predict not only that there will be a correlation, but the also direction the correlation will take, i.e. a positive correlation. If we were simply to state that there would be a correlation, but not specify the direction, positive or negative, then this would produce a two-tailed hypothesis.

You might be wondering why in this practical the research hypotheses are one-tailed. In making a decision about whether research hypotheses should be one or two tailed a psychologist is guided by prior research and/or theory. Eysenck has produced evidence to show that the forms A and B of the EPI have strong parallel form reliability, i.e. he found strong positive correlations between the two forms of the inventory. We would therefore **expect** any correlations we find to be positive. This is why the research hypotheses in this practical are both one tailed.

Method

Design
A number of books on research methodology talk about the **correlational design** and describe correlation as if it were a method of research in its own right.

Some authors have objected to this, claiming that correlation is a method of statistical analysis, not a method of collecting data. As usual, such debates leave students confused and pose difficulties for teachers! Given the lack of consensus among psychologists on this issue, it is acceptable for you to adopt either approach. Therefore, you may say either that a correlational design was used in this practical, or that two forms of a psychometric test were administered to subjects, and their scores were subjected to a correlational analysis.

Subjects
The subjects for this practical were fourteen full-time students at a college of further education, studying A level Psychology. There were eleven females and three males, all aged between sixteen and nineteen. Plus you!

Materials
Shortened versions of forms A and B of Eysenck's Personality Inventory, scoring sheets, and a list of thirty-two words taken from Eysenck's personality types.

Procedure
The procedure should describe how the practical was carried out as clearly and concisely as possible. Although you were a subject in

this practical, you still have to write it up as if you were the researcher. For example, you might say 'Each subject was asked to write a description of their own personality ... Then they were shown a list of thirty-two words and asked to pick any which they felt applied to them ... etc'. Notice that these examples use an impersonal style and the past tense. This is the style you need to use when writing your reports.

One precaution was taken when I asked my students to carry out the practical: half the students were given form A to complete and then form B, while the other half were asked to complete form B first and were then given form A.

This procedure is known as **counterbalancing** and is often used when carrying out experiments. I will explain its use in detail in Practical 3 (page 87). In this practical, counterbalancing was used as a precaution in case answering the first inventory influenced a subject's answers to the second inventory. Counterbalancing does not of course prevent this happening, it should mean, however, that any effect that the order of presentation might have will influence both inventories equally.

Results

You will need to put your table of pooled class data in the results. Place the means and standard deviations at the bottom of the table. The descriptive statistics for males and females will need to be presented in an additional table. You could also put your personality description and the words you picked to describe your own personality in this section; alternatively you could place these in an appendix.

Whichever method you choose, remember, when you come to discuss them to refer the reader to where they can be found.

Treatment of results

The treatment of results has already been discussed in some detail. In this section say briefly why Spearman's Rho was chosen to analyse the data, and give a summary table of the results as below.

	Observed Rho	Critical Rho	Size of N	Significance Level
E scores: form A with form B				
N scores: form A with form B				

Give the decision rule (the observed value of Rho must be equal to or greater than the critical value), then state for each of your research hypotheses, whether, in the light of the statistical analyses, they can be accepted or rejected.

Discussion

This practical has focused on two issues: the reliability of the EPI, and the validity of the EPI. It will probably be easier and clearer to keep the discussion of these two issues separate, at least to start with.

Reliability

You could begin this section by describing the reliability results. Discuss the raw data, descriptive statistics and scattergrams, as well as the correlation coefficients. Compare the reliability of the E scales and N scales. Eysenck found that both scales had parallel form reliability of 0.9, or above. How do your figures compare? If they are different, can you offer any explanation as to why this might be.

One important issue to consider is the difference between statistical significance and psychometric usefulness. Take the correlation coefficient of 0.56, which I obtained for the parallel form reliability of the E scale using my students' data. The correlation coefficient was shown to be statistically significant, but by psychometric standards it shows quite poor reliability. This can be seen more clearly if we work out the percentage association between the two sets of E scores. You can work this out by taking the correlation coefficient (0.56), moving the decimal point one place to the right (5.6), and squaring this number, which produces a figure of thirty-one per cent. You can do this with any correlation coefficient.

A thirty-one per cent agreement between the two E scales does not give much support to the claim that they are equivalent measures! If such a figure were to be found in a larger sample, then serious questions would be raised about the parallel form reliability of the EPI. So, it is very important to remember that statistical results do not speak for themselves, they have to be interpreted.

Validity

In this practical the validity of the EPI is not being examined in any statistical way. You might find it interesting, however, to try and assess how closely your own personality description fits the kind of personality indicated by your EPI scores. If you have described yourself as a sociable, outgoing type of person, and you obtained a high E score, then this would lend some support to the validity of the EPI since your subjective judgement and the objective score of the test are similar. Any major discrepancies between your own description and your EPI scores could raise interesting issues for discussion. One possible explanation is that the EPI is not a valid measure of personality. Of course an alternative explanation could be that people are not very accurate in assessing their own personality! You can discuss your own reaction, as a subject to the test. For example, a number of subjects find the fixed **yes** or **no** format too restrictive (this point is taken up by Alice Heim in her book, *Intelligence and Personality* – see the references section). However, do try to be objective in your assessment and remember that it is not appropriate to draw sweeping conclusions on the basis of the results of one subject.

Conclusion

In the conclusion you should state simply whether the null hypotheses were accepted or rejected. You can make some comments on the issue of the validity of the EPI shortened version but, as there was no statistical analysis of results, I suggest you are careful and tentative in how you phrase your conclusion. You could even say something like, 'In the light of the limitations of this study no firm conclusions can be drawn concerning the validity of the EPI . . .'.

References

Write the reference section up as shown in the AEB's Notes for Guidance (appendix B).

  You can find additional useful information in the following:

Atkinson, R.L., *et al.* (1990) *Introduction to Psychology* (10th ed.),
       New York: Harcourt Brace Jovanovich.
Chapter 14 in this widely available textbook has a good discussion of different methods of assessing personality. Earlier editions of the book also contain similar material.

Dey, I., (1993) *Qualitative Data Analysis*, London: Routledge.

Heim, A. (1970) *Intelligence and Personality: Their Assessment and Relationship*. London: Harmondsworth.
This book has a chapter which gives a critical appraisal of the EPI.

Webb, E.J., *et al.* (1972) *Unobtrusive Measures: Non-Reactive Research in the Social Sciences*, Chicago: Rand McNally.

Appendices

Put all your calculations in an appendix. You could also include in this appendix your own personality description and the words you selected to describe yourself.

 As this is your first report, you have had to cover a great deal of material quite quickly. You may be feeling a little swamped by it all. This is almost inevitable given the nature and organization of the A level course. Remember, however, that you will meet a lot of the basic ideas introduced here in subsequent practicals. Since you have covered so much ground in this chapter, it would be worth your while now to look back at the objectives for this chapter. If you are uncertain about an issue work through the relevant parts of the chapter again. Make sure that you have made the notes you need to make on the methodological ideas listed as key terms in the chapter objectives. You should also have learned a great deal about the theory of personality. Tidy up the notes you have made on personality for this practical and file them with your other notes on personality.

CHAPTER SUMMARY

In working through this chapter you should have become familiar with the idea of psychometric personality testing and be able to relate this to your studies of personality in general. You have also been introduced to a classification of different kinds of quantitative data, and to the considerations made in choosing an appropriate statistical test. Don't expect to remember all this now, you will be looking at this again and again later in the book.

This chapter gave you your first opportunity to write a practical report in the format required for the AEB. It probably took you a long time. In later chapters you will write other reports, but as you become familiar with the style you should find it takes less time.

Appendices for Practical 1

Table of pooled class results for the EPI

Table 4:1

Subject	Form A		Form B	
	E Score	N Score	E Score	N Score
1 (M)	10	3	5	3
2	11	3	12	2
3	6	6	6	7
4	4	9	7	8
5	10	8	9	8
6 (M)	6	3	11	4
7	9	7	4	10
8	4	10	2	8
9	7	5	6	6
10	3	6	3	5
11 (M)	9	6	9	4
12	6	9	5	9
13	8	7	8	7
14	5	6	4	6
15				

In the above table, (M) denotes the male subjects, all the other subjects are female.

You are subject fifteen, put your scores in the appropriate places.

Using the data for subjects one to fourteen, the coefficient obtained using Spearman's Rho to correlate the E scores on form A with the E scores on form B is 0.56.

The coefficient obtained by correlating the N scores on form A with the N scores for form B is 0.87.

When you add your scores to the above table and calculate the correlation coefficients with fifteen scores your results should not be drastically different from those above. If they are check your calculations.

The EPI – form A

Instructions

Here are some questions regarding the way you behave, feel and act. In the margin there is a space for answering **yes** or **no**.

Try to decide whether yes or no represents your usual way of acting or feeling. Then put a tick in the column headed **yes** or **no** in the margin. Work quickly, and don't spend too much time over any question; we want your first reaction, not a longdrawn out thought process. The whole questionnaire shouldn't take more than a few minutes. Be sure not to omit any questions.

Start now, work quickly, and remember to answer every question. There are no right or wrong answers, and this isn't a test of intelligence or ability, but simply a measure of the way you behave.

YES   **NO**

1   Do you often long for excitement?

2   Do you often need understanding friends to cheer you up?

3   Do you stop and think things over before doing anything?

4   If you say you will do something do you always keep your promise, no matter how inconvenient it might be to do so?

5   Do your moods go up and down?

6   Would you do almost anything for a dare?

7   Do you suddenly feel shy when you want to talk to an attractive stranger?

8   Once in a while do you lose your temper and get angry?

9   Generally, do you prefer reading or meeting people?

10   Are your feelings rather easily hurt?

11   Do you occasionally have thoughts and ideas that you would not like other people to know about?

12   Do you prefer to have few but special friends?

13   Do you daydream a lot?

14   Are all your habits good and desirable ones?

Eysenck Personality Inventory (EPI) material is copyright © H. J. Eysenck and S. B. G. Eysenck and is reproduced here by permission of Hodder & Stoughton.

	YES	NO

15 Can you usually let yourself go and enjoy yourself a lot at a lively party?

16 Would you call yourself tense or highly strung?

17 Are you mostly quiet when you are with other people?

18 Do you sometimes gossip?

19 Do ideas run through your head so that you cannot sleep?

20 Do you like the kind of work that you need to pay close attention to?

21 Do you get attacks of shaking or trembling?

22 Would you always declare everything at the customs, even if you knew that you could never be found out?

23 Do you like doing things in which you have to act quickly?

24 Do you worry about awful things that might happen?

25 Have you ever been late for an appointment or work?

26 Do you like talking to people so much that you never miss a chance of talking to a stranger?

27 Are you troubled by aches and pains?

28 Of all the people you know, are there some whom you definitely do not like?

29 Would you say that you were fairly self-confident?

30 Are you easily hurt when people find fault with you or your work?

31 Can you easily get some life into a dull party?

32 Do you sometimes talk about things you know nothing about?

33 Do you worry about your health?

YES	NO	**The EPI – form B**

The same instructions apply

1   Do you like plenty of excitement and bustle around you?

2   Have you often got restless feeling that you want something but do not know what?

3   Do you usually stay in the background at parties and 'get-to-gethers'?

4   As a child, did you always do as you were told immediately and without grumbling?

5   Do you sometimes sulk?

6   Do you like mixing with people?

7   Have you often lost sleep over your worries?

8   Do you sometimes get cross?

9   Do you like working alone?

10   Have you often felt listless and tired for no good reason?

11   Do you sometimes laugh at dirty jokes?

12   Do you feel uncomfortable in anything but your everyday clothes?

13   Can you put your thoughts into words quickly?

14   Are you often 'lost in thought'?

15   Are you completely free from prejudices of any kind?

16   Do you very much like good food?

17   When you get annoyed, do you need someone friendly to talk to about it?

18   Do you sometimes boast a little?

19   Would you rather be at home on your own than go to a boring party?

	YES	**NO**

20   Do you sometimes get so restless that you cannot sit long in a chair?

21   Do you always answer a personal letter as soon as you can after you have read it?

22   Can you usually do things better by figuring them out alone than by talking to others about it?

23   Do you ever get short of breath without having done heavy work?

24   Would you rather plan things than do things?

25   Do you sometimes put off until tomorrow what you ought to do today?

26   Do you get nervous in places like lifts, trains and tunnels?

27   Do you generally think that things will sort themselves out and come right in the end somehow?

28   Do you find it hard to fall asleep at bedtime?

29   Have you sometimes told lies in your life?

30   Do you usually keep 'yourself to yourself' except with very close friends?

31   Do you like cracking jokes and telling funny stories to your friends?

32   Would you rather win than lose a game?

33   Do you often feel self-conscious when you are with superiors?

Scoring for form A of the EPI

Check through your answers and place an E by the side of any answers which match those given in the E score table overleaf; if your answer does not match that in the table write nothing. For example if you have answered **yes** to question 1, place an E beside your answer. If, however, you answered **no**, write nothing and move on to score the next question.

Eysenck Personality Inventory (EPI) material is copyright © H. J. Eysenck and S. B. G. Eysenck and is reproduced here by permission of Hodder & Stoughton.

E score table for form A

Question number	Response
1	Yes
3	No
6	Yes
9	No
12	No
15	Yes
17	No
20	No
23	Yes
26	Yes
29	Yes
31	Yes

Count up the number of Es that you have and this gives you your E scale score for form A of the EPI.

Now score the N scale in the same way as the E score, but this time put an N next to any question which matches those in the N score table below.

N score table for form A

Question number	Response
2	Yes
5	Yes
7	Yes
10	Yes
13	Yes
16	Yes
19	Yes
21	Yes
24	Yes
27	Yes
30	Yes
33	Yes

Again, count the number of Ns you have and this gives you your N scale score for form A of the EPI.

Scoring for form B of the EPI

Obtain your E and N scale scores for form B in the same way as for form A, but use the tables below.

E score table for form B

Question number	Response
1	Yes
3	No
6	Yes
9	No
13	Yes
16	Yes
19	No
22	No
24	No
27	Yes
30	No
31	Yes

Add up the number of Es you have obtained to get your E scale score for form B of the EPI.

N score table for form B

Question number	Response
2	Yes
5	Yes
7	Yes
10	Yes
12	Yes
14	Yes
17	Yes
20	Yes
23	Yes
26	Yes
28	Yes
32	Yes

Add up the number of Ns you have obtained to get your N scale score for form B of the EPI.

The calculation of Spearman's Rho

To show you how to calculate Spearman's Rho (r_s), I have done the calculations using the extroversion scores on form A and the extroversion scores on form B (EA and EB) for the fourteen subjects in the pooled data. Since there are fifteen subjects in your data set, the numbers in your calculations will be slightly different.

Table 4. 2

Subject	Form A		Form B		d	d^2
	E Score	Rank	E Score	Rank		
1 (M)	10	12.5	5	5.5	7.0	49.0
2	11	14.0	12	14.0	0.0	0.0
3	6	6.0	6	7.5	−1.5	2.25
4	4	2.5	7	9.0	−6.5	42.25
5	10	12.5	9	11.5	1.0	1.0
6 (M)	6	6.0	11	13.0	−7.0	49.0
7	9	10.5	4	3.5	7.0	49.0
8	4	2.5	2	1.0	1.5	2.25
9	7	8.0	6	7.5	0.5	0.25
10	3	1.0	3	2.0	−1.0	1.0
11 (M)	9	10.5	9	11.5	−1.0	1.0
12	6	6.0	5	5.5	0.5	0.25
13	8	9.0	8	10.0	−1.0	1.0
14	5	4.0	4	3.5	0.5	0.25
					Σd^2 =	198.50

- **step 1** – rank each variable separately giving a rank of 1 to the lowest score – see Table 4.2. See the marginal note on how to deal with tied scores
- **step 2** – find the difference for each pair of ranks by taking the rank of the second variable from the rank of the first. See Table 4.2 column *d*

- **step 3** – square the differences found in step 2. See Table 4.2 column d^2
- **step 4** – sum (add up) the d^2s to give you Σd^2 – see Table 4.2
- **step 5** – let N = the number of pairs of scores. In this case $N = 14$
- **step 6** – insert the results of steps 4 and 5 into the formula below:

$$r_s = 1 - \frac{6\Sigma d^2}{N(N^2 - 1)}$$

$$r_s = 1 - \frac{6 \times 198.5}{14(14^2 - 1)}$$

$$r_s = 1 - \frac{1191}{14(196 - 1)}$$

$$r_s = 1 - \frac{1191}{2730}$$

$$r_s = 1 - 0.436 \text{ (correct to 3 decimal places)}$$

$$r_s = 0.56$$

- **step 7** – look up the value of rho in the critical values table in appendix D at the back of the book. This step is dealt with in the body of the chapter.

► **Ties in ranking**

Sometimes when ranking a set of scores, you have 2 or more scores with the same value. If this happens you have to average the ranks that the scores would have received had they been different. If you look at the scores for E on form A you can see the lowest score is 3, there are no other scores of 3 so this gets a rank of 1. However the next lowest score is 4 and there are 2 scores with this value. This means that ranks 2 and 3 need to be used. To share out these 2 ranks equally the average of the 2 ranks (2.5) is given to each of the scores. If there were three scores of the same value (score 6) then you give each score the average of the 3 ranks that would have been used if the scores were different (a rank of 6 has been given, the average of ranks 5, 6 and 7).

A survey into cognitive dissonance in smokers: the second practical

► Practical 2.

► This chapter contains materials you will need for the practical. Look to the end of the chapter to find them. They are:

● pooled data for Practical 2
● questionnaire for Practical 2
● calculations for Chi-square.

Chapter objectives

By the end of this chapter you should:

▌ have completed your second practical report

▌ have carried out a small scale survey

▌ have an understanding of Festinger's theory of cognitive dissonance

▌ be able to carry out a Chi-squared analysis

▌ know and be able to use the following terms key terms: hypothetico–deductive method, operational definition, questionnaire, sampling – quota and random.

INTRODUCTION

The aim of Practical 2 is to give you experience of one of the most frequently used methods of gathering data in the social sciences – the **survey**. Survey data can be collected, by either asking subjects to complete a questionnaire, or by interviewers asking subjects questions and recording their answers. In this practical you will be the interviewer. This method has often been used in social psychology and particularly in the study of beliefs, attitudes and attitude change. This practical will also introduce you to the **hypothetico-deductive method**; an idea fundamental to all scientific research – see boxed inset below.

► Survey method.

Once you have carried out the practical and gathered some data, you will use a number of simple descriptive statistics to summarize and display the data. You will also apply an inferential statistical test to the data.

► Before you proceed to the practical read the contents of the two boxed insets.

The hypothetico-deductive method

Psychologists put forward theories in an attempt to explain human behaviour; but how do we know whether we can trust these theories? The hypothetico-deductive method is a way of testing scientific theories. It involves deducing an hypothesis from a theory – a prediction that something will occur if the theory is valid – and then collecting evidence to test the hypothesis. For example, in this practical we are testing an hypothesis derived from cognitive dissonance theory. That is that smokers are more likely than non-smokers to deny, or play down, the health risks of smoking cigarettes. The aim of this practical is to gather evidence to test this hypothesis. If the results are as predicted this supports the theory; if the results are not as predicted then the theory may need to be modified or abandoned. This three stage process of theory, hypothesis, testing, is the basis of the hypothetico-deductive method.

► Attitudes are usually defined as, 'a relatively enduring organization of beliefs around an object or situation predisposing one to act in some preferential manner'. Rokeach (1965).

► Cognitions – used by Festinger to refer to thoughts, beliefs, attitudes, and also behaviours which a person is aware of.

Cognitive dissonance – a theory of attitude change

Social psychologists are interested in how people's **attitudes** are formed and change. One influential theory of attitude change is **cognitive dissonance** proposed by Festinger (1957). This theory suggests that when a person has two **cognitions** (sets of ideas) that are inconsistent they are likely to experience dissonance; a state of 'psychological discomfort or tension'. As dissonance is experienced as a negative drive state, a person is motivated to reduce or eliminate it.

Smoking is a behaviour which has frequently been used to illustrate the concept of dissonance. Most people, even smokers, wish to remain in good health; yet there is considerable evidence, from medical research, that smoking cigarettes seriously damages health. According to Festinger's theory people who smoke cigarettes are likely to experience dissonance. One way of removing this dissonance would be to give up smoking, but this can be difficult – some people enjoy smoking and do not wish to stop. Another way that smokers have of reducing dissonance is to deny, or at least to play down, the evidence that there are serious health risks attached to their habit. Festinger (1957) quotes a survey which found that twenty-nine per cent of non-smokers, twenty per cent of light smokers, but only seven per cent of heavy smokers believed that a link had been established between smoking and lung cancer.

Formulating an hypothesis

In this practical, you are going to be a member of a research team which is interested in testing the following hypothesis, derived from Festinger's theory of cognitive dissonance:

► The research hypothesis for testing using a survey technique.

► The null hypothesis will be that any differences recorded between smokers and non-smokers are merely due to chance.

Smokers are more likely than non-smokers to view smoking as having low health risks attached to it.

Non-smokers, on the other hand, are more likely to view the health risks as high. So how could we test such an hypothesis? The most direct way would be to question a group of smokers and a group of non-smokers about what they consider to be the health risks associated with smoking. Then examine the results to see if, as dissonance theory predicts, there is a difference in the beliefs of smokers and non-smokers about the risks.

This practical might seem very simple and straightforward to carry out but before you proceed there are a number of things you need to give careful consideration to. Firstly, who you are going to question? Secondly, exactly what questions are you going to ask them? I have made these decisions for you. The questions are in the questionnaire at the end of the chapter. The instructions for selecting people are in the text. However in order to understand how and why I made these decisions you will need to read the boxed insets headed: operational definitions (below); populations and samples; methods of sampling (page 61).

These contain information you need to know when you come to write up the practical.

► Who are you going to question?

Operational definitions

Before a psychologist can carry out research he/she must decide how to measure the variables that are to be studied. If we take this practical as an example then the first issue is to identify whether people are smokers or non-smokers. This might seem a fairly easy task, but how exactly do we define smoking? Do we include as smokers people who used to smoke but have now given up? Do we include someone who smokes occasionally? What people smoke might also be a complication. We can resolve the last issue by confining ourselves to the smoking of tobacco cigarettes.

On the question of classifying people as smokers or non-smokers, one major problem is that there is considerable variation in the quantity and frequency with which people smoke. Some people smoke a lot of cigarettes regularly, while other people smoke only a few cigarettes now and again. Do we define someone who only smokes a couple of cigarettes occasionally as a smoker? I hope that you are beginning to see that trying to **operationally define** smokers and non-smokers is not quite as simple as it first appeared. I have tried to get round some of the other problems by leaving it to the subjects themselves to define whether they are smokers or non-smokers. This relies on the subject's self-image, their view of themselves, and it can be argued, that how people define themselves might be more important in terms of their behaviour and beliefs than any judgement the researcher makes. You will have noticed that I have not tried to divide people into light smokers, heavy smokers, etc., but this is not to say how much people smoke will not affect their beliefs and the possible levels of dissonance they experience: common sense would suggest that it would. But again, to decide on some figure and say people who smoke more than this amount a day are heavy smokers would be rather arbitrary; we might define someone who smoked twenty cigarettes a day as a heavy smoker but they might consider themselves to be a light smoker!

I hope you can now see how important it is to formulate clear and precise operational definitions; without these the results of research may lack validity.

CARRYING OUT THE PRACTICAL

Ethical considerations

In Practical 1 you acted as a subject yourself, but in this practical you are going to ask other people to be subjects. The British Psychological Society has issued a document entitled, 'Ethical principles for conducting research with human participants', which is reprinted in appendix C.

Please read this appendix carefully before asking anyone to be a subject in your practical.

Selecting subjects

In this practical you will be testing a research hypothesis which relates to questions 1–4 of the questionnaire shown at the end of the chapter on page 74. I have emboldened the research hypothesis on page 58. Note that on the questionnaire, I have deliberately not numbered the opening question about whether or not the person smokes. This is because you may not actually need to ask this question; if you see someone smoking the question will be redundant. Also this numbering system will make it easier to relate the hypothesis to tables and charts that you will be required to construct.

To carry out this practical you need to interview eight people chosen on a **quota sample** (see boxed inset on page 62) basis using the questionnaire at the end of the chapter. The subjects should be picked by you but fit the following pattern:

- 1 male smoker who is 40 years of age or over
- 1 male smoker who is under 40 years of age
- 1 male non-smoker who is 40 years of age or over
- 1 male non-smoker who is under 40 years of age
- 1 female smoker who is 40 years of age or over
- 1 female smoker who is under 40 years of age
- 1 female non-smoker who is 40 years of age or over
- 1 female non-smoker who is under 40 years of age.

It is better to use people who you do not know if possible. If you approach people politely, explain that you are carrying out a survey on attitudes to smoking and that you have only four or five short questions you would like to ask them, I am sure you will have no problem finding eight willing subjects. People are **not** obliged to answer your questions, so if anyone appears reluctant or unwilling, do not try to persuade them, simply try someone else. (This is one advantage that a quota sampling method has over random sampling – see boxed inset overleaf). You will notice that I have included a question about age in the questionnaire, but it may not be necessary to ask this question. If you feel confident, when picking a person, that they are forty or over, or under forty, then just fill the answer box in yourself.

Finally, you might find it easier if you use a separate copy of the questionnaire for each subject you interview. If you have access to a photocopier you can make eight copies.

You can carry out the data gathering part of the practical now.

Populations and samples

In statistics the term **population** does not always apply to a group of people. It could refer to individuals, families, white rats, scores on a personality test or people's beliefs about the health risks of smoking. When carrying out research the term population refers to **all** the people, cases or situations that the psychologist wishes his hypothesis to apply to. Thus if I stated a hypothesis about the beliefs on the health risks of smoking of students at a college, the population would be the beliefs of all the students attending that college. However, if my hypothesis was broader and simply referred to the beliefs of students then my population would be **all** students (obviously the term 'student' would need to be operationally defined).

I am sure you can appreciate there are many reasons why it is rarely possible for psychologists to carry out research on whole populations; they are usually much too large. However, researchers want to go beyond what they actually study. They wish to generalize from the sample to the population. How can they do this? One approach is carefully to select a sample in an attempt to ensure that it contains a representative cross-section of the population. If the sample is representative then the researcher will have confidence in generalizing the results back to the population. For the methods of selecting a sample see the boxed inset on methods of sampling below.

Methods of sampling

There are a variety of methods for obtaining a sample but the four most common are:

1 **Simple random sampling** – this is where each member of the population has an equal chance of being selected for the final sample. To ensure true randomness the method of selection must be independent of human judgement. This is usually achieved by either:
- the lottery method – each member of the population is represented by a token, the tokens are placed in a container and

► Be careful – lists are rarely in a random order!

thoroughly mixed, and a sample of the required size is then selected. In this way it is simply chance that determines who is selected and who is not

- **random numbers** – computers can be programmed to generate numbers at random and statistics books often contain tables of random numbers. To use random number tables the population must first be numbered 1 to N. Having decided how large the sample is to be the researcher then selects the required numbers from the random number tables in any systematic and convenient way. The people/units corresponding to these numbers become the sample.

2 **Systematic sampling** – where existing lists are used a common and convenient method of sampling involves selecting, for example, every tenth name from the list. Strictly speaking this method is not random because each member of the population does not have an equal chance of being selected for the sample. If every tenth name is used, and your name is second, you have no chance of being selected. However, if a systematic sample is selected from a list which is itself arranged more or less at random, or when the method of organization is not related to the topic of the research, then it is called a **quasi-random sample**. Such a sample is similar to a simple random sample.

3 **Stratified random sampling** – this method involves dividing the population into strata first; then taking random samples, of the required size, from each stratum. For example, if a researcher is interested in how sex differences affect beliefs about the health risks of smoking they might want a random sample of fifty men and fifty women. A simple random sample of 100 adults from the general population would not guarantee an equal number of men and women. However, this can be ensured by dividing the population up into men and women, and then selecting a simple random sample of the required size from the men and for the women. A researcher can therefore use stratified sampling to ensure that different strata in the population (sexes, ages, IQs, etc.) are represented in the correct proportions in the sample. Or the researcher can manipulate the proportions to suit their research needs; a researcher might want an equal number of males and females in their sample even if there were more females than males in the general population.

4 **Quota sampling** – this is a controversial sampling technique commonly used by commercial market researchers but rarely used in scientific study. Its aim is to produce a representative sample quickly and cheaply. I will use a simple example to illustrate. If you were interested in how sex differences affect the choice of A level subjects among students at a particular college you might want to interview a sample of: twenty males studying two science subjects, twenty females studying two science subjects, twenty males studying two arts subjects and twenty females studying two arts subjects. How would you select such

a sample? One method would be some form of stratified sampling. However, this would probably involve obtaining the names of all the A level students at the college. Then having determined who was in the sample you would have to find those particular named individuals.

An alternative would be for you to approach students – say in the library or coffee bar – and enquire if they were studying A levels and if so which ones. Students with the relevant characteristics would be interviewed; others would not. You could proceed in this manner until you have interviewed your **quota** of students with the appropriate characteristics. This technique is not random because the final decision about who is selected for interview rests with the interviewer; it is not chance. You can see from this example that there are advantages, in terms of time and convenience, in quota sampling. There are, however, disadvantages in terms of a potential loss of accuracy and the inability to apply certain statistics. Such issues are beyond the scope of this book but I have included some references which give a more detailed discussion of sampling procedures and their advantages and disadvantages at the end of this chapter.

► Some textbooks refer to random sampling as probability sampling.

The sample for the practical

I have asked you to use a quota sample. In this practical we are interested in comparing the beliefs of smokers and non–smokers about the health risks of smoking. A representative sample of the adult population would therefore be ideal. However, on the basis of recent statistics you are only likely to find about a third of such a sample are smokers. As we want to compare the views of smokers and non-smokers it would be useful if our sample was fifty per cent smokers and fifty per cent non-smokers. This could be obtained by using a stratified random sample (explained in the boxed inset on sampling). However, drawing a random sample, particularly of the general population, can be an expensive and time-consuming business. With random samples it is usual to have named individuals to interview. Problems can arise if people are out when the interviewer calls, or refuse to take part. The great advantage of quota sampling is that it is a quick and cheap method – this is why it is so often used in market research. The idea behind quota sampling is that rather than interviewing named individuals, the interviewer has to interview a quota, or set number, of people with certain characteristics. The quota is based upon prior knowledge about the proportion of people in the population with the characteristics that are of interest to the researcher. An example might make this idea clearer. Let us say that as researchers, we want a sample that reflects the actual proportions in the general population of this country with respect to sex and class differences.

The most recent census might tell us that the population is approximately fifty per cent male and fifty per cent female and that forty per cent of people classify themselves as middle class and

sixty per cent as working class. (I have made these figures up for the purpose of this example.) If there was only the time and resources to interview 100 people, to ensure the sample matched the proportions for sex and class in the population, then the following quotas of people would need to be interviewed:

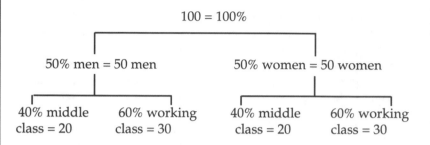

$$100 = 100\%$$

50% men = 50 men   50% women = 50 women

40% middle class = 20   60% working class = 30   40% middle class = 20   60% working class = 30

Analysing the data from your practical

Having gathered the responses from your eight subjects, the first thing that you need to do is to construct the tables shown below and fill in the appropriate numbers.

Table 5.1
Does smoking seriously damage people's health? (Q1)

	Yes	No	Total
Smokers	A	B	
Non-smokers	C	D	
Total			

To fill in this table you need to count how many of the smokers you interviewed said **yes** there are serious adverse health consequences from smoking. Put this number in box A. Then count the number of smokers you interviewed who said **no** to this question, put this number in box B. (If you have interviewed eight smokers then check that A + B = 8). Complete the tables below in the same way.

Table 5.2
Risks of developing lung cancer (Q2)

	Low risk	High risk	Total
Smokers			
Non-smokers			
Total			

Table 5.3
Risks of developing heart disease (Q3)

	Low risk	High risk	Total
Smokers			
Non-smokers			
Total			

	Yes	No	Total
Smokers			
Non-smokers			
Total			

Table 5.4
Harmful effects on the health of non-smokers (Q4)

The above results represent your data and the tables will need to be put in the **results** section of your practical report, (but I will explain how you write the report in detail later). As you are likely to be working on your own I only asked you to interview a small number of subjects. However I have included data gathered by some of my students using the same questionnaire and the same quota sampling procedure. You can therefore add your data to that shown in tables A to D at the end of the chapter and call it **pooled class data**.

Now that you have a full set of data (104 subjects in total; some in your own tables, some in the pooled data) you need to know how it relates to the research hypothesis. The first thing to do is simply to look carefully at the tables and see whether the data goes in the directions our research hypothesis predicts. For example, we are predicting that because of cognitive dissonance, smokers will tend to play down the adverse health consequences of smoking. Non-smokers, on the other hand, should not experience dissonance and thus are more likely to accept that smoking does have serious adverse health consequences.

► Eye-balling the data.

We would therefore expect the number in cell A of Table 5.1 to be smaller than the number in cell C, i.e. more non-smokers than smokers should agree that there are serious adverse health consequences from smoking. Similarly, the number in cell B should be larger than that in cell D, i.e. more smokers than non-smokers should say that there are no serious adverse health consequences from smoking.

Examine the tables for your subjects and the tables for the class results and see if this is the case.

 Given what you now know about cognitive dissonance, work out which cells you would expect to have the larger and which the smaller scores for Tables 5.2, 5.3 and 5.4. Does this accord with what the data actually shows?

Analysing the data statistically

What you have been dealing with so far is referred to as the **raw data**. This is the data directly generated from the research project. It has not been subjected to any kind of statistical analysis. Now we will begin the process of statistical analysis.

You have already examined the tables of data to see if the numbers in the various cells are in the direction that cognitive dissonance theory would predict, for example, more smokers than non-smokers saying **no** to the question about serious adverse health

► You will find it useful to re-read the sections in Chapter 2 on descriptive and inferential statistics (page 11). The example given in these sections is based upon this practical.

consequences from smoking. But the crucial question is, how do we decide whether the results support our **research hypothesis**? Could the results we have obtained be simply due to chance (the **null hypothesis**)? To help them answer this question, psychologists use inferential statistics. The mathematics of inferential statistics can be quite complex and is not of interest to most psychologists. However, psychologists do need to know how to select an appropriate inferential statistical test, apply it to their data and interpret the results. These are important skills which you will acquire as you carry out and analyse the data of your practicals.

Now the time has come to 'get your feet wet' and statistically analyse the data from your practical. If you have not already done so, fill the numbers in the appropriate cells for Tables 5.1 through to 5.4. Construct four identical Tables 5.5 to 5.8 for the class results in the following way:

Table 5.5: add scores for Table 5.1 to Table A
Table 5.6: add scores for Table 5.2 to Table B
Table 5.7: add scores for Table 5.3 to Table C
Table 5.8: add scores for Table 5.4 to Table D

Applying an appropriate statistical test to the data

As a psychologist you do need to learn how to select the appropriate statistical test to analyse the data from your research. Choosing an appropriate test involves making a number of decisions which are shown in Figure 4.2 on page 36 and discussed in the inset called 'Choosing a Test'.

If you look at Figure 4.2 you will see that:

- **decision number 1** concerns whether the hypothesis is predicting a difference or a correlation. In this practical guided by dissonance theory, we are predicting that there will be a **difference** in the responses of smokers and non-smokers to the questions we are asking them about the effects of smoking on health. You therefore need to follow the difference side of Figure 4.2
- **decision number 2** refers to the number of samples of scores that you have. If you look at Figure 4.2 you will see that there are some statistical tests for two samples of scores and different ones for k-samples (more than two sets of scores). In this practical there are two sets of scores; one for smokers and one for non-smokers.
- **decision number 3** concerns whether your research used has a related or unrelated design. I will explain in some detail the difference between these two designs in Practical 3, when you carry out a true experiment. In this practical you do not have an independent variable (a variable the researcher directly manipulates). Therefore it is not a true experiment.

► See 'Correlation and Experimentation' in Chapter 2 (pages 13–15).

In a related design, each subject appears in the different conditions of the research (or matched pairs of subjects are used). In an unrelated design, subjects only appear in one of the research conditions. In this practical, the two conditions are whether people are smokers or non-smokers. As each subject can only be a smoker **or** a non-smoker, they can only be in one of the two conditions. So this practical has an unrelated design.

- **decision number 4** concerns whether to use a parametric test or a non-parametric test. A key factor here is the level of the data obtained. There are four levels of measurement: nominal, ordinal, interval and ratio. Data needs to be at the interval or ratio level before a parametric test can be used. At this point you might like to quickly re-read the boxed insets on pages 35 and 37 in Chapter 4 but it is not essential that you do so.

► See 'Parametric and non-parametric tests' and 'Levels or scales of measurement' in Chapter 4 (page 37).

Where you are counting the frequency with which responses fall into named categories, such as smokers/non-smokers, then the data is considered to be nominal. There are non-parametric statistical tests specifically designed for use with such data. If you consult Figure 4.2 again you will see that the appropriate statistical test is Chi-square.

Remember that the reason for applying an inferential test like Chi-square to your data, is to establish whether or not the difference in responses for smokers and non-smokers is likely to have occurred by chance. You have four research tables, one for each question one, two, three and four. Therefore you need to perform the Chi-square test separately to the data in your Tables 5.5, 5.6, 5.7 and 5.8.

► You might find it helpful at this point to quickly re-read the section on inferential statistics in Chapter 2 (page 11).

Do the calculations now using the instructions given at the end of the chapter.

► Step by step instructions on how to calculate Chi-square are given at the end of the chapter (page 75).

Using the Chi-square tables

Having applied the Chi-square test to your data, you will have four Chi-square values, one for each of your questions. You have to compare your calculated values to the appropriate critical value, to be found in appendix D. To use this table you need to know how many **degrees of freedom (df)** your design has. To find this, apply the following formula:

► Degrees of freedom.

(number of rows minus one) × (number of columns minus one).

In your practical you have two rows (smokers and non-smokers) and two columns (a response of **Yes** or **No**, for questions one and four, responses of **Low** or **High** for questions two, three and five.) The number of degrees of freedom is therefore one for each of your questions.

Next you need to know whether your hypotheses are one or two tailed. You may remember this has to do with whether or not you are predicting the **direction** of difference beforehand, or just saying there will be a difference. In this practical, on the basis of dissonance theory, we are predicting that the proportion of smokers

► One and two-tailed hypotheses. See Chapter 2 page 9. You might like to re-read this now.

► Level of significance.

who replied **yes** to question one of the questionnaire will be lower than the proportion of non-smokers saying **yes**.

You are also expecting a higher proportion of smokers than non-smokers to respond with a **no** to question one. Therefore we are not just saying that there will be a difference in the responses of smokers and non-smokers, but we are predicting the direction these differences will take. So we are dealing with a one-tailed hypothesis.

Finally, to use the table of critical values in appendix D, a level of significance must be chosen. The convention is to start with a significance level of 0.05 (5 in 100). If a result is not significant at this level, then that is the end of the matter. You have to accept the null hypothesis; that the results are quite likely to have occurred by chance. If however, the results are found to be significant at the 0.05 level then you can proceed to see if they reach a higher level of significance, such as 0.01 (1 in 100).

Armed with this knowledge we can consult appendix D. The critical value shown for one degree of freedom, for a one-tailed hypothesis, at the minimum significance level of 0.05 is 2.71.

Level of significance for a one-tailed test

	0.10	0.05	0.025	0.01	0.005	0.0005
df 1	1.64	2.71	3.84	5.41	6.64	10.83

This is where you finally find out whether your results are statistically significant or not! If the values you have calculated by applying Chi-square to your data are equal to or greater than 2.71, then your results are statistically significant at the 0.05 level. This means that the probability of your results occurring by chance are less than 5 per cent, or 5 in 100 times. Or put another way, if you carried out the same procedures 100 times then these results might come up by chance five times. This is often written $p < 0.05$. This is usually considered sufficiently unlikely that you can reject the null hypothesis (that the results occurred by chance) and accept the research hypothesis. If you look at the critical values table shown above, you will see (reading from left to right) other critical values for more stringent levels of significance. Check to see if any of your calculated values are equal to or exceed these critical values. Remember to stay on the line for 1 df, and use the one-tailed significance levels. Identify the smallest level of significance for each of your calculated values.

For example, if you had calculated a Chi-square value of 7. 58, this exceeds the critical value of 6.64 at the 0.005 level of significance. However it is less than the critical value of 10.83 needed for the 0.0005 level of significance. The result can therefore be said to be statistically significant at the 0.005 (1 in 200 or $p < 0.005$) level but it is not significant at the extreme 0.0005 (1 in 2000) level.

► Significance levels become smaller as you move from left to right across the table.

WRITING UP YOUR PRACTICAL REPORT

Title
Something similar to that at the beginning of the chapter would be suitable.

Abstract
Remember this should be relatively short, approximately 100 words, and contain:

- a brief summary of your aims: your hypothesis
- the method and sample of subjects used
- the statistical test(s) that were applied to the data and whether they were found to be statistically significant or not
- conclusions drawn from the research.

Introduction
In this section of the report you need to introduce the reader to the topic area of your research and relevant psychological theories and research. It is helpful to think of the introduction as forming a funnel in which you start in broad, general terms and then focus more narrowly on the particular hypothesis you wish to test.

In the case of this practical, the introduction could be structured as follows:

► You will need to refer to a Psychology textbook to write this part of your report.

- briefly outline what attitudes are and the relationship between beliefs and behaviour
- introduce the notion of attitude change and different theories of attitude change
- explain what the consistency theories of attitude change are
- outline Festinger's theory of cognitive dissonance and give some examples of how it might operate in the case of smoking
- Festinger (1957) himself quotes a survey carried out in the USA which found that twenty-nine per cent of non-smokers, twenty per cent of light smokers but only seven per cent of heavy smokers believed that there was a link between smoking and lung cancer. This leads into the aim of this practical which is to investigate Festinger's theory by asking smokers and non-smokers about their beliefs on the health risks associated with smoking cigarettes
- the introductory section should end with a formal statement of the research and null hypothesis. It is clearer and makes marking easier if you use subheadings e.g.:

Research hypothesis
Smokers are more likely than non-smokers to view smoking as having low health risks attached to it.

Note: The above hypothesis states not only that there will be a difference in the beliefs of smokers and non-smokers but also the direction of the expected difference. Hence the hypothesis is one tailed.

Null hypothesis
Any difference in the beliefs of smokers and non-smokers on the health risks associated with smoking cigarettes are due to chance.

Method

In this section you need to explain to the reader how your practical was carried out. The golden rule is that you should write concisely but in enough detail so that the reader could carry out the practical exactly as you did. It will help you and the reader if you divide this section as follows: design, subjects, materials and procedure.

Design
This practical used a survey design with structured interviewing.

Subjects
Here you can explain the quota sampling procedure used. Say how many subjects you interviewed and that this data was pooled with data collected by twelve other researchers (these were my students, as I explained earlier).

Materials
Briefly explain the structure of the questionnaire, place a copy of the questionnaire in an appendix and refer your reader to it, e.g. 'a copy of the questionnaire can be found in appendix A'.

▶ Do not copy this into your own report. Use your own words.

Procedure
Explain how you obtained your subjects and what you said to them. For example you might say something like: 'The interviews took place in a shopping centre. The researcher approached people who appeared to meet the criteria of the quota sample and asked them if they would be prepared to take part in a small research project and answer a few questions about smoking and health. Those who agreed to take part were read the five questions and their replies were carefully recorded. Each subject who participated was thanked for their time and cooperation'.

Note that you do not write about the results or statistics in the method section but rather you explain how the data was obtained.

Results

In this section you need to summarize the data you have collected. Where there are large amounts of raw data these would normally be placed in an appendix, however, as you will be dealing with fairly small samples it is both reasonable and helpful to put tables of raw data in this section.

For this practical you can put the tables of your own subjects' responses and the pooled class data. These have been referred to earlier as Tables 5.1 to 5.8.

Treatment of results

In this section you need to explain briefly what kind of statistical analysis has been applied to the raw data and what the outcome was.

An explanation of why the Chi-square test was applied to the data is needed. You might say for example, 'As the design used was an independent design and the level of data was nominal, Chi-square was judged to be an appropriate test to use'. Then give a summary of the principal statistical findings. I think the clearest way to do this is in the form of a table as below:

Results of Chi-square analysis

	Calculated value	Observed value	Degrees of freedom	Significance level
Q1				
Q2				
Q3				
Q4				

Such a table should be followed by the decision rule which, in the case of Chi-square, is that the calculated value must be equal to, or greater than, the critical value to be statistically significant.

You can then state for each of your research questions whether, in the light of the statistical analyses, they can be accepted or rejected.

Remember, if a result is statistically significant, you are rejecting the null hypothesis i.e. saying that it is unlikely that the results have occurred by chance. Therefore you can accept the research hypothesis as a more plausible explanation of your results. However, it is very important for you to understand that even if a result is found to be highly statistically significant, this does not demonstrate unequivocally that the result did not occur by chance. Only that it was unlikely to have occurred by chance. Statistics deal with probabilities not certainties! This is why it is not appropriate to use the term **proved** when discussing the results of research.

NB you do not include the actual calculations here but in an appendix.

Discussion

As pointed out in Practical 1 this is an extremely important section of your report (see the 'AEB Marking Scheme for Coursework' in appendix B).

You should start this section by giving a detailed account of your results. Describe the pattern of your own subjects' results and the class data (pooled results). Are they similar or different? Refer to the tables; does the data support your research hypothesis?

Do not base your discussion on statistical analysis alone. This may indicate a statistically significant result but leave a number of interesting questions unresolved. For example, if you look at the results to question 1 in A, you will see that although more smokers than non-smokers replied **no**, as predicted by the research hypothesis, the majority of smokers replied '**yes**: smoking does seriously damage people's health'. Is this what would be expected on the basis of cognitive dissonance theory? Large numbers of smokers accepting that smoking does seriously damage people's health would seem to pose a problem for dissonance theory. Eiser (1978) has claimed that smokers who admit the health hazards of their behaviour may yet be reducing dissonance by other means. They may, for example, say, 'I am an addict, I know it adversely affects my health, but I cannot help it, there is nothing I can do about it', or, 'smoking may be bad for me but everyone dies of something and I know many smokers who have lived to a ripe old age'. If this were the case, what additional information would you need to obtain from your sample of smokers to investigate Eiser's claim?

An important limitation of cognitive dissonance theory is that dissonance itself cannot be measured directly. In this study you have measured the beliefs of smokers and non–smokers, not their experience of cognitive dissonance. A difference in beliefs about the health risks of smoking is used as the basis for inferring that smokers experience cognitive dissonance. However, this does not establish whether dissonance actually caused the difference in beliefs (I am assuming that you have found a statistically significant difference). You must therefore exercise caution in your interpretation of the results.

Describe and discuss the results for each of the research questions separately and in as much detail as possible. Compare your results with those of previous research and try to account for any differences.

Suggest any improvements or changes you would like to make. Acknowledging limitations in the design and implementation of your practical is a strength rather than a weakness.

Conclusion

In this section you simply say whether your research hypothesis has been accepted or rejected.

References

Remember that you should give a full reference to any research or researcher you have included in any part of your report. See the AEB 'Notes to be Issued to Candidates' (appendix B) on how to present your references.

Appendices

As usual, put all your calculations in an appendix. You need to show how the calculated values of Chi-square were obtained. It would also be appropriate to put a copy of the questionnaire in an appendix. Basically anything that it is important for the reader to see but would clutter the report itself should be placed in an appendix. In the report clearly indicate to the reader when additional material is in an appendix for example: 'a copy of the questionnaire is in appendix A'.

Again see the AEB 'Notes to be Issued to Candidates' for further guidance.

Now look back over your work. Make sure you have made the notes you need on the methodological ideas and statistical terms in this chapter. What have you learned about attitudes, cognition and cognitive change? Make sure you file your notes on these topics appropriately.

CHAPTER SUMMARY

In this chapter you have conducted a practical activity using a survey technique, with a questionnaire and a quota sample. You have analysed the results, first by eye and then by applying a non-parametric statistical test called Chi-square. You should have written up the results in the format required for Psychology practicals. I suggest you now look back over the chapter and over your research report and note down for yourself anything you remain unclear about. Try using this book and the reading given below to sort yourself out, and if that fails ask for advice from your tutor.

Further reading: Chapter 5

Aronson, E., (1984) *Social Animal*, W.H. Freeman.
    I suggest that you read Chapter 4 on Self-Justification.

Atkinson, R.L., *et al.* (1990) *Introduction to Psychology* (10th ed.), New York: Harcourt, Brace Jovanovich.

Moser, C.A. and Kalton, G., (1971) *Survey Methods in Social Investigation* (2nd ed.), Gower.
    This has a detailed description of sampling techniques.

Rokeach, M., (1965) *The Nature of Attitudes*. In Sills, D.L. (ed.), *International Encyclopedia of the Social Sciences*, New York: Macmillan Co. and the Free Press.

Wheldall, K., (1975) *Social Behaviour*, Methuen.
    Chapter 4 is a good introduction to the topics of **attitudes** and **prejudice**.

Appendices for Practical 2

Pooled Class Data

Table A
Does smoking seriously damage people's health? (Q1)

	Yes	No	Total
Smokers	35 (A)	13(B)	48
Non-smokers	46 (C)	2 (D)	48
Total	81	15	96

Table B
Risks of developing lung cancer (Q2)

	High risk	Low risk	Total
Smokers	30 (A)	18 (B)	48
Non-smokers	43 (C)	5 (D)	48
Total	73	23	96

Table C
Risks of developing heart disease (Q3)

	High risk	Low risk	Total
Smokers	14 (A)	34 (B)	48
Non-smokers	40 (C)	8 (D)	48
Total	54	42	96

Table D
Harmful effects on the health of non-smokers (Q4)

	Yes	No	Total
Smokers	16 (A)	32 (B)	48
Non-smokers	40 (C)	8 (D)	48
Total	56	40	96

The questionnaire for the practical

SURVEY ON SMOKING

Circle the appropriate response:

Male	Female
Over 40	Under 40

Determine whether the subject smokes or not by observation or ask:

Do you smoke cigarettes?

YES   NO

Question 1 Do you think that smoking cigarettes seriously damages people's health?

YES   NO

Question 2 Do you think that there is a high or low risk of developing lung cancer as a direct result of smoking cigarettes?

HIGH   LOW

Question 3 Do you think that there is a high or low risk of developing heart disease as a direct result of smoking cigarettes?

HIGH   LOW

Question 4 Do you think that the health of non-smokers can be damaged by breathing cigarette smoke?

YES   NO

The calculation of Chi-square

I will outline the general procedure for calculating Chi-square and then demonstrate by using the pooled class results for question 1 of the questionnaire.

When calculating χ^2 (Chi-square) the raw data is referred to as the **observed frequencies** and the cells in each table are labelled A, B, C and D as below.

- **step 1** – calculate an **expected frequency** for each cell using the formula:

$$\frac{R \times C}{G}$$

Where: R is a row total
       C is a column total
       G is the grand total

The observed frequencies are represented by O and the expected frequencies by E

- **step 2** – using the formula below:

$$\chi^2 = \frac{([O\text{-}E] - 0.5)^2}{E}$$

For cell A:
1 Subtract E from O.
2 Ignore any negative signs which result from taking E from O
3 Subtract a half (0.5) from the result of 2.
4 Square the result of 3.
5 Divide the result of 4 by E.
6 Repeat the above procedure for cells B, C and D.
7 Finally total the results for A, B, C and D

- **step 3** – calculate the number of degrees of freedom using the formula: (number of rows –1) × (number of columns –1)
- **step 4** – find the relevant critical value using the table in appendix D, this step is explained in the main text of the chapter.

► Subtracting 0.5 is known as Yate's correction. It is usually used when there is one degree of freedom. Strictly speaking χ^2 is unreliable if any E is less than 5.

Calculation of Chi-square with the pooled class data for question 1 on the questionnaire

	Yes	No	Total
Smokers	35 (A)	13 (B)	48
Non-smokers	46 (C)	2 (D)	48
Total	81	15	96

Table A
*Observed frequencies
– does smoking seriously damage people's health? (Q1)*

- **step 1** – calculation of expected frequencies:
  Cell A: $E = 48 \times 81 / 96 = 40.5$
  Cell B: $E = 48 \times 15 / 96 = 7.5$
  Cell C: $E = 48 \times 81 / 96 = 40.5$
  Cell D: $E = 48 \times 15 / 96 = 7.5$

- **step 2** – applying the formula:

	$[O - E]$	$[O - E] - 0.5$	$[O - E] - 0.5^2$	$\dfrac{[O - E] - 0.5^2}{E}$
Cell A 35 – 40.5 = 5.5	5	25	0.62
Cell B 13 – 7.5 = 5.5	5	25	3.33
Cell C 46 – 40.5 = 5.5	5	25	0.62
Cell D 2 – 7.5 = 5.5	5	25	3.33

- **step 3**
  $\chi^2 = 0.62 + 3.33 + 0.62 + 3.33 = 7.9.$

► The straight brackets mean that you ignore any minus signs: whatever the result you treat it as a positive number.

The experimental method

EXPERIMENTAL METHOD

In Practical 1 you used a psychometric test, and in Practical 2 the data was gathered by means of a survey. The next practical, which is in Chapter 7, asks you to use the experimental method. I have already given a brief outline of the experimental method in Chapter 2, on page 13, but before you carry out the next practical we need to examine this method of research in more detail.

The experiment has a special place in Psychology because it is the major way of testing theories that involve causal relationships.

Independent and dependent variables

An experiment was defined in Chapter 2 as a method of research that involves manipulating one variable (the independent variable or IV) and measuring the effect of this on another variable (the dependent variable or DV). Ideally all other variables (extraneous variables or EV) are held constant so that any change in the DV can be seen as being caused by the researchers manipulation of the IV. Unfortunately it is not possible to hold all extraneous variables constant. The aim in designing an experiment is therefore to try to remove or minimize the influence of extraneous variables so the researcher can see clearly whether or not the IV has caused some change in the DV. Let me illustrate some of these terms by examining the experiment described in Chapter 3. The details of the experiment are reproduced below.

An experiment into the effects of listening to music on the ability to solve mathematical problems

A researcher was interested in the effects of listening to music

► Independent variable – the variable directly manipulated by the researcher. The IV is the two or more conditions of the experiment.

► Dependent variable – this is usually a measure of your subjects' behaviour or performance.

► Extraneous variables – any variables, other than the IV, that can affect the DV. Extraneous variables can obscure or mask the effect of the IV on the DV. The researcher tries to eliminate or minimize their influence.

while studying. She predicted that listening to music would effect the number of mathematical problems that students could solve correctly. A group of twenty college students, all of whom were studying mathematics, were asked to take part in an experiment in which they had to solve as many mathematical problems as possible in thirty minutes. Ten of the students, picked at random, wore headphones and listened to a tape of music of their own choice. The other ten students wore headphones but heard no music. The results of the study are shown below.

The table shows the number of problems solved correctly by the two groups of students – the maximum score was sixty.

Table 6.1

Group 1 – who listened to music	Group 2 – without music
10	22
23	25
17	19
45	23
30	31
14	27
15	21
40	24
12	30
14	18

 For the above experiment what is the IV and what is the DV?

I will answer the above question for you now. The IV is the two or more conditions of the experiment, which the researcher directly manipulates. In this case it is whether the subjects listened to music or not. The DV is a measure of the subjects' behaviour or performance, in this experiment it is the number of mathematical problems that the subjects could correctly answer. Remember that you are looking to see if the IV causes some change in the DV. Whether students listen to music or not is supposed to cause a difference in the number of problems that they will solve correctly.

Extraneous variables

Let us now turn to the question of extraneous variables. There are broadly two types of extraneous variable – **subject extraneous** variables and **situational extraneous variables**.

Subject extraneous variables are the qualities or characteristics of the subjects which could affect the DV. In this experiment an example of a subject extraneous variable is the difference in the students' ability to solve mathematical problems.

► Sometimes extraneous variables are called irrelevant variables, but this implies that they are not important. They are very important. One of the skills in designing an experiment is to eradicate or minimize their influence.

Can you think of any other subject extraneous variables in this experiment?

► Answer this at the end of the chapter.

Situational extraneous variables are the factors to do with the situation or circumstances of the experiment, that might affect the DV. For example, one group of subjects may have the experiment in an uncomfortable room with many distractions, while the other group were in a comfortable room with no distractions.

When designing an experiment subject extraneous variables and situational extraneous variables are handled in different ways. Subject extraneous variables are dealt with by the choice of experimental design. There are various different experimental designs and I will outline three of the most commonly used designs below.

► Experimental design – refers to the different ways of dividing subjects between the conditions of the experiment.

Experimental design: controlling subject variables

In the following discussion of experimental design I will assume that there are only two conditions or levels of the IV. This is to make some of the points easier to explain.

► Experimental designs include:
● related measures
● matched pairs
● independent samples.

The repeated measures design
Given that subject extraneous variables can obscure the effect of the IV on the DV you might be wondering if it is possible to get rid of such variables altogether. This can be done by ensuring that each subject takes part in the two or more conditions of the experiment. In this way **all** subject extraneous variables are eliminated because you are comparing each subject's score under one condition of the IV with their score under the other condition.

However, this design raises a new extraneous variable; if each subject has to take part in both conditions of the experiment then one condition must be performed before the other. This raises the problem of **order effects** – see inset.

Order effects

Although the repeated measures design eliminates subject extraneous variables it has a potential problem with order effects. Let's imagine that we are going to carry out the experiment into the effects of listening to music on the ability of subjects to solve mathematical problems using a repeated measures design. This means each subject will solve problems with music and without music; they will take part in both conditions of the experiment. Can you see any potential problems with this? I can suggest two:

1 Practice – the subjects' performance could improve in the second (no music) condition because of practice in the first condition.

2 Fatigue – the subjects' performance could deteriorate in the second condition because of tiredness or difficulty maintaining concentration.

If we were to allow the experiment to go ahead without dealing with the problem of order effects then the results would be **confounded**. Confounding occurs when there is a systematic difference other than that caused by the IV. The consequence of confounding is that the results of your experiment cannot be interpreted. For example, if we found that subjects solved more problems without music (condition 2), could we be confident that it was a result of the IV (the presence/absence of music)? A sceptic might argue that the difference was simply a result of practice! In this situation the effects of the IV and the order effect (practice) cannot be disentangled.

When designing an experiment confounding must be avoided at all costs. So how do you deal with order effects? There are two widely used methods.

Counterbalancing
1 Counterbalancing involves alternating the order in which the subjects perform the conditions of the experiment. In the example we have been using this would mean:

- subject 1 – condition 1 (with music); condition 2 (without music)
- subject 2 – condition 2 (without music); condition 1 (with music)

This pattern is repeated for the remaining subjects.

Randomization
2 Randomization involves presenting the material for each of the experimental conditions in a random order. It cannot be used in this example but is discussed and illustrated in your next practical in Chapter 7.

Counterbalancing and randomization will usually mean that order effects are balanced across the conditions of the experiment. There are, however, some circumstances where neither of these techniques can be used. If, for example, you wanted to investigate the effects of alcohol on a driving skill. Subjects could be given a test of driving skill (on a simulator or test circuit) with and without alcohol. This would eliminate subject extraneous variables like the individual differences between subjects in their driving skill but could the conditions be counterbalanced for order effects? Half the subjects could perform the test with no alcohol and then with alcohol. However the other subjects could not perform the test with alcohol and then without, as the alcohol would still be in their bloodstream! The only solution to this is a long delay between performing the two conditions. Alternatively a different experimental design could be used.

The matched pairs design

The matched pairs design attempts to deal with subject extraneous variables by using subjects that are the same, or similar, regarding variables that may affect the DV. In the experiment on the effect of listening to music on solving mathematical problems we could give the students a mathematics test and then pair subjects on the basis of their test scores. One subject from each pair would then be randomly allocated to group 1 (with music) and the other would go into group 2 (without music). In this way subjects' ability at solving mathematical problems would be eliminated as a subject extraneous variable and there is no problem about order effects. The ideal experimental design you might think! Well, remember you have dealt with only one, albeit an important subject extraneous variable. What about other subject differences, motivation for example. Also before you can match subjects on a variable you need to be able to measure or test for it.

There are, however, many subject extraneous variables that are difficult, sometimes impossible, to test for. Also you need to take account of the practical difficulties in trying to match subjects; it could be very time-consuming.

The matched samples design is, therefore, a useful alternative to the repeated measures design but it has its own limitations.

The independent samples design

If order effects are a problem and matching is difficult a researcher can use the **independent samples design**. The subjects are allocated randomly to two groups and each group performs in only one condition of the experiment. The idea here is that any subject extraneous variables will be randomly spread between the two conditions and will therefore cancel each other out. **Random allocation** does not ensure that the two groups will be perfectly matched on all subject extraneous variables. It does, however, make it very unlikely that there would be any systematic bias.

The advantage of the independent samples design is that it can be used in virtually all experimental situations. The difficulty is that subject extraneous variables may be so great as to mask the effect of the IV on the DV. If you look at the results of the experiment on the effects of music on solving mathematical problems you can see that the two highest scores (forty-five and forty) are in group 1, with music. Yet the lowest scores are also in this group. How can we explain these apparently contradictory results? One explanation is that the subjects who achieved the highest scores are those who are simply very good at solving mathematical problems (a subject extraneous variable). The subjects with the low scores are those with the least ability in mathematics. The effect of the IV (the presence or

▶ Random sampling was discussed in Chapter 5. Random allocation of subjects to the different conditions of an experiment works on the same principle. Each subject has an equal chance of being allocated to one group or the other; by lottery for example.

▶ The researcher did use only subjects studying mathematics so a degree of control was exercised over the subjects' mathematical ability.

absence of music) may not be strong enough to overcome the individual variation in mathematical ability.

► The answer is at the end of the chapter.

 Can you think of any other explanation for the results of this experiment?

Situational extraneous variables: controlling the situation

Subject extraneous variables are not the only factors which can affect the results of your experiment: how do you deal with situational extraneous variables? There are many factors to do with the situation (background noise, the instructions the experimenter gives, personal qualities of the experimenter, etc.) that could affect subject performance. If such factors are not considered and dealt with carefully the results of an experiment could be confounded, or any effect of the IV could be obscured.

The ideal answer to the problem of situational extraneous variables is to hold them constant; if background noise was a potential problem, in an experiment, you could make sure the experiment was carried out somewhere quiet. However, there are some situational extraneous variables which you may not be able to hold constant. An experiment may, because of the number of subjects used, require two or more experimenters. How can you deal with the possible effect of differences in the personality and characteristics of the experimenters? One solution is to adopt a procedure similar to counterbalancing (see boxed inset on order effects). Thus in the Listening to Music experiment if two experimenters were needed you could organize it as below:

	group 1	group 2
experimenter 1	5 subjects	5 subjects
experimenter 2	5 subjects	5 subjects

It is important to remember that, as with counterbalancing for order effects, the above procedure does not remove the possible effects of having different experimenters. It does mean, however, that situational extraneous variables dealt with in this way will not confound the experiment. They will not produce systematic differences in the DV.

There are many potential situational extraneous variables and the techniques outlined above can only realistically be used to deal with a few of them. Researchers use the technique of randomization to clear up any remaining problems. In the Listening to Music experiment each group of subjects was given sixty mathematical problems to solve. Since this was not a repeated measures design, and each subject was only tested under one experimental condition, the same sixty questions could be given to all of them. But if it had been a repeated measures design it would have been necessary to give each subject two sets of sixty questions, one set for each condition. An important situational extraneous variable here is the level of difficulty of the problems; some problems may be more difficult than others. How can the researcher ensure that subjects get problems of the same level of difficulty under each experimental condition? Firstly, the researcher can select 120 problems of roughly the same level of difficulty. These 120 problems can then be randomly divided into two sets of sixty. Subjects could then be allocated one set or the other at random for their first experimental condition, which would automatically decide which set they received for their second test. Much the same result would be achieved by counterbalancing, with each subject being given their sets of problems in an alternating pattern as described in the inset on order effects.

Unfortunately it is not possible to eliminate all situational extraneous variables. When designing an experiment the researcher's primary goal is to avoid any systematic effects that will confound the results. The secondary goal is to remove or minimize the effects of extraneous variables which will obscure the effect of the IV on the DV. Finally, the researcher can only hope that the effect of the IV is strong enough to overcome the 'noise' created by extraneous variables.

 Now check that you understand all the key terms listed in the chapter objectives, and have made notes on them where you need to.

Activity Answers
Activity on page 79
The results could reflect the fact that some students find music an aid to concentration, listening to music therefore improves their performance. Other students, however, find music a distraction and listening to music has an adverse effect on their performance.

Activity on page 82
Another possibility is that personal taste in music had a confounding effect on the results. Perhaps those who liked the music played performed better at the calculations. Or, those who liked the music best were more distracted by it, or those who didn't like the music chosen were irritated by it in a way that distracted them.

CHAPTER SUMMARY

In this chapter I have introduced you to some of the most important features of experimentation. You will have seen that they are all about control. That is setting up conditions under which the connections between independent and dependent variables can be demonstrated – if such connections exist. Then trying to exclude extraneous variables so that they do not obscure the connections. From this discussion you should now have a good grasp of the problems you would face in trying to design an experiment of your own, and of some techniques of minimizing these problems. In the next chapter you will meet some of the same problems again because it is a practical which involves the experimental method.

Further reading: Chapter 6

Two useful introductions to the experimental method:

Miller, S., (1975) *Experimental Design and Statistics*, London: Methuen.

Coolican, H., (1990) *Research Methods and Statistics in Psychology*, London: Hodder & Stoughton.

An experiment to investigate the effectiveness of imagery and rehearsal as methods of recalling word-pairs: the third practical

► Practical 3.

► There are materials at the end of this chapter which you will need for the practical. Look through the chapter appendices now to familiarize yourself with these.
  They are:

● pooled class data for Practical 3
● word-pairs for use in Practical 3
● pro-forma for collating the results of Practical 3
● calculation of the Wilcoxon signed ranks test
● a reading on imagery and memory.

Chapter objectives

By the end of this chapter you should:

▌ have completed a third practical report

▌ understand what has been claimed about the role of rehearsal and imagery for recall, and the theoretical background to this

▌ be able to draw a frequency histogram

▌ have had further practice in understanding experimental design and in choosing appropriate statistical tests

▌ have carried out a Wilcoxon signed ranks test

▌ be able to define the following key terms and use them appropriately: rehearsal, mnemonic system, imagery, frequency histogram, related test.

IMAGERY AND REHEARSAL IN MEMORY

The experiment is probably the most frequently used method of research in Psychology. The principal aim of the practical in this chapter is to give you experience of the experimental method, building on what you learned in Chapter 6.

The topic area for this practical is memory and I have included some background material and references to help you.

As the title suggests the aim of this practical is to compare two methods for remembering pairs of words. One of the methods, **rehearsal**, you have probably used yourself many times. It is a technique commonly used by people when they need to remember verbal material (words, numbers, sentences etc.). Imagine you are asked to learn the lines of a poem, or the words of a part in a play. What would you do? You may not need to imagine, if you have actually been faced with such a task. I know that when I have been in such a situation I have usually resorted to repeating the words over and over again, until I could recall them without error.

Another **mnemonic system** (method of aiding memory) is called the method of loci. This method uses imagery and is particularly effective when you need to recall an ordered sequence of arbitrary items, like unrelated words. First you need to memorize an ordered sequence of locations (loci is Latin for 'places') for example the route from your front door to your bedroom. When you have a clear mental picture of this journey you can memorize unrelated words as objects and places you pass on your mental walk. You form an image which relates the first word you have to remember to the first location, the second word to the second location, etc. Atkinson et al., (1985) give the following example:

> 'If the words are items on a shopping list – for example, bread, eggs, beer, milk, and bacon – you might imagine a slice of bread nailed to your front door, an egg hanging from the light cord in the hallway . . .'

Once the words have been memorized in this way they can be recalled by taking your mental walk again. Each location will retrieve an image, and each image will retrieve a word.

One serious educational application of **imagery** as a mnemonic device is the keyword method for learning the vocabulary of a foreign language. With this method you first need to find a part of a foreign word that sounds like an English word. For example, the French word for window is **fenêtre**, this contains the English sounding word **net**. The next step is to form a mental image connecting the keyword and the English equivalent – for example a man falling out of a window and being caught in a net. This should establish a meaningful connection between the French and English words. To remember the French word for **window** you would first retrieve the image involving the man falling out of the window, thus recalling the word **net** which serves as a retrieval cue for fenêtre.

The study of memory, and in particular ways of improving memory, can therefore have important practical applications.

So far I have presented matters as simply a comparison between two methods of remembering material, the results of which may have some practical application. However, underlying this there are important theoretical issues concerning the way information is stored and retrieved from memory. There is an offprint which summarizes these issues at the end of the chapter (beginning on page 100) and I will give you advice about how to incorporate this material in the introduction and discussion sections of your report later.

INTRODUCING THE PRACTICAL

Dealing with extraneous variables

Having read Chapter 6 you will be aware that each of the experimental designs has its own advantages and disadvantages; there is no single **best** design. A major problem when designing an experiment is how to deal with subject extraneous variables. These are variables, other than the IV, which can affect the DV.

In this experiment you wish to test the effectiveness of two memory techniques (the IV) on subjects' ability to recall word-pairs (the DV). Think for a moment what other variable might affect the subjects' ability to recall word-pairs?

▶ The IV: two mnemonic techniques. The DV: ability to recall.

One factor that you may have thought of is the initial memory ability of subjects. There is no doubt that people differ in terms of their ability to recall information. Thus a subject's initial memory ability will influence the number of word-pairs that they recall independent of the memory techniques. Extraneous variables, like initial memory ability, are known as subject extraneous variables because they are associated with the subject.

Another extraneous variable you might have thought of is noise. If some subjects have to do the experiment in a noisy room then this can act as a distraction and impair their performance. This kind of extraneous variable is, not surprisingly, called a situational extraneous variable.

The crucial point about the different experimental designs is that they represent alternative ways of dealing with subject extraneous variables.

Given that subject extraneous variables can affect the DV and therefore should be eliminated if possible, the natural first choice as an experimental design is the repeated measures design. With this design each subject performs under the two (or more) conditions of the experiment. Therefore you are comparing each subject's performance in one condition with their performance in the other condition. Since you are, in effect, comparing each subject with themselves, differences **between** subjects are not important.

▶ Using a repeated measure design to control subject variables.

However, the repeated measures design is not without problems of its own. In particular if all subjects have to do all the conditions of an experiment then they cannot do them at the same time. This creates the problem of **order effects**. What would the consequence be in this experiment if all the subjects were to learn a list of word-pairs using rehearsal and then a list of word-pairs using imagery? The result, I am afraid, would be that the experiment would be confounded. This is because it would not be possible to say that any difference in performance was due to the IV alone i.e. the two memory techniques. It could be the case that practice on the rehearsal list leads subjects to do better on the imagery list. You would not know that this was the case, but then you could not rule out the possibility. Let us assume for the moment that practice does have an effect; how could we deal with it? Choose another design is one answer; but let's not give up on the repeated measures design just yet! There are two techniques which are commonly used by researchers to deal with order effects: counterbalancing and randomization.

Counterbalancing would give us an experimental procedure like this:

▶ Counterbalancing is a technique used to deal with order effects by alternating the order of presentation of the experimental conditions.

Order of presentation		
	first	**second**
Subject 1	condition A (imagery)	condition B (rehearsal)
Subject 2	condition B (rehearsal)	condition A (imagery)

► Randomization: presenting the material from the two or more experimental conditions in a random order, to control for order effects.

This pattern is continued for the remaining subjects.

To use randomization we might proceed as follows: if subjects are asked to try to recall twenty word-pairs, ten using imagery and ten using rehearsal, then each word-pair needs to be randomly assigned to one of the two memory techniques. Also the techniques need to be presented in a randomly determined sequence. This could be achieved in the following way:

1 You take twenty pieces of paper and write one word-pair on each. These are then placed in box A and mixed.

2 You take twenty pieces of paper and write the word **image** on ten of them and **rehearse** on the other ten. These are placed in box B and mixed.

3 You take one piece of paper from box A, this will be the first word-pair that you will present to your subjects. You then take a piece of paper from box B, this will determine which technique subjects will use to try to recall the word-pair. You continue this process until all the word-pairs have been linked to one of the two memory techniques.

In this way you ensure that the word-pairs are randomly assigned to the techniques, and the order in which the subjects are given the techniques is random.

It is important to remember that if an order effect, such as that resulting from practice occurs, then neither counterbalancing nor randomization will get rid of it. What they will do, however, is to ensure that practice affects both conditions to the same extent.

You might have guessed that I would suggest the use of the repeated measures design for this experiment.

 Read through the details on how to carry out the experiment, look at the materials involved and identify if you can, what method has been used to deal with order effects.

CARRYING OUT THE PRACTICAL

You will probably be relieved to hear that you are going to act as an experimenter, rather than subject, in this practical! Familiarize yourself with the procedure for carrying out the experiment, outlined overleaf. Then find two subjects; they can be male or female and of any age over twelve years. Members of your family or friends are fine. You cannot, however, carry out the experiment with both subjects at the same time.

Procedure

- **step 1** – read the following standardized instructions on the subject:

Instructions for the subjects

'The purpose of this experiment is to investigate two different techniques for memorizing word-pairs. I will read you a list of word-pairs, one at a time. Your task is to learn the pair so that later, when I give you the first word of the pair, you will be able to tell me the word that goes with it. There are two memory techniques I want you to use. For some pairs you are to repeat the two words in a quiet voice four times.

For other words you are to remain silent while forming a mental image or picture in which the two words are associated or interacting in some way; the more vivid or unusual the better. For example, if I gave the word-pair **clown – bicycle**, the mental picture you form might be of a clown riding a bicycle.

Just before I give you each word-pair I will tell you which method of memorizing to use by saying either **repeat** or **image**. After you have been given all twenty word-pairs, I will say **count**, and you are to count backwards from ninety-nine until I tell you to stop.

I will then test your memory by saying the first word in each pair, and you have to try to tell me the word that goes with it. Any questions?'

Allow subjects ten seconds for each word-pair.

- **step 2** – read out the technique and word-pairs given at the end of the chapter
- **step 3** – now say **count** – let subjects count backwards for thirty seconds
- **step 4** – read out the first word of each word-pair, as shown in the table at the end of the chapter (on page 97) and record the subjects' responses. You can check to see whether their responses are correct or not at the end
- **step 5** – finally, thank each of your subjects for participating in the experiment. Then debrief them about the purpose of the experiment and ask them for any comments about how they undertook the task. One point of particular interest is whether subjects found that they tended to form mental images even when they were asked to repeat.

Keep a note of any comments your subjects make as these may be used when writing the discussion section of your report.

Analysing the results

Add the results of your subjects to the table of pooled class data at the end of the chapter. Place them in the space provided for subjects fifteen and sixteen.

Now that you have the raw data examine it carefully. The aim of the experiment was to see whether there was any difference in the effectiveness of the two memory techniques. Can you answer this question from an examination of the raw data? I do not know what the scores for your two subjects were, but looking at subjects one – fourteen the answer seems quite clear. Every subject, except number six, recalled more word-pairs correctly using imagery than rehearsal. The differences in performance were very large for some subjects e.g. subject twelve recalled all ten of the imagery word-pairs, but only one using rehearsal. While the results do seem clear-cut it is still necessary to summarize them and present them to the reader of the report in a clear, accessible format.

Expressing the central tendency

As you are comparing the performance of subjects using the two techniques it would be useful to have a measure of central tendency for each condition. Which measure of central tendency do you think would be most appropriate? Consult Chapter 3 if in any doubt.

Drawing a histogram

It would also be helpful, for the reader of your report, to have the data presented graphically so the results can be seen at a glance. One way of doing this is to construct **frequency histograms**.

► Measures of central tendency include the mean, the median and the mode.

Drawing frequency histograms

If you drew a frequency histogram for the pooled data it would look like Figure 7. 1. Your own will look slightly different because you have added some more data.

Figure 7.1

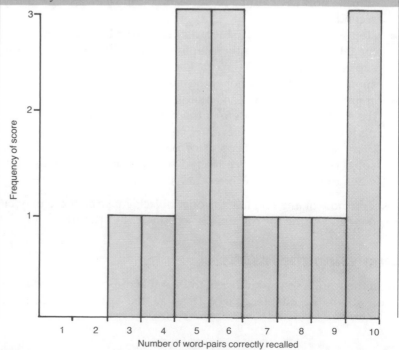

The first step is to draw two axes, and mark them with appropriate intervals. It is conventional to make the vertical (or *y*) axis that for frequency. The *x* or horizontal axis represents the scores grouped into categories. In our case the categories are simply units: one, two, three etc., word-pairs correctly recalled. However with large sets of data, or data spread thinly over a long range the data can be grouped into categories. For example all between one and three, between four and six and so on, as long as each category is the same size.

The bars on the histogram show how many scores fell into each category marked on the *x* axis. Since each bar is of the same width the **area** of each column is proportional to the number of cases it represents. Note that in a histogram categories for which there are no scores are still included – as is the case with one or two word-pairs remembered on our histogram.

You will need to draw two frequency histograms, one for the rehearsal scores and one for the imagery scores. I have included an example in Figure 7.1 using the class data for imagery. Remember your histograms will be slightly different because of the inclusion of your own two subjects' scores.

Finally, despite the clear-cut superiority of the imagery technique shown in the results, you must establish the probability of these results occurring by chance. To do this you need to select and apply an appropriate statistical test.

Applying an appropriate statistical test

To decide which is the most appropriate test to apply to the data let's return to Figure 4.2. You should be getting quite familiar with this chart by now! Starting with decision number one; I think it should be clear that a test of **difference** is needed, so let us move to the difference side of the chart.

Decision two – number of samples of scores. In this experiment there are **two** sets of scores: the imagery scores and the rehearsal scores.

Note that although there is only one group of subjects each subject is giving you two scores.

You have now progressed to decision number three. This concerns the design of the experiment. Fortunately this is an easy decision to make: the experiment used the repeated measures design therefore a **related test** is required. The repeated measures and matched samples designs are grouped together and known as related designs, while the independent and single subjects designs are known as unrelated designs. As you have used a repeated measures design for this experiment it is clear you need to use a related statistical test.

▶ Repeated measures. Related tests.

Levels of data
The final decision, number four, concerns whether to use a

► Nominal; ordinal; interval; ratio.

► Levels of data are dealt with in Chapter 4.

parametric or non-parametric test. To answer this question you need to consider a number of other factors. The first concerns what the level of data in this experiment is. You may remember that there are four levels of measurement: nominal, ordinal, interval and ratio, and that they form a hierarchy, with nominal being the lowest and ratio the highest level of measurement.

 Try to decide yourself what the level of data in this practical generates. Remember it is the DV that you measure in an experiment; in this case the number of word-pairs correctly recalled.

Unfortunately, as with Practical 1, there are arguments **for** and **against** calling the data of this experiment ordinal, interval and even ratio! Let's go through these. Firstly, I do not think there is any doubt that the data are of at least ordinal level. It makes perfect sense to rank order the scores. For example, in the rehearsal condition, subject six achieved the highest score, five word-pairs recalled out of ten, subjects two and five got the second highest score of four out of ten etc. However, do the data qualify for an interval scale? An interval scale requires units of measurement indicating not only that one subject has scored more than another, but how much more. It does seem reasonable in this experiment to say that subject six in the rehearsal condition not only remembered more than subjects two and seven but that he/she remembered one more word-pair. Can we say that each word-pair represents units of memory like each degree centigrade represents units of temperature? This is obviously a more difficult problem to resolve, you can probably think of arguments yourself in favour of and against considering word-pairs to be equal units of measurement. The reason why this decision is important is because it influences whether or not you can use more powerful statistical tests, called parametric tests or whether you must use slightly less powerful non-parametric statistical tests.

► **Powerful** means a statistical test's ability to detect a significant difference between sets of scores.

It is sensible for the researcher to use the most powerful test(s) available. But parametric tests require that the data being analysed be of an interval or ratio level of measurement. This is the dilemma in this experiment. Do you assume the data are interval or ratio level, so that a parametric test can be considered. Or do you settle for a non-parametric test on the basis that the data are certainly of at least ordinal level. Being a cautious Capricorn I suggest you play safe and use a non-parametric test. This has one distinct advantage in that the mathematics involved are much simpler. However, a parametric test awaits you in the next practical!

After that rather lengthy discussion of levels of measurement, let us return to Figure 4.2. If you examine this figure you will see that the appropriate two sample, non-parametric difference test is the **Wilcoxon signed ranks test**.

► Test of difference; repeated measures; two sample; ordinal; level; non-parametric; Wilcoxon signed ranks test.

Step by step instructions on how to carry out the Wilcoxon signed ranks test can be found at the end of this chapter.

Read through the calculations and then do them for your own data set.

► **Do the calculations now.**

WRITING UP THE PRACTICAL

I am sure you are getting the basic idea of how to write practical reports by now and so I will only include comments on things not covered before. Remember to use the format shown in the Notes for Guidance (see appendix B).

Title
Make up your own.

Abstract
Remember to keep within a word limit of about 100 words.

Introduction
You could start this section with a short, general introduction to the study of memory. Explain the ideas regarding short and long-term memory, and the processes of encoding, storage and retrieval.

You then need to put the experiment into its theoretical context. Use the information contained in the offprint at the end of the chapter to outline the dual-code theory and include some of the arguments and evidence for and against Paivio's ideas. Include some examples of the use of imagery and rehearsal and conclude with a statement of the aim of the experiment. The aim should be clearly expressed in the title.

Experimental hypothesis
Is there any reason to expect that one of the memory techniques used will be better than the other? What would you expect on the basis of the dual-code theory? Frame a one or two-tailed experimental hypothesis on the basis of your answers to these questions.

I will not give you the experimental hypothesis, you must make up your own. Remember that it should predict what you expect the outcome of the experiment to be and it should be specific.

► **Hint** – the names of the two techniques (the IV) will need to appear in the experimental hypothesis as will the DV (the number of word-pairs correctly recalled).

Null hypothesis
Again I will leave you to frame this yourself but again remember to be specific.

METHOD

Design
As you already know the design used in this experiment was a repeated measures design. Explain briefly why this design was chosen and say something about order effects and how they were dealt with.

Subjects
I will leave this to you.

Materials
Put a copy of the word-pairs in an appendix and refer the reader to it.

Procedure
Explain, step by step, how you carried out the experiment. You will need to include the instructions you read to the subjects, the counting backwards procedure and how the subjects' ability to recall the word-pairs was tested. Remember to use the past tense and an impersonal style, 'The experimenter read the following instructions to each subject . . . '.

► The golden rule is that someone reading the procedure section should be able to carry out the experiment exactly as you did. They should be able to **replicate** your study.

Results

Include the table created in step 4 of 'Carrying out the Practical' and the table of pooled class results in this section.

Treatment of results

Put your frequency histograms here and then briefly explain why the Wilcoxon signed ranks test was used to analyse the data. Put the results of the statistical analysis into a table as below:

Observed value of T	Critical value of T	Significance level	N

► The decision rules for significance levels are dealt with in Chapter 2.

Remember your significance level will depend on whether you decided on a one or two-tailed experimental hypothesis.

 Give the decision rule and state whether, in the light of the statistical analysis, your hypothesis can be accepted or rejected.

Discussion

As stated before, start this section with a detailed description of your results. This should include reference to your own subjects' scores, the pooled class data, the histograms and the results of the statistical test.

 Now try to relate your findings to those of previous studies. To what extent are they similar or different? Do they lend support to any particular theory mentioned in the introduction section?

 Were there any particular problems in carrying out the experiment? Can you think of any ways in which the design or implementation of the experiment could be improved? One issue which has come up when my students have carried out this experiment is that a number of subjects have found it difficult not to form mental images when asked to repeat the word-pairs. This difficulty raises some interesting questions about the design of the experiment. Did either of your subjects report a similar difficulty? Can you think of any ways of overcoming or reducing this problem? Assuming at least some subjects experience this difficulty, does it affect the interpretation of the results? As you can see research often raises more questions than it answers! Don't be put off by all the questions I have included, they are only suggestions for issues you **could** discuss, they should not be taken as a list of things you must include.

Conclusion

In this section simply state whether or not you have accepted or rejected your null hypothesis.

References

Don't forget to include references to any research or researcher you have included in your report.

Appendices

Put your calculations here.

CHAPTER SUMMARY

Using this chapter you have carried out an experiment on memorizing, using a design chosen to control subject extraneous variables – a repeated measures design. The pooled data you incorporated into your results was produced using a technique of randomization to control order effects. You expressed the results in a frequency histogram and subjected them to a non-parametric statistical test of difference called the Wilcoxon signed ranks test. You should have learned a lot about the experimental method, and in passing about theories of memory too.

Further reading: Chapter 7

There is some useful general material on memory in:

Gross, R., (1992) *Psychology: The Science of Mind and Behaviour* (2nd ed.), Chapter 12, Sevenoaks: Hodder & Stoughton.

There is also a good introduction to the topic of memory in:

Atkinson, R.L., *et al.* (1990) *Introduction to Psychology* (10th ed.), Chapter 8, New York: Harcourt Brace Janovich.

Useful introductions to statistics are in:

Miller, S., (1975) *Experimental Design and Statistics*, London: Methuen.

Coolican, H., (1991) *Research Methods and Statistics in Psychology*, Sevenoaks: Hodder & Stoughton.

Appendices for Practical 3

Table of pooled class data

Record your own results for subjects fifteen and sixteen. Use this table also to calculate the first two steps of the Wilcoxon signed ranks test.

Subject no.	Image score	Repeat score	Difference	Rank
1	10	3		
2	10	4		
3	5	0		
4	6	3		
5	8	3		
6	5	5		
7	9	4		
8	6	1		
9	4	0		
10	5	3		
11	3	0		
12	10	1		
13	7	2		
14	6	2		
15				
16				

Word-pairs

Where word-pairs are marked **repeat** ask the subject to memorize using rehearsal. Where they are marked **image** ask the subject to memorize using imagery. Allow about ten seconds for each word-pair.

Technique	Word-pairs
repeat	rabbit – house
repeat	boy – rope
image	shoe – mountain
repeat	table – skull
image	doctor – flag
image	book – fish
repeat	slave – party
image	lamp – bird
image	heart – water
repeat	ladder – baby
repeat	teacher – pudding
image	mule – dress
repeat	kettle – fox
image	snake – fire
image	tree – queen

Technique	Word-pairs
repeat	flower – money
image	harp – elephant
repeat	bear – candle
repeat	clock – moon
image	horse – potato

Proforma for recording results

During the experiment write in the actual response. Mark them correct or incorrect later.

First words	Subject 1		Subject 2	
	Response	Correct/ incorrect	Response	Correct/ incorrect
clock				
table				
snake				
shoe				
flower				
lamp				
boy				
horse				
book				
rabbit				
harp				
slave				
mule				
heart				
bear				
ladder				
doctor				
kettle				
teacher				
tree				

Calculation of Wilcoxon signed ranks test

- **step 1** – calculate the difference between each pair of scores, d, ($x_a - x_b$). Do the subtraction consistently and record any minus signs
- **step 2** – rank the differences, d, from the smallest (rank 1) to the largest (rank N). You must ignore any minus signs when ranking the differences: thus -7 will be higher than $+5$. Where $d = 0$ see Note 1. Where there are identical scores (ds) see note 2
- **step 3** – add together the **ranks** of the differences with the **less** frequent sign (this might be plus or it might be minus). This is called T
- **step 4** – look up the critical value of T in appendix D and if the observed value is equal to or less than your calculated value, the results are statistically significant at the level shown in the

table. Remember to check the five per cent significance level first, and if the results are significant at this level, then check more stringent levels. When you write up the practical use the most stringent level of significance that your results achieve.

▶ If a pair of scores is tied (you have a *d* of 0) then these scores are dropped from the statistical analysis and *N*, the size of the sample, is reduced by one.

If two or more of the differences are the same then you give each of them the average of the ranks which would have otherwise been used.

Ranking

Ranking often causes confusion where there are equal scores. These are the rules. Give the lowest rank to the lowest score. Suppose that the lowest score is 2, then the rank is 1. Then suppose that the next score is 4, and that there are 3 people with that score. The ranks available for them to occupy are ranks 2, 3, and 4. Give them all rank 3. The formula is:

The sum of the ranks needed to accommodate

$$\frac{\text{that number of scores}}{\text{the number of scores}}$$

$$\frac{2+3+4}{3} = \frac{9}{3} = 3$$

You have now ranked 4 scores so the next rank is 5.

Sometimes using this formula will result in ranks with figures behind the decimal point.

If you are still unclear about ranking, work out how the ranks were assigned in the worked example.

Wilcoxon signed ranks – worked example

Subject no.	Image score x_a	Repeat score x_b	Difference	Rank
1	10	3	7	12.0
2	10	4	6	11.0
3	5	0	5	8.0
4	6	3	3	2.5
5	8	3	5	8.0
6	5	5	0	*
7	9	4	5	8.0
8	6	1	5	8.0
9	4	0	4	4.5
10	5	3	2	1.0
11	3	0	3	2.5
12	10	1	9	13.0
13	7	2	5	8.0
14	6	2	4	4.5

*See marginal note above

The table above shows the results of steps 1 and 2.

- **step 3** – the sum of the ranks for the least frequent sign is 0, the least frequent sign is negative as all the differences are positive;

there are no negative values at all. The observed or calculated value of T is therefore 0. This is because in these results each subject performed better with the image method than with the rehearsal method

- **step 4** – if you consult the critical values of T in the Wilcoxon signed ranks test in appendix D you can find the appropriate critical value of T. In this example the are thirteen pairs of scores (remember one pair has been dropped from the analysis because they were tied and $d = 0$). Look at the left hand column to where $N = 13$. The numbers in this row represent the critical values at different levels of statistical significance. You need to start at the 0.05 level as this is the minimum level, if your result is not significant at this level it will not be significant at a more stringent level of significance. However, before you can select the correct critical value you must decide whether your hypothesis is one or two tailed. In this example I will predict, on the basis of the dual-code theory, that imagery scores will be higher than rehearsal scores and therefore the hypothesis is one tailed. The critical value at the 0.05 level, with a one-tailed hypothesis is 21. The decision rule for this statistical test is that the observed value of T must be equal to or less than the critical value for the result to be significant. As 0 is less than 21, the result is significant at the 0.05 level and you can reject the null hypothesis. Having established that your result is significant at the minimum 0.05 level you can now check to see if your results are significant at a more stringent level. Look across the row and see if your observed value is equal to or less than the critical values shown. If it is use the highest or most stringent level of significance available. In this case you can go to the highest level in the table, the 0.001 level (1 chance in 1000). As your result (0) is less than critical value (4) the results are highly significant – very unlikely to have occurred by chance. This is the value to use in your treatment of results table.

Levels of significance

One-tailed test

	0.05	0.025	0.01	0.001
Sample size 13	21	17	12	4

With samples of more than twenty-five pairs
If you have more than twenty-five pairs of scores then the distribution of T approximates that of the normal distribution. There is a formula available to transform T into a Z score – this formula can be found in more specialist books on statistics. I have given you two references to such texts in the further reading section for the chapter (see page 95).

Reading for Chapter 7

Imagery and memory

Supposing I asked you to tell me how many tables you have in your house. You may know the total number and show no hesitation in replying to the question. On the other hand, you might not know the total, but you might be able to work it out. If you are like me, you would probably try to visualize each room in your house, in a very methodical manner, focusing on the tables in each room, counting them as you go through all the rooms. An example might be: 'Let me see . . . in the kitchen I have two . . . in the dining room I have one, so that's three . . . in the sitting room I have two – no, with the small one in the corner there are three . . . so three plus three is . . . '. While counting I would **see** the actual tables in my head as visible images.

Based on reports of this sort it would seem that we can store information in long-term memory (LTM) about the visual characteristics of experiences we have had. These experiences include faces we have seen, maps we have studied, scenes we have witnessed, and so on. Further, there is evidence that the visual information stored in LTM in some form resembles a picture. The question is not about whether we can remember pictures. The important question is: do we store actual images of things we see or do we store something else in memory such as an abstraction or abstract description of our visual experiences? How is this visual information represented in memory? The theories and experimental evidence presented in this section are directly related to this question.

The idea, that images may serve as an alternative to verbal codes as a means of representing information in LTM, has received a great deal of experimental support over the past fifteen years. One of the foremost proponents of this view is Alan Paivio (1969, 1971) who advocates a theory known as dual-coding or dual system.

Essentially, dual-coding theory assumes that there are two basic ways of representing information in memory; two coding systems. One is verbal, or linguistic; the other is non-verbal. The latter coding system may be called imaginal, and it includes the types of visual images discussed above. Paivio considers the two coding systems to be strongly connected, so that it is possible to derive an image from a verbal label, and vice versa.

Evidence for the dual-code theory

The basis for the dual-code hypothesis comes from a series of experiments by Begg and Paivio (1969), in which the main variable being manipulated was the classification of words into **concrete** or **abstract**. Their results show that when subjects are given instructions to make imagery connections for concrete and abstract words they make these connections faster for concrete than for abstract words, and recall more concrete than abstract words. This would seem to indicate that the better performance with concrete words is due to the fact that pictorial representation of concrete words is easier than for abstract words because: (a) images of concrete objects are already stored in LTM, and therefore (b) the recall of concrete words is facilitated because subjects can use the information available in two coded forms (imaginal and verbal) to aid them during the learning phase. One of the main implications of the dual-coding view of memory is that information that can be stored as both a verbal and imaginal code should be more accessible than information held in just one coding system. The reason for this is that dual-coded information can be accessed by either a verbal or non-verbal retrieval process. In a sense, there is twice as much information about a twice-coded item than about an item that exists only in one coded form.

The notion of picture-like codes in LTM has been supported by the work of other researchers. Frost (1972) carried out an experiment which also lends support to the existence of a separate code in LTM for pictorial information. She presented subjects with a set of sixteen drawings of common objects. The drawings could be categorized on a semantic basis – the objects were from one of the four categories; animals, articles of clothing, vehicles, and furniture. Alternatively, they could be categorized on a visual basis – the objects were at four orientations: the long axis could be vertical, horizontal, tilted right, or tilted left. One group of subjects was led to expect a recognition test after studying the drawings, and another to expect a free-recall test on the object names. However, both groups were given a free-recall test. Frost's results showed that the free recall of the group of subjects who expected to recall showed clustering on the basis of semantic category. That is, the objects from the same semantic category tended to be recalled together. In contrast, the group expecting a recognition test recalled in cluster based on both semantic and visual characteristics. These results suggest that subjects who expected the recognition task stored a visual representation of the objects in LTM. They used this representation as well as a semantic representation in the recall task. Whereas subjects expecting free recall only organized the material in terms of semantic categories and therefore did not produce visually determined clusters. This hypothesis is also supported by Frost's other results. For example, she found that subjects who expected recognition were efficient on a visual recognition task, whereas those who expected recall were more efficient at name-recognition.

In a free-recall test subjects are given material to learn and are then asked to remember it unaided in any order. For example, subjects could be given a list of twenty words to learn. Then they are asked to write down, in any order, as many of the words as they can.

Evidence for the dual-code theory has also come from the study of memory for natural language, in particular, memory for sentences. When subjects are asked to remember sentences they often have difficulty recalling the actual wording, but seldom forget the mean-

► In a recognition test subjects are given some material to learn. This original material is then mixed in with new material and the subjects' task is to identify (recognize) the original material. For example, subjects might be given a list of twenty words to learn. They are then presented with a list of eighty words (the twenty original words plus sixty new words mixed together randomly). The subjects are asked to identify the twenty words they were given to learn.

In a free-recall test subjects are given material to learn and are then asked to remember it unaided in any order. For example, subjects could be given a list of twenty words to learn. Then they are asked to write down, in any order, as many of the words as they can.

ing. An experiment by Sachs (1967) showed that subjects did not notice whether a sentence had been changed from active to passive as much as they noticed a change in meaning. For example, changing a positive sentence to its negative. Begg and Paivio (1969) extended this study, by using both abstract and concrete sentences. A typical concrete sentence, one that involves concrete nouns, is 'The spirited leader slapped a mournful hostage'. An abstract sentence is 'The arbitrary regulation provoked a civil complaint'. These two types of sentences were presented to subjects in a short text, after which subjects were given a recognition test. Each distracter sentence on the recognition test resembled one of the original sentences, but was changed either in wording alone or in meaning. For example, a wording only change in the concrete sentence given above might be 'The spirited leader slapped a mournful captive'. A semantic change might be 'The spirited hostage slapped a mournful leader'. Begg and Paivio found that Sachs' results held for the concrete sentences, but not for the abstract sentences. For concrete sentences, subjects recognized changes in meaning better than changes in wording alone. But for abstract sentences, word changes were recognized better than meaning changes.

Paivio interprets these findings in terms of the dual-code theory. He believes that the meaning of concrete sentences is stored more in the form of images than by words. Hence, changing the wording in such a sentence, but leaving the meaning intact, will not affect the image representation of the sentence and the change will not be noticed. On the other hand, an image is not an effective way to store the meaning of an abstract sentence; a verbal representation is much more efficient. Hence, for abstract sentences, changes in wording are noticed. Based on this sort of evidence, Paivio (1971) has suggested that imagery plays an important role in language comprehension. We understand linguistic inputs in terms of the images they convey, particularly when the linguistic material contains a high percentage of concrete words.

The evidence outlined above seems to provide overwhelming support in favour of picture-like representations in LTM. However, the problem is not actually that straightforward.

Arguments and evidence against the dual-code hypothesis

The argument against the dual-code hypothesis centres on a vital question – what are these pictorial representations in LTM like? Are they exactly like our perceptions of the outside world? If they are, argues Pylyshyn (1973), then the dual-code hypothesis seems highly implausible. For example, consider the amount of storage required to store detailed copies of everything we see.

According to Pylyshyn the memory capacity required would be unlimited. Another point to consider is how we would use such stored scenes. The images would somehow have to be retrieved, which would entail re-perceiving and analysing them to **see** what was there. Such a system would be totally inefficient because if the stored pictures have to be re-perceived before they can be used, they may as well be stored as already perceived entities rather than exact copies of visual events. A further problem is how to get access to a picture through a word. In most cases, a word corresponds to several pictures. Which picture should we select? Take as an example the word **rose**. Rose corresponds to many possible pictures: large, small, button, pink, yellow, etc. Which of these pictures is the right one to select for the word rose?

Pylyshyn argues that in view of the above difficulties, the images, or pictures, must exist in memory as **analysed entities**, that is, in the form of general descriptions rather than as **raw sensory** material or pictures of the outside world. But what about the images we are able to construct inside our heads? There is no denying the subjective experience associated with mental images. Pylyshyn agrees that people experience mental images, but he points out that the occurrence of such experiences is a separate issue from the debate about whether we store picture-like codes in LTM. The fact that we have a subjective impression of forming images does not mean that we do this because we have the actual pictures stored. We should be equally able to reconstruct these pictures from stored abstract, general descriptions. Thus, the impression that we have pictures stored just because we can evoke them is misleading.

The hypothesis which can be derived from Pylyshyn's arguments is that representation of pictorial knowledge about the world is no different from the type of representation achieved by means of language. There is experimental evidence favouring this unitary theory of imagery and verbal processes.

One experiment by Bower and Winzenz (1970) compared the efficiency of different learning strategies in a paired-associate learning task. Subjects were instructed to construct either sentences or images to link the pair of associated words in order to improve their recall. They found that both learning strategies improved recall.

Bower suggests that, with both image and sentence mediation instructions, the subject is forced to search for and encode meaningful relationships between the word pairs. He argues that it is the formation of semantic relationships that facilitates the recall of the paired associates, rather than the construction of a mental picture. However, these results are open to more than one interpretation.

The idea that imagery forms a basis for language comprehension has also been challenged by more recent experimental work. Specifically, the hypotheses of Begg and Paivio (1969) that concrete sentences might be represented in memory by imagery, and abstract sentences by words, has been attacked. An experiment by Franks and Bransford (1972) cast doubt on this hypothesis. In an earlier study (Bransford and Franks, 1971) they had shown subjects groups of sentences formed by combining four simple sentences in various ways. When the subjects were tested later, they tended to recognize test sentences on the basis of how many of the four simple ideas they combined, rather than on whether or not they had actually been presented. Franks and Bransford concluded from this that when they were given the initial group of sentences, the subjects integrated the information contained in them and stored this integrated knowledge in memory. The subjects' recognition judgements were then based on that integration. So that the greater the number of initial simple ideas a test sentence contained (and therefore the more it resembled the integrated form), the more likely it was to be recognized as one of the originally presented sentences.

In this early study, Bransford and Franks used concrete sentences, and according to the ideas of Begg and Paivio (1969), their results should not extend to abstract sentences. The reason for this is that, according to Begg and Paivio, abstract sentences are stored verbally, which implies that changes in wording should be more recognizable and changes in meaning less so. Thus, using abstract sentences in the Franks and Bransford experiment should enable subjects to be more accurate with their recognition judgements because they can detect changes in the wording of the test sentences. Unfortunately for the dual-code hypothesis, however, Franks and Bransford (1972) showed that their initial results were replicated regardless of whether abstract or concrete sentences were used. This finding implies that concrete and abstract sentences are processed in the same way in memory.

Two codes or one?

The evidence presented above seems to indicate that it is not fruitful to postulate the existence of two separate codes for pictorial and verbal information both on logical and empirical grounds. But how can we explain such phenomena as the strong subjective impression of using imagery and the effects of imagery on memory tasks?

Anderson and Bower (1973) suggest that both visual and verbal information are represented in LTM by means of a single abstract code, and that the distinction between pictorial and verbal codes is a quantitative difference rather than a qualitative difference. They argue that when subjects use images to remember paired-associates or to comprehend sentences, a richer, more conceptually detailed body of information is encoded and stored in memory. Thus, the difference between imaginal and verbal storage is really a difference in the richness of the presentation, rather than a qualitative difference between pictures and words. The semantically richer representations associated with the use of images are more efficiently retrieved, resulting in the imagery effects in verbal learning tasks.

The argument above is not the final solution to the dual-code/unitary-code controversy, but it does provide a possible solution which can be pursued. It would seem that visual experience is not represented in LTM in full pictorial detail, but certain information about visual events must be stored in LTM, in order for us to recognize patterns and remember things previously seen. What has yet to be determined is just how visual information, or the images generated from that information, is stored in LTM.

References

Allen, M., (1968) 'Rehearsal strategies and response cueing as determinants of organization in free recall', *Journal of Verbal Learning and Verbal Behavior*, Vol. 7, p. 58.

Anders, J.R. and Bower, G.H., (1973) *Human Associative Memory*, Washington D C: Winston & Sons.

Bousfield, W.A., (1953) 'The occurrence of clustering in the recall of randomly arranged associates', *Journal of General Psychology*, Vol. 49, p. 229.

Bower, G.H., (1970) 'Organisational factors in memory', *Cognitive Psychology*, Vol. 1, p. 18.

Bower, G.H., *et al.,* (1969) 'Hierarchical retrieval schemes in recall of categorised word lists', *Journal of Verbal Learning and Verbal Behavior*, Vol. 8, p. 323.

Bower, G.H., and Winzenz, D., (1970) 'Comparison of associative learning strategies', *Psychonomic Science*, Vol. 20, p. 119.

Bransford, J.D., and Franks, J.J., (1971) 'The abstraction of linguistic ideas', *Cognitive Psychology*, Vol. 2, p. 331.

Cofer, C.N., Bruce, D.R., and Reicher, G.M., (1966) 'Clustering in free recall as a function of certain methodological variations', *Journal of Experimental Psychology*, Vol. 7, p. 858.

Delin, P.S., (1969) 'The learning to criterion of a serial list with and without mnemonic instructions', *Psychonomic Science*, Vol. 16, p. 169.

Franks, J.J., and Bransford, J.D., (1972) 'The acquisition of abstract idea', *Journal of Verbal Learning and Verbal Behavior*, Vol. 11, p. 311.

Frost, N., (1972) 'Encoding and retrieval in visual memory tasks', *Journal of Experimental Psychology*, Vol. 95, p. 317.

Kellas, G., *et al.,* (1973) 'Temporal aspects of storage and retrieval in free recall of categorized lists', *Journal of Verbal Learning and Verbal Behavior*, Vol. 12, p. 499.

Mandler, G., and Pearlstone, Z., (1966) 'Free and constrained concept learning and subsequent recall', *Journal of Verbal Learning and Verbal Behavior*, Vol. 5, p. 126.

Paivio, A., (1969) 'Mental imagery in associative learning and memory', *Psychological Review*, Vol. 76, p. 241.

Paivio, A. (1971) Imagery and verbal process, New York: Holt, Rinehart & Winston.

Pylyshin, Z.W., (1973) 'What the mind's eye tells the mind's brain: a critique of mental imagery', *Psychological Bulletin*, Vol. 80, p. 1.

Sachs, J.D., (1967) 'Recognition memory for syntactic and semantic aspects of connected discourse', *Perception and Psychophysics*, Vol. 2, p. 437.

Tulving, E., (1962) 'Subjective organisation in free recall of 'unrelated' words', *Psychological Review*, Vol. 69, p. 344.

Tulving, E., and Pearlstone, E., (1966) 'Availability versus accessibility of information in memory for words', *Journal of Verbal Learning and Verbal Behavior*, Vol. 5, p. 381.

Winograd, E., and Lynn, D.S., (1979) 'Role of contextual imagery in associative recall', *Memory and Cognition*, Vol. 7, p. 29.

An experiment to investigate the Stroop effect: the fourth practical

▶ Practical 4.

▶ This chapter contains materials you will need for Practical 4. Check through the chapter appendices before you proceed to familiarize yourself with these materials which are:

● table of pooled class data for Practical 4
● Stroop effect materials for Practical 4
● Calculations for the related t test.

You will need a stop-watch for the practical.

INTRODUCTION

The aim of the practical in this chapter is to reinforce ideas presented in the previous practical concerning experimental design and to introduce you to a parametric statistical test. The topic for this experiment is attention. Below I give you an introduction to this topic; more detailed discussion can be found in the books listed in the further reading for the chapter (page 119).

Attention

Parkin (1987) says attention can be thought of in two ways: as an ability to avoid distraction, and as the capacity to sustain concentration over a period of time.

Researchers interested in attention have suggested a distinction between **automatic** and **controlled processing** (Posner and Snyder, 1975). The basic idea is that some mental and physical processes are under an individual's conscious control, while others tend to occur automatically – without conscious awareness or intention.

A frequently quoted example of this is learning to drive a car. When you first learn to drive, such things as steering, braking, and

▶ Automatic and controlled processing.

changing gear, all require a great deal of concentration. Problems often arise for the learner driver when they are required to do two or more things at once e.g. brake and change down gears. Also, as any driving instructor will tell you, learner drivers can become so engrossed in such things as changing gear that they fail to attend to what is happening on the road in front of them! Yet to drive competently, let alone skilfully, frequently requires a driver to do two, three or more things virtually simultaneously.

How does the transformation from learner to expert occur? The concepts of automatic and controlled processing, introduced above, have been used to explain this transformation. The basic idea is simple, and familiar to you I am sure. With practice, skills which initially required a considerable amount of attention become virtually automatic. Thus for the experienced driver, car handling and an awareness of other road users can take up so little of their attention that they can also hold a conversation or listen to the radio etc. Of course if required, for instance if a dog ran into the road, the experienced driver can snap out of this **automatic pilot** state and concentrate all their attentional resources on taking avoiding action.

The development of automatic processing has a major advantage in that it reduces the number and amount of things that we have to attend to consciously. Thus it releases the scarce resource of conscious attention for other tasks.

The Stroop effect

► The Stroop effect.

Psychologists such as Gleitman (1981) have pointed out that automatic processing can produce interference which actually lowers performance on certain tasks. A classic example of this is the **Stroop effect**, named after J.R. Stroop who devised a colour naming experiment.

The experiment involved subjects naming colours as quickly as possible. In one condition subjects named patches of colour. In a second condition subjects named the ink colour in which words were printed. In a third condition subjects had to name the ink colour in which words were printed, but the words themselves were colour names. For example, subjects would see the word **blue** but it would be written in red ink and their task was to say **red**. Stroop found that subjects were much slower at naming the ink colours when the stimuli were themselves colour words (condition three above). To see just how difficult and frustrating it can be, time yourself on one of the colour word lists which you will find on page 120 at the end of the chapter (details on how to construct them can be found in the methods section under the heading 'Conducting the practical', overleaf).

One explanation for the Stroop effect is that we automatically process the meaning of words. Thus when a subject sees the word **blue** but is supposed to respond to the ink colour and say **red**, the name of the word is automatically processed. This interferes with the subject's ability to process and say the word **red** thus delaying their response. In particular it has been suggested that the Stroop effect produces a mental race between the processes involved in naming the colour and reading the word. As people have much greater practice in reading than in naming colours, the reading response wins the race and slows colour naming. The difficulty experienced in naming the ink colour of the colour words is therefore the consequence of an over-learned skill, and cannot be brought under conscious control.

CARRYING OUT THE PRACTICAL

Experimental design

I have included details of how to construct the materials for this experiment at the end of the chapter (page 120). Turn to them now and you will see that they follow Stroop's original experiment quite closely, in that there are lists of neutral words and colour words. A decision has to be made about what is the most effective experimental design to use: repeated measures, matched samples, independent samples or single subject.

► Choosing the experimental design:

● repeated measures
● matched samples
● independent samples.

 What do you think would be the most appropriate design to use? Keep in mind the problem of subject extraneous variables discussed in the previous practical. You might like to refer back to Chapter 6, pp. 79–82, and Chapter 7, pp. 86–8, on the advantages and disadvantages of the different designs.

I think the repeated measures design is the most appropriate because of its ability to eliminate subject extraneous variables. There are however, disadvantages in using this design, in particular the problem of order effects. If you use the repeated measures design, then each subject must do both conditions i.e. they must name the ink colour of neutral and colour words lists.

► Order effects problems.

As they will be timed on how long it takes them to name the ink colours in each type of list, the method of dealing with order effects used in the previous practical, randomization, cannot be used. So how can you deal with order effects?.

Counterbalancing would appear to be a reasonable solution. With this technique half of the subjects would be presented with the neutral word lists, followed by the colour word lists, and the other half would be presented with the lists the other way round. The idea is that if there are any order effects, such as improved performance due to practice, it will affect both of the experimental conditions equally.

► Counterbalancing see Chapter 6, pp. 80–1, and Chapter 7, pp. 87–8

Having chosen the repeated measures design (I hope it was the one you chose too) you can proceed to carry out the experiment. As in previous practicals I will give you some step by step guidance.

Conducting the practical

For this experiment you will need to find at least two **willing**

► Selecting the subjects.

subjects (you can use more if you choose). There are a couple of re-strictions on who you can use. Your subjects need to be fluent read-ers of English and must not be colour blind! If they normally wear glasses for reading then they should wear them during the experi-ment.

▶ Making the materials.

- **step 1** – you need to prepare six lists of words as shown at the end of the chapter (page 120). To do this cut a sheet of lined paper into six strips approximately three cms. wide; each strip will need to have at least sixteen lines. Then print the words carefully, one per line, using felt-tip pens or coloured pencils. Number them on the back one to six.

▶ Counterbalancing the presentation.

- **step 2** – the subjects need to be presented with the lists of words in a counterbalanced order. As there are six lists (three of neu-tral words and three of colour words), and you have two sub-jects, I would suggest presenting the lists as follows:

  subject 1 – order of list presentation – 1, 4, 2, 5, 3, 6

  subject 2 – order of list presentation – 4, 1, 5, 2, 6, 3

▶ Instructing the subjects.

- **step 3** – read the following set of instructions to the subject: 'I am going to present you with six lists of words, one at a time. Your task is to say aloud the ink colour in which each word is written, starting at the top of the list and working down to the bottom. You will be timed for each list and should try to name the ink colours as quickly, but accurately, as possible. Do you have any questions? Here is the first list (place it in front of them, but upside down so they cannot see the words). When I say **go** turn it over and name the ink colour in which the words are written. **Go**

▶ Recording the results.

- **step 4** – use a stop-watch to time how long it takes the subject to name the ink colours. Make a note of the time taken, (round times up or down to the nearest whole second), and the list number. Then place the next list in front of your subject and re-peat the procedure. It is important to know if a subject makes any errors, and if so, how many. The best way to measure errors is for you to have a list of the correct ink colours to be named for each experimental list and monitor each subjects' responses, placing a cross by any mistakes

▶ Introspective accounts.

- **step 5** – do not forget to ask your subjects for an introspective report. Their comments on how they carried out the task may provide interesting information for the discussion section of you report.

Thank your subjects for their cooperation.

Analysing the results

Put you results into the table overleaf.

Time taken in seconds						
	List 1	List 2	List 3	List 4	List 5	List 6
Subject 1						
Subject 2						

A copy of this table will need to be put in an appendix to your report.

Calculating means and medians
Before you can add your subjects' scores to the table of pooled class results, shown at the end of the chapter, you must calculate your subjects' mean and median times for each condition. To calculate the mean times using the table above, add up each subject's times for lists one, two and three (the neutral word lists) and divide this total by three. Then add up each subject's times for lists four, five, and six (the colour word lists) and again divide the total by three.

To find the median for each condition, arrange the three times in order from quickest to slowest. The median is the middle time. If two of the times are the same e.g. if one of your subjects got scores of ten, ten, and twelve seconds for lists one, two and three, then their median time for the neutral words condition would be ten seconds.

A graphical presentation of the data would be useful. You could, as in Practical 3, draw frequency histograms using the pooled class results. You would need two histograms, one for each of the experimental conditions. An alternative, which might be useful in this practical, is to draw a **frequency polygon**. However, one thing you must decide before you can construct your frequency polygon is whether you are going to use the mean or median scores. There are advantages and disadvantages with both of these measures of central tendency (discussed in Chapter 3). The mean, being the most sensitive measure of central tendency, would normally be used. However, if there are extreme scores then the median can be a more accurate indicator of central tendency.

Look at the data from your subjects to see if, out of the three times for each type of list, there are any which are considerably higher or lower. You cannot see the raw scores for subjects one to eight, but a good indicator of the existence of extreme scores, is the difference between the subject's mean and median **within** each list type. A large difference would indicate the existence of extreme scores.

If you examine the pooled class data at the end of the chapter I think you will agree that the differences between means and medians within each list type are very small. You could therefore use either the mean or the median scores. However, one advantage with using the median scores in this experiment is that they are whole numbers. This makes the construction of the frequency polygon easier. Using whole numbers also makes the calculations easier when you come to apply a statistical test.

► Consult Chapter 3 if you have any difficulty calculating the means or the medians.

► Deciding between the mean and the median.

Drawing frequency polygons

Frequency polygons are constructed like frequency histograms with the vertical axis indicating the frequency of the scores, and with the scores being marked off on the horizontal axis. However, instead of bars, frequency polygons use points which are joined together by straight lines. The advantage of this approach is that you can plot the results of more than one set of scores on a single graph. This is particularly useful where you want a visual comparison between two or more sets of scores. I have included an example of a frequency polygon overleaf constructed using the median scores for the pooled class data. Study this carefully before you draw your own.

Grouped data

If your raw data consists mainly of different scores that occur with a low frequency then the resulting histogram or polygon can be difficult to interpret. In such circumstances it can be helpful to **group** the raw data into classes. To do this find the range of the scores and divide this up in to a convenient number of equal width classes. Look carefully at Table 8. 1 below and then at the polygon.

Table 8.1
Data for frequency polygon (see Figure 8.1)

Class	Mid-point	Frequency median in secs. Colour words	Frequency median in secs. Neutral words
0– 2	1	0	0
3– 5	4	0	0
6– 8	7	5	0
9–11	10	3	2
12–14	13	0	4
14–17	15	0	0
18–20	19	0	2
21–23	22	0	0

Note: when drawing a frequency histogram with grouped data the width of each bar represents the class. However, when drawing a frequency polygon you do not plot a bar but a single point. This raises the questions as to where exactly the point should be placed. The logical answer to this question is at the midpoint of the group of scores. Therefore when drawing a frequency polygon with data grouped into classes you mark off the horizontal axis in class midpoints. I have shown the class midpoints in column two of Table 8.1 and they are marked on the polygon (Figure 8.1)

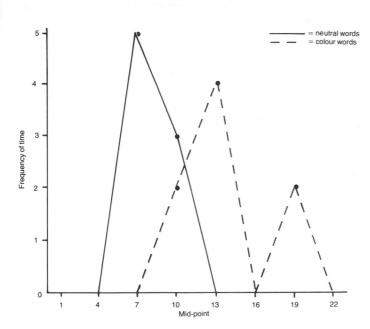

Figure 8.1
*Frequency polygon drawn from
data in Table 8.1*

Applying an appropriate statistical test

Once again to decide what is the most appropriate test to apply to the data we need to consult Figure 4.2, in Chapter 4.

- **decision 1** – are you predicting a difference or a correlation?

Clearly a difference is being predicted so let us move down to decision 2 on the difference side of the chart:

- **decision 2** – how many samples of scores do you have?

In this experiment there are three sets of scores for each of the two conditions. However, you have calculated the mean and median scores for each condition and are going to see if there is a statistically significant difference between the median scores. How many sets of medians are there? The answer is two, therefore you need a two sample statistical test

- **decision 3** – do you need a related or unrelated statistical test?

As you know from the previous practical to answer this question you need to know what experimental design was used. In this experiment a repeated measures design was used and therefore a related statistical test is required

- **decision 4** – can a parametric statistical test be used?

As I have mentioned in previous practicals, parametric statistical tests are powerful tests, but their use is somewhat restricted because they are based upon certain assumptions about the data to be analysed. I have summarized these assumptions for you in the following inset. Please read this now.

> ### *Assumptions underlying use of parametric tests*
> Parametric tests are powerful statistical tests but their use is restricted because they are based on a number of assumptions, these assumptions are summarized below:
>
> 1 The level of the data needs to be ratio or interval.
> 2 The data should be drawn from a population of scores that is normally distributed.
> 3 The populations from which the scores are drawn should have homogeneous (similar) variances.

As you can see from the inset the decision as to whether or not you can use a parametric test involves answering three more questions! I will go through these questions as they apply to this experiment and have provided some more boxed insets to explain the more general points.

▶ Level of data.

The first question concerns the level of data. I hope you are becoming familiar with the idea of levels of data and I suggest you decide for yourself what level of data you think we have in this experiment. Remember the dependent variable in this experiment is the time taken (measured in seconds) to name the ink colour of the word lists.

I think the question of what level of data we have in this experiment is quite clear cut – for a change! The measurement of time in seconds has a true zero – zero literally means no time. Also there are clearly equal units of measurement – one second is equal to any other second. The data level is therefore ratio level. The first obstacle to using a parametric test has been overcome; let us move on to the next question.

▶ Normally distributed variable.

The second question is whether the population(s) from which the scores to be analysed have been drawn is **normally distributed** (see inset on the normal distribution overleaf). To answer this question you need to establish whether or not the samples of scores come from a population(s) which is normally distributed. Unfortunately there is no very satisfactory way of doing this! However, before you throw your hands up in despair, there is some good news. Statisticians have examined this assumption and concluded that it can be violated without seriously affecting the accuracy of the results. Technically, parametric tests are said to be **robust** regarding this assumption. It has been claimed (Coyle, 1980), that as long as it is reasonable to assume that if you had a large number of scores, the majority would form a central hump in the middle of the distribution with the higher and lower scores trailing off at each end, then this is good enough.

▶ Robustness – parametric statistical tests are said to be robust when the assumptions on which they are based can be broken without adversely affecting the accuracy of the results.

The third question is whether the scores are drawn from

populations that have equal or homogeneous variance (see inset on homogeneous variance overleaf). As you will know from previous reading (Chapter 3) variance is a statistical measure of the spread or distribution of a set of scores. So this assumption is simply that the populations, from which the samples of scores were drawn, have a similar amount of spread. To test this assumption you could calculate the variances of your samples of scores. If they were similar then you might feel that it is safe to use a parametric test. However, you need to be careful because the assumption is that the samples of scores come from **populations** with equal variance, not that the samples themselves have equal amounts of variance. While it is quite easy to calculate the variance of your samples of scores it is difficult to establish whether two populations of scores have equal variance. Again statisticians have tested this assumption and found parametric tests to be robust – provided that you have the same number of scores in each condition.

To conclude this rather technical discussion it is fair to say that in practice, rather than trying to establish that the assumptions underlying parametric tests have been met, many psychologists tend to use parametric tests unless there is some clear and obvious reason to indicate they should not.

So, in this experiment, I think it is quite reasonable to assume that the scores come from a population that is at least approximately normally distributed. Therefore a parametric test is justified. As a repeated measures design was used in this experiment then a related parametric test is required. If you look at Figure 4.2 again you can see that a related *t* test is recommended.

► Equal or homogeneous variance.

► If, as in this experiment, you have a repeated measures design, you will be dealing with a single set of difference scores and therefore the equal variance assumption is not involved. If, however, you had used an independent samples design, and therefore you were considering using the independent *t* test (or an *F* test), this assumption would have to be considered.

► In practice many psychologists use parametric tests unless there is an obvious reason not to.

► Test of difference; repeated measures; two samples; parametric test; related *t* test.

The normal distribution
If you were to take a very large sample of people, measure their height and plot the resulting scores on a frequency histogram the result would look something like Figure 8.2, below.

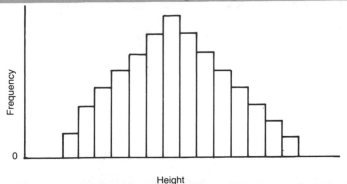

Height

Figure 8.2
Frequency histogram for height in an adult population

Notice the shape of the distribution; it is like a bell, with most scores falling in the middle and the rest tailing off evenly on either side. This shape corresponds closely to the so-called normal distribution curve shown in Figure 8.3 overleaf.

Figure 8. 3
The normal distribution curve

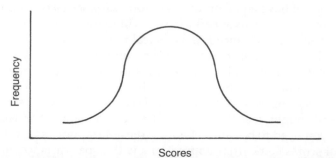

The normal distribution is important for a number of reasons. Firstly, there are many variables in psychology that have been found to be normally distributed e.g. intelligence test scores.

Secondly, the normal distribution has been found to possess a number of very useful mathematical properties. For example, the mean, median and mode are all the same and occur at the apex of the curve. If you know the mean and standard deviation of a variable that is normally distributed then you have a complete description of the distribution. You can draw the curve and calculate what proportion of the scores fall above, below, or in between any two scores that you specify. This is a very useful tool which I will illustrate and explain further in Chapter 11 on revising for the statistics and methodology section of the A level exam.

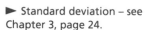

► Standard deviation – see Chapter 3, page 24.

Homogeneous variance

Variance is a measure of the amount of dispersion or spread in a set of scores. Its use as a descriptive statistic is discussed in Chapter 3. The idea of homogeneous or equal variance is easy to understand if you look at the frequency graphs shown below and overleaf.

If two populations of scores had equal variance then they might look something like Figure 8.4.

Figure 8.4

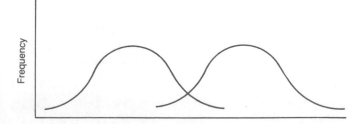

Two populations of scores with different amounts of variance might look like Figure 8.5.

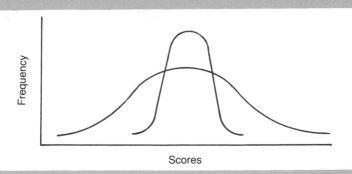

Figure 8.5

I will discuss this assumption in more detail in Chapter 11 which deals with revising for the methodology and statistics questions in the A level examination.

Using the related t test

As I suggested, when discussing the frequency polygon, you could use either the mean or median scores for the *t* test. It makes the calculations slightly easier, however, if you use the medians as these are whole numbers. The instructions on how to do the related *t* test are at the end of the chapter (page 121). Turn to them now, read them through and then do the calculations for your own data set. It is a good idea to double check your results at each stage, as it is very easy to make a mistake when entering numbers into a calculator.

► **Do the calculations now.**

Using the table of critical values for t

When you have obtained your observed value for *t*, you will need to find the relevant critical value. To do this consult appendix D for the critical values for related *t*. You, will have nine degrees of freedom (if you have added your two subjects' scores to the eight in the table of pooled class results). This is because the number of degrees of freedom is *N* (ten) minus one, which gives nine. You must also decide if the experimental hypothesis is one or two tailed.

► Degrees of freedom.

► One tail or two?.

I will leave you to decide this! Finally, look at the decision rule carefully, it states that the observed value of *t* must be equal to or **exceed** the critical value. (This is different from the Wilcoxon signed ranks test where the observed value must be equal to or **less** than the critical value).

WRITING UP THE PRACTICAL

As you have written up several practical reports by now, I will only comment on those sections where you might need a little help. But remember to include all the sections in the AEB format (see page 167).

Introduction

I have included quite a lot of information on the Stroop effect in my introduction to this practical. You can use any of this material you find helpful in writing your own introduction. It would be useful to add to this a brief account of some of the theories and research on selective attention. I have given you a number of sources for such information in the further reading for the chapter (overleaf).

Experimental hypothesis

I will leave it to you to formulate an appropriate hypothesis. It needs to be a clear, specific prediction about what you expect the outcome of the experiment to be. Take into account relevant theory and the results of previous research when deciding if your hypothesis is going to be one or two tailed.

Results

Put the raw data from your two subjects in an appendix and the table of pooled class data in the results section.

Treatment of results

Include your frequency polygon and give a brief explanation of which test was used to analyse the results and why. Put the observed and critical values of *t* in a table as in Practical 3.

Discussion

You need to describe your results in detail and then relate them to the theories and findings outlined in the introduction. Here are six points you could consider:

1 Did your results confirm the existence of the Stroop effect?

2 Can you comment on the speed/accuracy data? Usually the colour words have longer times and more errors, which is an indirect indication of the greater cognitive demands of this task.

3 Can you explain your results in terms of current theories of selective attention? You could consider, for example, Broadbent's single-channel model and Triesman's attenuator model in terms of their ability to explain the results of your experiment?

4 Do your results say anything about the role of automatic processes in complex tasks like reading?

5 Do your subjects' introspective reports say anything of interest about the processes involved or the methodology of the experiment? For example, I have found a number of subjects comment on the difficulty of reading words printed in yellow. Another subject, who appeared to do very well, when questioned, admitted to deliberately not focusing her eyes when naming the ink colour in the colour word condition, or only focusing on the first or last letter of the word.

6 Can you suggest any improvements in the design of the

experiment? Would it be better to have more lists, or fewer lists? Could you include other conditions e.g. colour-suggesting words like sky or grass? What about the errors? Did subjects make any? If they did were there more on the neutral word lists or the colour word lists? What are the implications of errors for your results?

References

These are some references you might like to consult. If you consult them you can put them in the reference section of your report.

Gleitman, H., (1981) *Psychology*, New York: Norton.

Parkin, A.J., (1987) *Memory and Amnesia: An Introduction*, Oxford: Blackwell.

Posner, M.I., and Synder, C.R., (1975) 'Attention and cognitive control', in Solo, R.L., *Information Processing and Cognition*, New Jersey: Erlbaum.

Coyle, J., 'Experimental Design', in Radford, J., and Govier, E. (eds), (1980) *A Textbook of Psychology*, London: Sheldon Press

Stroop, J.R., (1935) 'Studies of Interference', *Serial Verbal Reactions, Journal of Experimental Psychology*, Vol. 6, pp. 643–61.

NEC, (1990) 'Cognitive Psychology Module', *A Level Psychology Course*, Unit 2, Cambridge: National Extension College.

Broadbent, D., (1958) *Perception and Communication*, Oxford: Pergamon.

Treisman, A., (1960) 'Contextual clues in selective listening', *Quarterly Journal of Experimental Psychology*, Vol. 12, pp. 242–8.

CHAPTER SUMMARY

In this chapter you will have learned something about selective attention which you can add to your other studies of selective perception. You should also have increased your knowledge of how to choose a statistical test by learning about the assumptions which have to be met for a parametric test to be used.

Appendices for Practical 4

Table of pooled class data

Subject	Neutral words Mean	Median	Colour words Mean	Median
1	6.0	6	9.0	9
2	6.3	6	11.0	12
3	8.0	8	12.3	12
4	7.3	7	12.3	12
5	11.3	11	21.0	20
6	7.3	7	9.3	9
7	10.0	10	14.3	13
8	11.3	11	17.7	18
9				
10				

The scores are all times in seconds.

The Stroop effect materials

Write the following words in each strip in the colour denoted by the letter in brackets which follows it.

Strip 1	Strip 2	Strip 3	Strip 4	Strip 5	Strip 6
Art (Y)	Cave (R)	Art (G)	Red (Y)	Blue (R)	Red (G)
Stove (B)	Stove (G)	Bottle (Y)	Green (B)	Blue (G)	Green (Y)
Art (G)	Bottle (R)	Stove (R)	Red (G)	Yellow (R)	Green (R)
Cave (R)	Art (B)	Bottle (G)	Blue (R)	Red (B)	Yellow (G)
Bottle (R)	Stove (B)	Cave (R)	Yellow (R)	Green (B)	Blue (R)
Stove (Y)	Art (G)	Stove (B)	Green (Y)	Red (G)	Green (B)
Stove (G)	Cave (Y)	Art (Y)	Yellow (G)	Blue (Y)	Red (Y)
Art (B)	Bottle (G)	Bottle (B)	Red (B)	Yellow (G)	Yellow (B)
Cave (Y)	Stove (R)	Art (B)	Blue (Y)	Green (R)	Red (B)
Art (R)	Cave (B)	Stove (Y)	Green (R)	Red (B)	Green (Y)
Bottle (G)	Art (Y)	Cave (B)	Yellow (G)	Red (Y)	Red (B)
Cave (B)	Bottle (Y)	Bottle (R)	Green (B)	Red (Y)	Yellow (R)
Stove (R)	Art (R)	Stove (G)	Green (R)	Blue (R)	Yellow (G)
Bottle (Y)	Cave (G)	Cave (Y)	Blue (Y)	Blue (G)	Blue (Y)
Cave (G)	Bottle (B)	Art (R)	Blue (G)	Yellow (B)	Green (R)
Bottle (B)	Stove (Y)	Cave (G)	Yellow (B)	Green (Y)	Blue (G)

B = Blue, R = Red, Y = Yellow, G = Green

Calculation of the related t test
The median scores for the colour and neutral word lists

Subject	Colour medians A	Neutral medians B	d Step 3	d^2 Step 4
1	9	6	3	9
2	12	6	6	36
3	12	8	4	16
4	12	7	5	25
5	20	11	9	81
6	9	7	2	4
7	13	10	3	9
8	18	11	7	49
			$\Sigma d = 39$	$\Sigma d^2 = 229$

- **step 1** – calculate the medians (or the means) for the two sets of scores. These are shown in the table above
- **step 2** – arrange the scores in a table such that the condition with the highest total comes first (column A), call the other condition column B

  I have arranged the table above as described in step 2
- **step 3** – calculate the difference between each subject's scores by taking the score in column B from the score in column A
- **step 4** – square the difference (d) for each subject
- **step 5** – add up all the ds (Σd)

  $\Sigma d = 39$
- **step 6** – add up all the d^2s (Σd^2)

  $\Sigma d^2 = 229$
- **step 7** – substitute the numbers calculated in steps 5 and 6 in the formula below:

$$t = \frac{\Sigma d}{\sqrt{\dfrac{\Sigma d^2 - (\Sigma d)^2}{N-1}}}$$

Proceed with the calculations as follows:
- **step 8** – $N\Sigma d^2$ – this means multiply Σd^2 by N (the number of pairs of scores). In this experiment $N = 8$

  $N\Sigma d^2 = 1832$
- **step 9** – $[\Sigma d]^2$ – this tells you to square Σd

  $[\Sigma d]^2 = 1521$
- **step 10** – subtract $[\Sigma d]^2$ from $N\Sigma d^2$

  $1832 - 1521 = 311$
- **step 11** – divide the result of step 10 by $N - 1$ ($N - 1 = 7$)

  $311 \div 7 = 44.43$
- **step 12** – square root the answer of step 11

  $\sqrt{44.43} = 6.67$

- **step 13** – divide Σd by the result of step 12 to give you the observed value of t:
  $39 \div 6.67 = 5.85$
  Therefore $t = 5.85$

That is the worst of it over; all you have to do now is find out whether your result is statistically significant. To do this, as in the other statistical tests we have carried out, you need to look up the appropriate critical value for the test in question. If you now turn to appendix D you will see that in order to select the correct critical value you need to know:

1 How many degrees of freedom there are ($N - 1$). You already know that there are 8 subjects (N) so $N - 1$ is 7.
2 Whether your hypothesis is one or two tailed. I will assume in this case that a one-tailed hypothesis has been made.
3 What significance level you feel is suitable. It is usual to check to see if results are significant at the 0.05 level first and if they are go on to more stringent levels of significance.

With this information we can consult the table of critical values in appendix D. You will see that the critical value for a one-tailed hypothesis with 7 degrees of freedom is 1.895 at the 0.05 level of significance.

Levels of significance for a one-tailed test

	0.05	0.025	0.01	0.005
Degrees of freedom 7	1.895	2.365	2.998	3.499

The decision rule states that the observed value of t must be equal to, or exceed the critical value for significance to be established. In this case the observed value (5.85) clearly exceeds the critical value (1.895) therefore the results are significant at the 0.05 level; the null hypothesis can be rejected and the experimental hypothesis accepted.

Notice that the results are also significant at the 0.005 level. This is the value you would put in your treatment of results as p≤0.005.

► p≤0.005 means that the probability of the results occurring by chance is equal to, or less than 1 in 200.

An experiment into the role of organization in memory: the fifth practical

► Practical 5.

► This chapter contains materials for Practical 5. Look at the chapter appendices. The materials are:

● pooled data for Practical 5
● stimulus sheets A and B for Practical 5
● Calculation for the Mann-Whitney U test.

You will need a stop-watch to conduct the practical.

Chapter objectives

By the end of this chapter you will:

▌ have completed a fifth practical report

▌ be aware of the role of organization in long-term memory

▌ understand what an asymmetrical order effect is

▌ gain further practice in experimental design and in choosing an appropriate statistical test

▌ carry out a Mann-Whitney test

▌ know and be able to use the following key terms; organized and random format and asymetrical order effect.

INTRODUCTION

The practical in this chapter introduces you to a different experimental design and to a statistical test that you have not used so far. I will provide you with a short introduction and some references, but as you are now quite practised in writing practicals I will keep my comments fairly brief.

The role of organization in memory

For this practical we will return to the topic area, memory. In particular this practical will focus on the role of organization in memory. The experiment that you will carry out is based on research carried out by Bower, Clark, Winzenz and Lesgold (1969). They presented two groups of subjects with identical sets of words to learn but the words were organized differently. For one group the words were organized in the form of an associative hierarchy. This was formed by choosing a starting word, written at the top of the hierarchy, and then placing three different but strong verbal associatives to it at the next level in the hierarchy. Each of these words was then used in turn to generate two more verbal associates, which formed the third level of the hierarchy. Finally, two associates were generated below each third level word, thus giving a five level hierarchy with a total of twenty-two words. You can see what this looks like by looking at stimulus sheet A at the end of the chapter (page 130).

The associations in stimulus sheet A are purely intuitive and the connections between distant words in the hierarchy are understandable only in terms of the intervening associations in the chain.

If you examine stimulus sheet B at the end of the chapter (page 130) you will notice that the words are the same as those in stimulus sheet A, except that they have a random rather than organized format. Stimulus sheet A is therefore called the **organized** format and stimulus sheet B the **random** format.

Bower *et al.*'s major finding was that subjects given the words in the organized format had better recall than subjects given the words in the random format. How might we explain this finding?

Bower *et al.* suggest that many subjects, when given the words in an organized format, commented upon the construction principle used to generate the associative hierarchy. They used this principle to reconstruct the word list from memory. When the words were presented in the random format subjects do not appear to have been able to work out the construction principle and therefore it was not used to aid recall. Bower *et al.* argue that recall in the organized condition is a two stage process. If subjects can remember some of the words, particularly at the top of the hierarchy, they can then generate associations to these words and check to see if they recognize them as being on the original sheet. Some subjects in Bower *et al.*'s experiment recalled words not on the original sheet; these words were often false recognitions of words generated as associations to previously recalled items. Therefore, Bower *et al.* claim that recall with the organized format consists of the generation of word associates and the recognition of them as being on the stimulus sheet.

With the random format, subjects cannot establish a similar simple rule to help them generate possible words. The original experiment conducted by Bower *et al.* was more extensive and complex than I have outlined here, but the aim of the practical is to try to replicate the major finding of their work.

► Stimulus sheet A – the organized format and stimulus sheet B – the random format.

► The construction principle refers to how the words are linked in the association hierarchy. In this experiment cheese is the keyword at the top of the hierarchy. Below this are the associated words, mouse, bread and yellow; followed at the next level by the words associated with them.

CARRYING OUT THE PRACTICAL

Experimental design

Please read this section through carefully before attempting to carry out the experiment.

In this experiment you will be trying to find out if subjects will recall more words when the words are presented in an organized format in comparison to a random format.

 What are the independent and dependent variables in this experiment?

► Deciding the experimental design.

The first thing that you need to decide is what experimental design to use. I have argued, in previous practicals, that the most powerful design is repeated measures, because it eliminates extraneous subject variables. But, given the aim of this experiment, is this an appropriate design to use? Can you think of any problems with using a repeated measures design?

One problem I would suggest, is that if each subject is to do both conditions, as is the case with the repeated measures design, then you have to do something to deal with order effects. In previous practicals you have used randomization or counterbalancing to deal with order effects. In a practical such as this, however, randomization is not possible. Think back to the imagery versus rehearsal practical (Chapter 7), where randomization was used. Consider why this technique for dealing with order effects cannot be used here.

► Dealing with order effects.

Counterbalancing (which was used in the Stroop experiment, Chapter 8) cannot be used either. A person could be presented with the words in the random format and then the organized format. But what would happen if subjects were presented with the words in the organized format first? They could use the information gained from using the organized format to aid their recall when given the same words in a random format.

The situation described above is an example of what is called an **asymmetrical order effect**. An example of such an effect was discussed in Chapter 6, on pp. 80–1. The example given concerned an experiment on the effects of drinking alcohol on driving ability. It would be difficult to use a repeated measures design in such an experiment because you could not counterbalance the conditions. Half of the subject could do a driving test without alcohol and then do the test again having consumed some alcohol. However, the other subjects could not do the test in reverse because the alcohol would be in the bloodstream for quite a long period of time.

► An asymmetrical order effect.

This seems to be a situation where the repeated measures design simply cannot be used and you must therefore consider the alternatives. A design which avoids the problem of order effects and is simple to organize is the independent samples design. With this design subjects are randomly assigned to one or other of the experimental conditions and it is hoped that any subject extraneous variables will cancel each other out.

► Independent sample design.

A matched-pairs design could be considered and does have the advantage of eliminating subject extraneous variables on which subjects have been matched. But in practical terms matching can be a difficult and time-consuming process, so despite its advantages it will not be used in this experiment.

► Matched-pairs design.

Conducting the experiment

Having decided on the design, how is the experiment to be carried out? I have included the materials for the experiment at the end of the chapter as stimulus sheet A and Stimulus Sheet B (page 130). As you can see each stimulus sheet has the same twenty-two words, but in stimulus sheet A they are organized into an associative hierarchy, whereas in stimulus sheet B they have been randomly allocated to their positions. You will also need a stop watch and four sheets of blank paper headed:

response sheet 1 A
response sheet 2 A
response sheet 1 B
response sheet 2 B

You will need to find two subjects and carry out the experiment on one subject at a time. Toss a coin to decide which stimulus sheet your first subject will be given, A or B, and give your second subject the other.

● **step 1** – read the following instructions to your subject:

'This is a two trial experiment. During each trial you will be given the same sheet of words, which you should try to learn. You will be given sixty seconds to study the sheet, it will then be removed and you will be given a sheet of paper on which to write down as many of the words as you can in any order. You will have two minutes in which to recall the words. You will then be presented with the sheet of words again and have another sixty seconds to study them. The words will be taken away and you will have a further two minutes in which to write down the words'

● **step 2** – follow the procedure below:

Place the stimulus sheet, upside down, in front of your subject so they cannot see the words. Tell them to turn over the stimulus sheet and start to learn the words. Start timing.

After sixty seconds tell the subject to stop, take away the stimulus sheet and give them response sheet 1 (A or B depending on which condition the subject is doing).

Start timing, give the subject two minutes to free recall the words, that is write down the words in any order.

Take away the the response sheet and give them the same stimulus sheet again. Start timing.

After sixty seconds, remove the stimulus sheet and give response sheet 2 (A or B). Give the subject two minutes to recall the words.

Thank the subject for their participation.

Repeat this procedure for subject two but using the other stimulus sheet and response sheets.

Analysing the results

Work out the number of correctly recalled words from the response sheets and add your subjects' scores to the table of pooled class results at the end of the chapter. Your subjects will be; subject ten, for the 'organized' format and subject twenty, for the random format.

You will now need to take each subject's two scores (response sheet one score and response sheet two score) and calculate the mean score. Place each subject's mean score in the appropriate column in the table of pooled class results.

Consider an appropriate way of presenting the subjects' mean scores graphically. I will leave it up to you to choose what type of graph to use but remember to draw it/them neatly and label the axes clearly. Look back at the graphs used in previous practicals.

► For calculating means see Chapter 3.

► Chapter 7 for histograms
Chapter 8 for frequency polygons.

Applying an appropriate statistical test

It is decision time again. What would be an appropriate test to use on the subjects' mean scores? Look back at Figure 4.2 Chapter 4, page 36.

- **decision 1** – seems fairly clear-cut; we are clearly predicting a difference in the mean scores between the two conditions
- **decision 2** – this again is quite straight forward, we are comparing two sets of scores so we require a two sample test
- **decision 3** – this experiment used an independent samples design therefore you need an unrelated statistical test
- **decision 4** – can you use a parametric test or do you need to use a non-parametric test? Look back at the discussion of this issue in Chapter 8. The first issue concerns the level of data you have in this experiment. Your dependent variable is the number of words the subjects recalled correctly. In the imagery verses rehearsal practical, Chapter 7, I argued that it is difficult to decide exactly what level of measurement you have when dealing with things like the number of words recalled. You certainly have an ordinal level of measurement and therefore it is probably best to play safe and use a non-parametric test.

► Test of difference two samples independent design non-parametric Mann-Whitney U test.

If you follow Figure 4.2 you will see that the recommended statistical test is the Mann-Whitney U test.

I have given you step by step instructions on how to carry out the Mann-Whitney test and a worked example at the end of the chapter (page 130), you will need to look at this now. Then do your own calculations.

► You might be wondering why the mean values are being used if the data is ordinal level. With ordinal level data the medians would normally be calculated. However, if there are only two scores, as here, the mean and the medians will be the same.

► **Do the calculations now.**

Extending the practical

You do not need to do this as part of your practical but you might be interested to see if subjects' performances improve from response sheet 1 to response sheet 2. What statistical test could you use to find out if there is a significant improvement in the scores?

NB If you do attempt this think carefully about the experimental design involved.

WRITING UP THE PRACTICAL

As you have written up several practical reports by now I will only comment on those sections where you might need a little additional help. Remember to include all the sections included in the AEB format, see appendix B (page 167).

Introduction

I have described the work of Bower *et al.* (1969) in my introduction and you will find the issue of organization in memory discussed in Gross, R.D., (1992) *Psychology: The Science of Mind and Behaviour*, Chapter 12. Davenport, G., (1992) *Essential Psychology*, describes Bower *et al.*'s experiment in Chapter 6, page 145. The cognitive psychology modul of the NEC A level Psychology course also has relevant material.

You might like to start your introduction section with a broader discussion of memory and recall before focusing on Bower *et al.*'s research.

Experimental hypothesis

The experimental hypothesis is left up to you, but remember what is needed is a clear, specific prediction about what you expect the outcome of the experiment to be. Does existing theory and/or prior research suggest that subjects with the organized format will recall more words than subjects given the words in a random format? The answer to this question should determine whether your hypothesis is one or two tailed.

If you do decide to analyse the results to see if there is an improvement in recall from stimulus sheets 1 to stimulus sheets 2, then you will need two additional hypotheses. One for improvement in the organized format words, and one for improvement in the random format words. Remember, however, that you are not required to do this, it is an optional extra!

Null hypothesis

The null hypothesis is also left to you.

Results

You can put the table of pooled class data in the results section with your own additions.

Treatment of results

Include your graphical presentation of the subjects' mean scores in the treatment of results. Give a brief explanation of which statistical test(s) were used and why. Put the results of your statistical analysis in a table, as shown in previous practicals, and make it clear to the reader whether or not your null hypothesis is accepted or rejected.

Discussion

Begin your discussion by describing the results of your experiment in as much detail as you can. Do not forget to include any comments that your subjects may have made which are relevant to your findings or methodology. Here are some points to consider:

1 Do your results confirm those of Bower *et al.*? If they do not you should try to offer some explanation for your results.
2 Is there any information from your study which supports, or goes against, Bower *et al.*'s explanation of their results? You could examine the response sheets to see the kind of words that subjects recalled by mistake. Do subjects in the organized format condition have more **false recognitions** than subjects in the random format condition?
3 You may not have carried out a statistical analysis but you can still comment on any difference in recall between the response

sheets 1 and 2. If there is a difference does it apply to both the organized and random conditions?

4 Comment, if appropriate, on the design, materials and procedure used in the experiment. If you were to repeat the experiment would you make any changes? If 'yes', what would they be and why would you make them?

References
Do not forget to include references!

Appendices
You know the kind of things to put in appendices – copies of the stimulus sheets, the calculations etc.

 Now look back through what you have done. Is there anything you want to add to your notes on methodology and statistics? If so do it now before you forget.

Make sure you file the notes on organization and memory you used for the practical with your other notes on memory.

CHAPTER SUMMARY

In working through this chapter you will have learned something about the role of organization in memory and you will have conducted an experiment using an independent measures design. You will have subjected your results to statistical analysis using a non-parametric test of difference suitable for independent designs, called the Mann-Whitney U test.

Further reading: Chapter 9

Anderson, L.K., (1980) *Cognitive Psychology*, New York: W.H. Freeman. I suggest you read Chapter 7.

Atkinson, R.L., *et al.*, (1990) *Introduction to Psychology*, New York: Harcourt Brace Jovanovich. I suggest you look at Chapter 8, pp. 309–10.

Bower, G.H., *et al.*, (1969) 'Hierarchical retrieval schemes in recall of categorical word lists', *Journal of Verbal Learning and Verbal Behaviour*, Vol. 8, pp. 323–43. This is the original article and is rather heavy going.

Gross, R.D., (1992) *Psychology: The Science of Mind and Behaviour* (2nd Ed.), Chapter 12, Sevenoaks: Hodder & Stoughton.

Davenport, G., (1992) *Essential Psychology*, London: CollinsEducational. Describes Bower *et al.*'s experiment in Chapter 6, page 145.

Appendices for Practical 5

Table of pooled class data

Condition A				Condition B			
(Organized format)				(Random format)			
Subject	Trial 1	Trial 2	Mean	Subject	Trial 1	Trial 2	Mean
1	15	17	16.0	11	11	13	12.0
2	16	16	16.0	12	9	13	11.0
3	18	20	19.0	13	9	12	10.5
4	14	16	15.0	14	8	10	9.0
5	12	15	13.5	15	10	13	11.5
6	9	14	11.5	16	12	14	13.0
7	14	17	15.5	17	12	14	13.0
8	11	15	13.0	18	8	10	9.0
9	16	20	18.0	19	7	12	9.5
10				20			

Stimulus sheet A

CHEESE

BREAD		MOUSE		YELLOW	
milk	wheat	cat	trap	sun	butterfly
cow	germ	eyes	bear	hot	moth
butter	field	tiger	cage	tan	net

Stimulus sheet B

TIGER

TAN		SUN		BEAR	
germ	trap	moth	mouse	eyes	butter
net	yellow	bread	milk	wheat	cat
field	cow	cage	butterfly	cheese	hot

The calculation of the Mann-Whitney test

- step 1 – if the two groups are different in size let N_a be the size of the smaller group and let N_b be the size of the larger group. If both groups have the same number of subjects it does not matter which you call N_a and N_b
- step 2 – rank the combined set of scores $(N_a + N_b)$ giving a rank of one to the lowest score, two for the next lowest score etc. Where two or more scores are the same (tied) you give each score the average of the ranks which would have been used if they had not been tied. See Chapter 7, p. 98 for more information about ties
- step 3 – find the sum of the ranks for N_a and call this R_a

- **step 4** –substitute the values of N_a, N_b and R_a into the formula below and calculate U:

$$U = N_aN_b + \frac{N_a(N_a + 1)}{2} - R_a$$

- **step 5** – substitute the values of U, N_a and N_b into the formula below and calculate U':

$$U' = N_aN_b - U$$

- **step 6** – look up the appropriate critical value in the table of critical values for the Mann-Whitney U test in appendix D. To do this you need to know N_a, N_b, whether your hypothesis was one or two tailed and the desired level of significance
- **step 7** – the decision rule states that you can reject the null hypothesis if the observed value of U or U' (whichever is the smaller) is equal to, or less than the critical value.

Worked example of the Mann-Whitney U test

- steps 1 and 2

	Condition A			Condition B	
Subject	N_a Mean	Rank	Subject	N_b Mean	Rank
1	16.0	15.5	11	12.0	8.0
2	16.0	15.5	12	11.0	5.0
3	19.0	18.0	13	10.5	4.0
4	15.0	13.0	14	9.0	1.5
5	13.5	12.0	15	11.5	6.5
6	11.5	6.5	16	13.0	10.0
7	15.5	14.0	17	13.0	10.0
8	13.0	10.0	18	9.0	1.5
9	18.0	17.0	19	9.5	3.0

- **step 3** – sum of ranks for $N_a = R_a = 121.5$
- **step 4** – $U = N_aN_b + \frac{N_a(N_a+1)}{2} - R_a$

$$U = 9 \times 9 + \frac{9(9 + 1)}{2} - 121.5$$

$$U = 81 + 45 - 121.5$$

$$U = 126 - 121.5$$

$$U = 4.5$$

- **step 5** – calculate U' using the formula $U' = N_aN_b - U$
  $U' = 9 \times 9 - 4.5$
  $U' = 81 - 4.5$
  $U' = 76.5$

- **step 6** – for a one-tailed hypothesis at the 0.05 level of significance where $N_a = 9$ and $N_b = 9$ the critical value is 21.

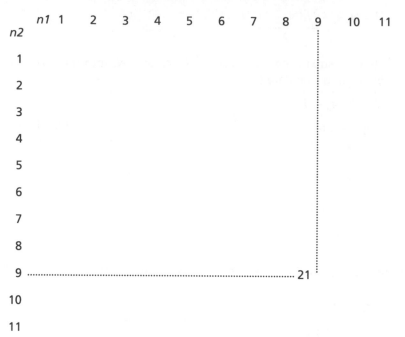

- **step 7** – the decision rule for significance states that if the observed value of U or U', whichever is the smaller (so it's $U = 4.5$) is equal to or less than the critical value (21) you can reject the null hypothesis. So, on the basis of the data provided, the result is significant at the 0.05 level: $p < 0.05$.

Some further practicals

WHY MORE PRACTICALS?

In the book so far I have described in detail how to carry out, analyse and write reports for five practicals. I have included five practicals because this is the number of practicals that the AEB require you to submit for assessment. (In September 1995 this is likely to change to four.) Each of these practicals is given a mark out of twenty, thus the maximum mark you can achieve for the coursework is 100, twenty for each of the five practicals (see appendix B, 'Marking Scheme for Coursework'). In this chapter I am going to outline three further practicals that you might consider doing.

Why should I attempt another practical?

There are several answers to this question:

1 You may find that having carried out a couple of the practicals that you would like to have more control over the design and implementation of a practical. You might want more **say** in a practical and an opportunity to try out some of your newly acquired skills in methodology and statistics.

2 You can carry out and write up more than five practicals, but use the five with the highest marks as your coursework. I would suggest, however, that you weigh up carefully any anticipated improvement in marks against the time and effort required to carry out an extra practical.

3 On a less positive note you may encounter problems with one of the practicals I have already described and decide that rather than struggle on with it you would rather tackle a new practical. So you can substitute one of the practicals here for one of those in the previous chapters. However, I would advise you not to substitute more than one practical in this way.

Can I improve my marks by doing another practical?

Bonus marks, up to a maximum of three, are available for practicals that are largely designed and carried out by students themselves. These bonus marks, however, only count if your total score for the five practicals is less than 100. Thus if you carried out five totally original and brilliant practicals, and each was given a mark of twenty-three, you would still only be credited with a total coursework mark of 100. On the other hand if you had four practicals, three with marks of twenty and one with a mark of seventeen, then a fifth practical with a mark of twenty-three would raise your coursework mark to the maximum of 100.

▶ It seems probable that, with effect from the 1995 exam, these marking arrangements will change. You should check with the board.

Do I have to do more than five practicals?

There are a number of reasons, outlined above, for considering the possibility of designing and carrying out a practical of your own. Do not, however, think that this is something you **have** to do; it is not. What you should do is five practicals, and the five in Chapters 4, 5, 7, 8 and 9 will get you full marks if use them as the basis for producing first class practical reports.

How much help can I expect?

If you do decide to carry out one of the practicals outlined in this section do not forget that you will need access to subjects as there is no pooled class data provided. Also to gain bonus marks you must design and write up the report with a minimum of assistance.

I will, therefore, only give you a brief outline of topics you could investigate and leave most of the design and reporting decisions up to you.

Can I do a practical of my own?

If you are feeling really adventurous and have a great idea for a practical of your own, fine but you **must** operate within the British Psychological Society's Principles for Conducting Research with Human Participants. These are printed in appendix C and you should read them carefully before undertaking any research of your own. If you have any doubts about the ethics of a practical you are thinking of doing, **do not do it!**

PROJECT 1 – INTERPERSONAL ATTRACTION: THE MATCHING HYPOTHESIS

Interpersonal attraction

A number of studies have found that dating and married couples are usually closely matched in terms of their rated level of physical attractiveness (Berscheid and Walster 1974).

For example, a study by Murstein (1972) asked people to rate the physical attractiveness of photographs of each partner of ninety-nine couples without knowing who was paired with whom. The physical attractiveness ratings of the couples matched each other significantly more closely than did the ratings of photographs of those that were randomly paired into couples. Silverman found similar results in a real-life field study in which separate observers rated the physical attractiveness of couples in bars, theatre lobbies and other social events. A recent study by Folkes (1982) of a video dating service in the USA found that men and women tended to choose as dates people who matched them in physical attractiveness.

As a lot of the research on the **matching hypothesis** has been carried out on married couples let us take this as our starting point. On the basis of the matching hypothesis men and women who are married to each other should have a similar level of physical attractiveness.

One possible way of testing this aspect of the matching hypothesis would be to obtain photographs of married couples and then separate the pictures of the husbands from their wives. Then subjects could be asked to rate the level of physical attractiveness of each of the women and the same, or a different group of subjects, could rate the physical attractiveness of the men. The scores for each couple could then be paired and a correlation analysis carried out. On the basis of the matching hypothesis it would be predicted that there should be a positive correlation, with women rated as highly attractive being married to men rated as highly attractive; and women rated low on physical attractiveness being married to men rated low on physical attractiveness.

Carrying out the project

This is reasonably straight forward. The major decision is whether you ask the same subjects to rate both the husbands and wives or have one set of subjects rate the husbands and a different group rate the wives. There are, as always, advantages and disadvantages with both methods. Think about them carefully and make your choice.

Subjects

You will have to generate your own data by finding subjects. The number of subjects you need will depend on the design decisions you make, but between ten and twenty subjects would be ideal. Ten would be acceptable if you chose to use a related design (each subject rates all of the photographs). However, more than this would be needed if you decided in favour of an unrelated design (if, for example, you asked male subjects to rate the photographs of the brides and you asked female subjects to rate the photographs of the grooms).

Materials

Local newspapers often contain photographs of recently married couples; you could use these as the material for your practical.

You will also need to develop a rating scale, this could simply involve asking subjects to rate the photographs for physical attractiveness on a scale from one to ten, with one being defined as unattractive and ten highly attractive. See below:

Unattractive							Highly Attractive		
1	2	3	4	5	6	7	8	9	10

Procedure

Subjects would be shown the photographs in a random order and asked to rate them for physical attractiveness. You would need a record of each subjects' ratings for subsequent statistical analysis.

Analysing the results

To analyse the results, firstly, you could find the mean or median attractiveness rating for each photograph. These ratings would then need to be paired for each married couple and a correlation analysis carried out. Do not forget to include a graphical presentation of your data.

Applying an appropriate statistical test

The main consideration when applying an appropriate statistical test is the level of data. The level of data will be the major determinant of whether you use a parametric or non-parametric test of correlation. Once you have decided on the appropriate test and carried out the calculations you will need to see if the resulting correlation coefficient is statistically significant. Look back to the first practical in Chapter 4 to see how you do this.

Writing up the practical

I cannot give you any real assistance in writing up the practical if you are to obtain bonus marks, but as you should have written several practical reports by now you should have a good idea about the kind of things that need to be included under the relevant report headings.

Introduction

See the introduction to this project. There is some useful information on the matching hypothesis in Gross, R., (1992) *Psychology: The Science of Mind and Behaviour*, Chapter 18, pp. 494–7.

Hypothesis

You are given a strong hint as to what the hypothesis could be in my passages on interpersonal attraction.

Results

A clearly labelled table of results will be needed.

Treatment of results

See the Treatment of Results section for Practical 1 which also used a correlation analysis.

Discussion

In your discussion remember to describe your results in as much detail as possible and then go on to relate them to the theories and studies you have described in your background section.

References

Do not forget to include references at the end of your report.
My references for this project are listed below.

Berscheid, E., and Walster, E., (1974) 'Physical Attractiveness', in Berkowitz, L. (ed.), *Advances in Experimental Social Psychology*, New York: Academic Press.

Folkes, V.S., (1982) 'Forming Relationships and the Matching Hypothesis', *Personality and Social Psychology Bulletin*, Vol. 8, pp. 631–6.

Murstein, B.I., (1972) 'Physical Attractiveness and Marital Choice', *Journal of Personality and Social Psychology*, Vol. 22, pp. 8–12.

Silverman, I., (1971) 'Physical Attractiveness and Courtship', *Sexual Behavior*, Vol.1, pp. 21–5.

Further Reading: Project 1

Davenport, G.C., (1992) *Essential Psychology*, London: Collins Educational.
Chapter 8, 'Social influence and interpersonal perception' has a good summary of the factors influencing interpersonal attraction.

Gross R.D., (1992) *Psychology, The Science of Mind and Behaviour*, Sevenoaks: Hodder & Stoughton.
I have already mentioned that there is a useful discussion of the matching hypothesis on pp. 494–7, Chapter 18.

Pennington D., (1986) *Essential Social Psychology*, London: Edward Arnold.

Berscheid, E., and Walster E.H., (1978) *Interpersonal Attraction*, California: Addison Wesley.

PROJECT 2 – THE COGNITIVE DEVELOPMENT OF YOUNG CHILDREN

Cognitive development in childhoood

One of the most well-known theories of children's cognitive development is that of J. Piaget. He believed that children's thinking develops through a fixed sequence of stages – sensori-motor, pre-operational, concrete operations and formal operations.

These stages are described in most of the introductory Psychology textbooks already referred to: Davenport, G., (1992) *Essential Psychology*, Chapter 4, pp. 74–82; Gross, R.D., (1992) *Psychology: The Science of Mind and Behaviour*, Chapter 25, pp. 740–55.

Piaget claims that a major feature of the thinking of children at the pre-operational stage is an inability to conserve. Piaget demonstrated this by asking children questions about a series of **tasks**. These tasks could form the basis of a project if you have access to a reasonable number of children in the age range four to nine.

Use a textbook to find out about the tasks:

1 The conservation of liquid.
2 The conservation of amount/substance.
3 The conservation of number.

Carrying out the project

One project could consist of a straightforward replication of Piaget's work. Using one or more of the tasks; conservation of liquid quantity, substance and number. You could test the hypothesis that more children at the pre-operational stage (four to six) will fail to conserve than children at the concrete operational stage (seven to nine). You would need to administer the tasks to the children and count the number of children at each stage who were able to conserve. The data could then be put in to a two by two table, as shown below.

	Age 4 to 6	Age 7 to 9	Total
Conserved			
Failed to Conserve			
Total			

I will use the conservation of liquid quantity as an example to explain the procedure you should adopt.

1 Having selected a child to work with, spend some time getting to know them – do not rush into the task. Only begin the task when you feel you have established a friendly rapport with the child.

2 You might introduce the task(s) to the child as a game which you want them to help you with.

Decide what you are going to use as liquid. Water would be fine but it might be nice to use lemonade or coke, which the child could drink afterwards as a reward! The child must agree that there is the same amount of liquid in container A and B before you proceed to pour the liquid in container B into container C.

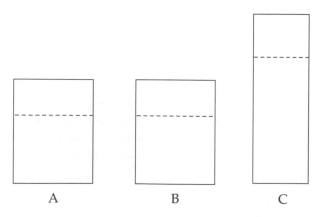

A   B   C

3 The child is asked, 'Is there the same amount of water in this container (point to A) as there is in this container (point to C)'? It is important not to suggest to the child that there is a right and a wrong answer.
4 Record the answer and ask the child to explain the reason for their decision. Keep a record of what each child says, if possible.
5 The same basic procedure should be used for all the children and can, with minor modification, be used for the other conservation tasks.

Analysing the results
The analysis of results would consist of simply completing the table on page 138. Consider what type of graph would be the most effective way of presenting your results.
Hint: the data are similar to that in Practical 2, Chapter 5.

Applying an appropriate statistical test
Work through the decisions in Figure 4.2, Chapter 4 (page 36).
Hint: This project is not a true experiment, as the IV is age and this cannot be directly manipulated by the researcher. However, you are still predicting a difference between the performance of two groups and each subject can only take part in one of the two conditions. So what is the design? The data consists of a frequency count using named categories, so what is the data level? See Practical 2 (Chapter 5).
There are two tests suitable for analysing the data from a practical such as this. Chi-square, which was used in Practical 2, is described in Chapter 5. Unfortunately, for this test to be reliable you will need a minimum of ten children in each age group, four to six years old and seven to nine years old. If you cannot manage this number of subjects you can analyse the data using a test called Fischer's Exact Test, but you will have to refer to another book to get the instructions for this (see Further reading on page 140).

Writing up the report

Introduction
There is quite a lot of material on Piaget, the stages of cognitive development and conservation, in the books I have already referred you to: Davenport, G.C., (1992) *Essential Psychology*, and Gross, R.D., (1992) *Psychology: The Science of Mind and Behaviour*. Other useful sources of information are given in the further reading section overleaf.
Be careful not to spend too much time describing Piaget's theory as a whole. Provide the reader with an outline of Piaget's ideas and then focus on the issue of conservation and the pre-operational and concrete operational stages.

Hypothesis
I have suggested a suitable hypothesis in the section entitled **Carrying out the project**.

Results

Put the table of results in this section. The children's explanations of their decisions can be considered data and put in an appendix.

Treatment of results

See the Treatment of Results section in Practical 2, Chapter 5.

Discussion

In your discussion you will need to describe your results in as much detail as possible and then go on to relate them to theories and studies you have described in your background section. Do not forget to describe and discuss the reasons children give for their answers.

References

Do not forget to include these after your conclusion. My references for this project are listed below:

Davenport, G.C., (1992) *Essential Psychology*, London: Collins Educational.

Gross, R.D., (1992), *Psychology: The Science of Mind and Behaviour*, Sevenoaks: Hodder & Stoughton.

Further reading: Project 2

A book with a clear account and critical evaluation of Piaget's ideas is:

Donaldson, M., (1978) *Children's Minds*, London: Fontana.

A detailed account of the reasoning behind the use of Fisher's Exact Test is to be found in:

Siegel, S., (1956) *Non-Parametric Statistics*, Maidenhead: McGraw-Hill.

PROJECT 3 – AN OBSERVATIONAL STUDY OF PROSOCIAL BEHAVIOUR AT PEDESTRIAN CROSSINGS

Prosocial behaviour

Over the last twenty years there has been a growing interest among social psychologists in the topic of prosocial or helping behaviour. One variable which has been found to influence prosocial behaviour is the sex of the person needing help or assistance. In the USA Pomazal and Clore (1973), for example, set up an experiment in which a car was parked at the side of the road and either a male or a female confederate pretended to be jacking up the car to change a flat tyre. The confederate did not look in the direction of passing cars or make any gestures for them to stop. The researchers found that the female confederate was offered assistance by approximately one in four of the cars passing. The male confeder- ate was offered assistance by only one in fifty of the cars passing. Those stopping to help were almost all males. Another study by West, Whitney and Schnedler (1975) used a car by the side of the road with the bonnet raised. Again females were offered assistance much more frequently than males and almost all of the people who stopped to assist were males.

Similar results have been found in studies of hitchhiking. Pomazal and Clore (1973) found that out of every 100 passing cars, on aver- age nineteen stopped for a female hitchhiker and only six for a male. Only one of the drivers who stopped to offer a lift was fe- male. A study by Snyder, Grether, and Keller (1974) compared the help given to a male, female and a couple; it was found again the lone female was much more likely to be offered a lift.

These studies, while interesting, have a number of limitations for interpreting sex differences in prosocial behaviour. In the case of offering assistance to someone with a flat tyre, or whose car has broken down, many women drivers might feel that they do not have the technical ability to be of any real assistance. In the case of hitchhiking there are obvious dangers in women offering men a lift. The finding that males are much more likely to offer assistance to females, than other males, could be interpreted as indicating some sexual overtones. It could also be the case that male drivers are re- sponding to gender stereotypes, with females being viewed as needing assistance with a broken down car or a flat tyre. Whereas men judge other men to be capable or overcoming these difficulties themselves.

It would be interesting to investigate sex differences in prosocial behaviour in an essentially neutral situation. One such situation is when a driver stops to allow someone to use a pedestrian crossing. Another would be drivers stopping to allow another driver to enter a line of traffic or turn right across a flow of traffic.

Carrying out the project

One advantage of a study like this is that it does not require you to get subjects directly. However, to investigate sex differences in prosocial behaviour effectively you must think carefully about the design of the study and what data you need to collect. Below are four suggestions:

1 A basic study could involve you positioning yourself near a zebra crossing and simply recording the number of male and fe- male drivers who stop to allow a person to use the crossing. One problem with this study is that it does not take into account the number of male and female drivers passing the crossing. If most of the cars passing the crossing are driven by men then simply on a chance basis more men are likely to stop than women. One way to overcome this problem is to position yourself so that you can ob- serve the sex of drivers approaching the crossing. You could then

▶ Controlling for subject variables.

► Controlling for situational variables.

take the first twenty male drivers who approach the crossing while somebody is waiting to cross and count how many stop. Then do the same for twenty female drivers.

2 There are a number of uncontrolled variables in the study outlined above. For example, the number of people at the crossing, the sex of the person(s) at the crossing, where people stand at the crossing etc. You could overcome some of these problems by taking the role of the pedestrian yourself. You could wait for male/female drivers to approach the crossing and then walk to the edge and see whether they stop or not. Again, you could use twenty male and twenty female drivers.

3 One variable of interest, in the light of the research quoted above, is the sex of the pedestrian. Are male drivers more likely to stop to allow female pedestrians to cross than males pedestrians? You could add this hypothesis to your study by recording the sex of people waiting to cross or by enlisting the assistance of a confederate of the opposite sex to yourself.

4 There is a certain pressure on drivers to stop at zebra crossings and therefore it could be argued that this is not a real test of altruism. You could use one of the other traffic situations mentioned above e.g. stopping to allow someone to turn right, either instead of, or to compare with the prosocial behaviour at crossings.

Analysing the results

The analysis of results would consist of constructing suitable tables and graphs. Consider carefully what would be the most effective way of presenting your results.

Applying an appropriate statistical test

This will depend to some extent on exactly what study you decide to carry out. But you will need to work through the decisions in Figure 4.2 in Chapter 4, page 36 to select an appropriate statistical test.

Hint: This project is not a true experiment, as the IV is sex and this can not be directly manipulated by the researcher. However, you are still predicting a difference between the behaviour of two groups and each subject can only take part in one of the two conditions. So what is the design? The data consist of a frequency count using named categories, so what is the data level? See Practical 2, Chapter 5.

Writing up the report

Introduction
I have given you some information on sex differences in prosocial behaviour; you can find a general discussion of this topic in:

Gross R.D., (1992), *Psychology: The Science of Mind and Behaviour*, London: Hodder & Stoughton.

NEC, (1990) 'Social Psychology Module', *A Level Psychology Course*, Unit 4, Cambridge: National Extension College.

Hypothesis
Again the hypothesis will depend upon what exactly you decide to do but it is likely to be something along the lines of, 'There will be a difference in the number of male and female drivers who . . .'.

Results
Put suitable table(s) of results in this section.

Treatment of results
For treatment of results see the section in Practical 2, Chapter 5.

Discussion
In your discussion you will need to describe your results in as much detail as possible and then go on to relate them to theories and studies you have described in your background section. Remember to discuss any methodological problems that may have arisen during the project.

References
Do not forget to include your references. My references for this project are listed below:

Osman, L.M., (1982) 'Conformity or Compliance? A study of sex differences in pedestrian behaviour', *British Journal of Social Psychology*, Vol. 21, pp. 19–21.

Pomazal, R.J., and Clore, G.L., (1973) 'Helping on the highway: The effects of dependency and sex', *Journal of Applied Social Psychology*, Vol. 3 pp. 150–64.

Snyder, M., Grether, J., and Keller, K., (1974) 'Staring and compliance: A field study on hitchhiking', *Journal of Applied Social Psychology*, Vol. 4, pp. 165–70.

West, S.G., Whitney, G., and Schnedler, R., (1975) 'Helping motorists in distress: The effect of sex, race and neighbourhood', *Journal of Personality and Social Psychology*, Vol. 31 pp. 691–8.

Further reading: Project 3

A social psychology textbook with a good chapter on prosocial behaviour is:

Baron, R.A., and Byrne, D., (1977) *Social Psychology: Understanding Human Interaction*, Boston: Allyn & Bacon.

CHAPTER SUMMARY

This chapter gave you an opportunity to carry out a further practical which you might use as an alternative to one of the five given in the previous chapters. Less guidance was given, so if you did carry out one of these projects you will have had to rely on your own resources to a greater extent. Even if you didn't carry out any of these projects, you may have found them interesting reading, since they tell you about the kinds of research which lies behind topics which you will study elsewhere in your Psychology course.

Statistics and methodology questions

Chapter objectives:

By the end of this chapter you should:

▌ have worked your way through some methodology and statistics questions from past A level Psychology examinations

▌ have identified concepts which you now understand and are able to apply in answering examination questions

▌ have identified concepts which you still feel uncertain about, and have made a plan to revise them further

▌ have practiced examination technique with regard to short answer examination questions.

INTRODUCTION

In Paper 2 of the AEB A level Psychology examination, section A contains a compulsory question on methodology and statistics. In the AEB A/S level Psychology examination there is only one paper but section A is also a compulsory question on methodology and statistics. In both the A level and A/S level you will be presented with a description of a piece of research followed by a series of questions relating to it. These questions focus on issues that you have met in the course of carrying out and writing up your practical reports. Therefore revising for this part of the examination should not require you to learn much new material. However, I think it will help your revision if you see what this part of the examination looks like. I have therefore included some past A level questions. To gain maximum benefit you should spend some time revising and then try to answer these questions under examination conditions. Yes, that does mean **no** looking at this book! Also allow yourself forty-five minutes – the time allowed in the examination. I have provided what I think would be suitable answers to the questions and references to the relevant sections in this book.

The answers I have given in this chapter are often more detailed than those you would need to write in the examination. This is because I am not just trying to answer the questions but also explain some of the terms and concepts. In the examination use the marks allocated to each question as your guide on how much to write. A question for which there is only one mark might well be answered in a sentence. A question worth three marks is likely to need a short paragraph. Once you have tried a couple of the past questions I am sure you will start to get a feel for the kind of questions you are likely to face in your examination. At this point you could start to take notes from some of the chapters in the book. To help you do this I have given a list below of the major terms and concepts that I think you should be familiar with. I do not guarantee that this will cover every question you could be asked in the examination but I would be surprised if it does not cover eighty to ninety per cent of the questions.

To help you organize your revision I will divide the statistics and methodology material into four sections:

1 research methods and experimental design,
2 descriptive statistics,
3 inferential statistics
4 correlational research

What you need to know about research methods and experimental design

1 You need to be able to identify the major types of research design (experimental, correlational, survey, observation study) and briefly state their advantages and disadvantages.
2 If the study described in the examination question is an experiment, you must be able to identify which design it is: repeated measures, matched samples, independent samples or single subject. You also need to know what the advantages and disadvantages of these different designs are.
3 Following on from (2), you need to be able to explain what order effects are, how they arise, and how they can be dealt with (counterbalancing and randomization).
4 You should understand what the term confounding means and how confounding can occur (constant and random errors).
5 You may be asked to write a research or null hypothesis.
6 Related to (5) you may be asked if a stated hypothesis is one or two tailed or to write a one- or two-tailed research hypothesis.
7 Sampling – you need to know what a random sample is, and how to produce a random sample. Why are samples used? What factors could lead to a biased sample.

What you need to know about descriptive statistics

1 You need to know what the major descriptive statistics are and their advantages and disadvantages:

- central tendency – mean, median and mode
- dispersion – range, interquartile range, variance and standard deviation.

Note: it is very unlikely that you will be asked to calculate any of these statistics.

2 You should know what a normal distribution curve looks like (you might be asked to make a sketch of one). You could also be asked where the mean, median and mode fall on a normal distribution curve. A fixed percentage of scores fall between +1 and –1, +2 and –2 and +3 and –3 standard deviations on a normal distribution curve. You should know what these percentage figures are.

What you need to know about inferential statistics

1 It is almost guaranteed that you will be asked in some way about the meaning of the term **statistically significant**.
2 You should be aware of the different levels of significance and why different levels of significance are sometimes set.
3 You need to know what a Type 1 and a Type 2 error are and how the possibility of such errors can be reduced.
4 Students are frequently asked to either:

- pick an appropriate statistical test to apply to the data presented in the examination question

OR

- to say what test has been applied to the data and to explain why that particular test was used.

Note: To answer questions such as those above you need to be able to make the decisions shown in Figure 4.2, Chapter 4, page 36. This means you must know:

- the assumptions underlying the use of parametric tests
- the different levels of measurement
- the different types of research and experimental design
- the names of the tests themselves.

 The following tests are the ones you are most likely to be asked about:

Tests of difference

	Parametric	**Non-parametric**
Related design	Related *t* test (interval level data or above)	Mann-Whitney (ordinal level data or above) sign test (nominal data or above)
Non-related design	independent *t* (interval level data or above)	Wilcoxon rank sum (ordinal data or above) Chi-square (nominal data or above)

Tests of correlation

Parametric	Non-parametric
Pearson's product moment correlation (interval level data or above)	Spearman's Rho (ordinal level data)

NB You will **not** actually be asked to use any of these tests in the examination room!

Correlation

1 You should know what correlation is a measure of and the strengths and weaknesses of the correlational design.

2 You need to understand the difference between a positive and negative correlation.

3 A question may present you with a correlation coefficient and ask you to explain what it shows.

4 You could be asked to interpret scattergrams.

5 How do you establish whether a correlation coefficient is statistically significant or not? What exactly does it mean if a correlation coefficient is found to be statistically significant?

The above lists may seem quite daunting but you have already come across many of these terms and concepts whilst carrying out and writing up your practical reports. There are obviously some points, however, that you will need to check in previous chapters of the book. If you work your way through the past questions given on pp. 150–9 and check your answers with those in appendix E this will give you a good idea of the things you need to check up on. Good Luck!

WORKING WITH PAST EXAMINATION PAPERS

Below the following guidance notes are five past examination questions, and in appendix E, you will find some notes on how I would have answered them. I strongly recommend that you **do not turn** straight to my answers, but instead set aside periods of forty-five minutes for each, attempt your own answers, and then check them with the notes in appendix E. Use this activity also to develop your examination technique

- read the question thoroughly. For this kind of examination question you need to gain a good understanding of the research described before you can answer the questions
- make rough notes towards the answers of all the questions before you answer them properly. Do this because you will sometimes be in a better position to answer the earlier questions,

▶ Develop your examination technique.

▶ For more examination guidance turn to appendix F (pp. 197–200).

when you have done the thinking to answer the later ones. Avoid the temptation to rush into answering the first question first. For these kinds of examination questions thinking is more important than writing

- usually forty-five minutes are available for a question, plan to spend ten on planning, and five on reading and correcting your answer. That is thirty minutes writing time. However with these kinds of short answer questions you can afford even more time planning and checking

- review your plan and make sure that it answers the question. The major reason why candidates do badly in examinations is not because they don't know the answers, but because they don't answer the question the examiner set

- write the answer, keeping a check on your timing. Pay attention to presentation. If the examiner can't read what you have written, or if it is presented in an illogical way, he/she will find it difficult to award you marks

- leave time for reading over the answer you have written and correcting it. In a real examination this is probably better done when you have answered all the questions and you can return to earlier ones with some new thoughts.

Before you check your responses with my notes, answer the following questions:

- how well do you think you did? You'll find out in a minute but being able to diagnose your own performance is an important examination skill

- how well did you manage your time? Did you spend too long on sections carrying a few marks, and not enough on sections carrying many marks? Did you spend too long planning and not enough time writing? Did you leave enough time to check through the answer at the end?

If you identify problems here, these are things you should concentrate on improving.

When you check your answers with mine, remember that there are many different ways of answering correctly. My notes only give one way. Don't try to match your answers with mine word for word. Instead ask yourself four kinds of questions:

- did I interpret the question correctly?
- did I understand the terms and concepts in the question correctly and did I use them accurately in my answer?
- did I recognize and introduce into my answer the terms and concepts the examiner was looking for?
- did I spend an appropriate amount of time, and write an appropriate number of words for each section of the answer?

Make a list of the areas where your answer fell short and use the list to check back in the book for further revision.

▶ Don't make the mistake of thinking that you can pass examinations by learning model answers by heart. Examiners take great pains to avoid setting the same question twice. But questions refer to the same ideas year after year. Focus your revision on the key concepts which examiners use. These are the ones identified earlier in the chapter (page 146).

► To pass examinations you need to be able to think like an examiner.

When you have exhausted the examination questions in this book, try your hand at setting your own examination questions, in the same format. You might try using your own practical reports as the basis for similar kinds of question.

PAST A LEVEL QUESTIONS

(Notes on answering these questions appear in appendix E (pp. 186–96). I recommend that you try answering them, before you look at the answer notes.)

AEB Psychology A level, Paper 2, June 1987
Answer **all** parts of the question.

The marks allocated to each part of the question are shown in brackets at the end of each part of the question.

1 Read carefully the details below of an investigation. Answer each of the questions that follow.

Many GCE A level candidates claim that they are able to work more effectively when they have music as a background noise. Other candidates agree that silence is a more effective background for study purposes.

An experimenter decides to investigate these claims. An independent measures design is used on a group of 40 subjects who are randomly selected from a population of A level students. The test comprises of a list of 30 carefully chosen 7 letter anagrams, which the subjects have to try to solve in 15 minutes. The experimental group of subjects is allocated to a noise condition; they wear headphones which are attached to a central tape recorder that plays popular music to each subject. The control group also wears headphones, but the silence condition is maintained by not having a tape on the tape recorder. When the results are collected for each condition, showing the number of correct solutions, they display homogeneity of variance and exhibit near normal distributions.

(a) What advantage would there be in using a repeated measures design?

(1 mark)

(b) What would **two** of the distadvantages be if a repeated measures design were to be used?

(2 marks)

(c) Write down a null hypothesis for this experiment.

(2 marks)

(d) Explain why the experimental hypothesis should be two tailed.

(1 mark)

(e) State an alternative sampling technique to random sampling that might give a more representative sample of A level students. Briefly explain why your alternative method may be more advantageous for this experiment.

(3 marks)

(f) State briefly why 40 is a reasonable number of subjects for this experiment.

(2 marks)

(g) The list of anagrams was made from seven-letter words which were 'carefully chosen'. Identify **two** variables which the experimenter should have taken into account in making this choice.

(2 marks)

(h) Write down brief instructions that the experimenter might give to the subject.

(2 marks)

(i) Give an example of a random error that may confound the experiment.

(1 mark)

(j) Briefly describe what is meant by 'demand characteristics'. How may these be shown by subjects in this case?

(2 marks)

(k) Explain why the control group also needs to wear headphones.

(1 mark)

(l) What criteria should be met before a parametric test is applied?

(3 marks)

(m) Assuming that the criteria are all met, what statistical test would you use in this experiment?

(1 mark)

(n) A 0.001 level of significance was proposed in order to judge the difference in results. Discuss briefly why this proposal may lead to a type 2 error.

(2 marks)

AEB Psychology A level, Paper 2, June 1988, Section A
Answer **all** the parts of the question.

The marks allocated to each part of the question are shown in brackets at the end of each part of the question.

1 You wish to discover if the IQ scores of ten pupils are related to their academic position in class. The academic position is calculated from the marks obtained in several academic subjects. The

marks have been totalled for each pupil and from these results, they have been placed in rank order from 1 to 10.

Pupil	Rank order in academic subjects	IQ score
Barbara	10	110
Fiona	1	140
Oliver	2	140
Gareth	7	100
Norman	8	102
John	9	80
Miranda	3	115
Clare	6	110
Nathan	4	132
Daphne	5	110

You decide to use a rank order correlation coefficient to discover the relation between IQ scores and rank order in academic subjects. The rank order correlation coefficient is calculated as +0.85.

(a) What level of measurement is used in the table above in the column headed 'rank order in academic subjects'?

(1 mark)

(b) Write down the IQ scores in descending order and assign a rank order to each score.

(2 marks)

(c) What is meant by the term 'standard deviation'?

(2 marks)

(d) Make a freehand sketch of a normal distribution curve and mark on it the position of
  (i) the mean
  (ii) one standard deviation each side of the mean.

(2 marks)

(e) In the total population of the UK, the arithmetic mean of IQ scores is 100, and the standard deviation is 15.
  (i) What approximate percentage of the UK population have IQ scores between 100 and 115?
  (ii) What approximate percentage of the UK population have IQ scores above 130?

(2 marks)

(f) The following shortened table shows critical values for rank correlation coefficients at the 0.05 and 0.01 levels of significance.

N	0.05	0.01
5	1.000	–
6	0.886	1.000
7	0.786	0.929
8	0.738	0.881
9	0.683	0.833
10	0.591	0.794
11	0.544	0.714

You have already decided to use the 0.05 level of significance. Use the table to answer the following.

Is the result of +0.85 significant at the 0.05 level? Give a brief reason for your answer.

(2 marks)

(g) What is meant by the phrase 'the result is significant at the 0.05 level'?

(2 marks)

(h) Under what circumstances would you prefer to use an 0.01 level of significance in preference to an 0.05 level?

(2 marks)

(i) Explain what is meant by the following levels of measurement:

(i) interval

(ii) nominal.

(2 marks)

(j) Suggest two ways in which the reliability of IQ tests may be demonstrated.

(2 marks)

(k) (i) Explain briefly the difference between a one-tailed and a two-tailed hypothesis.
(ii) Write down a suitable two-tailed hypothesis for the investigation mentioned at the beginning of this section.

(3 marks)

(l) If you wanted to select a random sample of 30 children from one school that had a total population of 500 children, what would be the most efficient method of doing this, assuming you had access to all of the class registers?

(3 marks)

AEB Psychology A level, Paper 2, June 1989 Section A
Answer **all** parts of the question.

1 A team of four Psychology students aim to investigate rough and tumble play in a primary school and they formulate two hypotheses:

(a) The number of girls engaging in rough and tumble play is significantly different from the number of boys engaging in rough and tumble play.

(b) The number of 5/6 year old children engaging in rough and tumble play is significantly different from the number of 9/10 year olds engaging in rough and tumble play.

The Psychology students do a pilot study in which they categorize rough and tumble play as either play hitting accompanied by laughing or smiling or play wrestling accommpanied by laughing or smiling or play pushing accompanied by laughing or smiling.

The primary school that the Psychology students chose for their main investigation has staggered playtimes; 5/6 year olds play at a different time to 9/10 year olds.

The Psychology students decide to work in teams of two – one, one acting as observer and the other as recorder. They make their observations during breaktimes.

The data they collect is as follows (each child appears in only one category):

Table 1

Sex	Number of children engaging in rough and tumble play	Number of children not engaging in rough and tumble play
Girls	40	58
Boys	59	76

Table 2

Age(years)	Number of children engaging in rough and tumble play	Number of children not engaging in rough and tumble play
5/6	58	70
9/10	41	64

To test their hypotheses the students employ two Chi-square tests and use a significance level of $p < 0.05$. When calculated the test results are not significant.

(a) Briefly state **two** reasons for using a pilot study in this case, before carrying out the main investigation.

(2 marks)

(b) Give **two** reasons why it is necessary for the investigators to have good inter-observer reliability.

(*2 marks*)

(c) Another category of rough and tumble play could possibly have been used. This was 'play chasing accompanied by laughter or smiling'. The investigators decided not to use this category since they considered it lacked face validity. What is meant by face validity and why does this category appear to lack face validity?

(*2 marks*)

(d) Give **two** reasons why the Chi-squared test is an appropriate test to use in this investigation.

(*2 marks*)

(e) Give **two** reasons why it is useful to choose a school with staggered playtimes for observation.

(*2 marks*)

(f) Explain why it is advantageous to have each team with one student observing and the other recording the data.

(*1 mark*)

(g) The children in the playground may react to the presence of the investigators so that they behave in uncharacteristic ways. Suggest **two** ways in which this problem may be minimized.

(*2 marks*)

(h) Why is it preferable that a minimum significance level be decided before the main investigation commences?

(*2 marks*)

(i) What is meant by the statement that the result is not significant at the $p < 0.05$ level?

(*2 marks*)

(j) The hypothesis (a) mentioned at the beginning of the question is concerned with rough and tumble play in boys and girls. What is the appropriate null hypothesis?

(*2 marks*)

(k) Chi-squared is a non-parametric test. What three criteria must be satisfied before a parametric test is used?

(*3 marks*)

(l) The results suggest that there are no significant age or sex differences in rough and tumble play. How might the categorization system in Tables 1 and 2 mask sex/age differences in the frequency of such play?

(*3 marks*)

AEB Psychology A level, Paper 2, June 1990, Section A
Answer **all** parts of the question.

1 A controversy surrounds the apparent advantages in using word processors to write course work for GCSE English Language examinations compared to traditional pen and paper methods.

You decide to run a controlled study for a period of one academic year, using 30 matched pairs of students, in a large comprehensive school.

You are able to match the students in each pair according to your chosen criteria. As there is a sufficient number of students, they are able to be formed into two classes or sets, with 30 in each. By spinning a coin, one class is assigned to be experimental subjects whilst the other class act as their controls. The same teacher takes both experimental and control classes for lessons for the whole of the academic year. Both classes are taught the same material and the teacher takes particular care to avoid any bias towards experimental or control classes when teaching.

The only difference between the two classes is that the experimental students do all their written work by using word processors. These are made available for their use both inside and outside of lesson times. The control class students do all of their work by traditional pen and paper method.

All of the course work of both classes is assessed by an experienced teacher from another school. To ensure that no bias takes place, each piece of hand written work produced by the control group, unknown to the students, is copied word for word on a similar word processor to those used by the experimental class. The printed copy of the work from both classes is secretly coded and shuffled together before being sent to the teacher for assessment.

At the end of the academic year, the results for the experimental and control classes are made known. The median score for each student over the academic year is calculated and these sets of scores are compared for the matched pairs in each group. Since the data do not fulfil the criteria for a parametric test, a Wilcoxon matched pairs signed ranks test is applied.

(a) State a null hypothesis appropriate to this study.

(2 marks)

(b) You have good cause to think that the experimental group, using the word processors, will do better in their GCSE course work than the control group. State a relevant one-tailed experimental hypothesis which would take account of your prediction.

(2 marks)

(c) State the level of significance appropriate to this hypothesis and **briefly** indicate why you would use this level.

(2 marks)

(d) What test would have been appropriate had the data fulfilled the criteria for a parametric test?

(2 *marks*)

(e) Give two criteria which the investigator might have taken into account in order to have arrived at the Wilcoxon matched pairs signed ranks test as being the most appropriate test for this study.

(2 *marks*)

(f) In relation to this study:

(i) state one advantage of using a matched subjects design.

(1 *mark*)

(ii) state one disadvantage of using a matched subjects design.

(1*mark*)

(g) In this study what is (i) the independent variable?

(1 *mark*)

(ii) the dependent variable?

(1 *mark*)

(h) Briefly describe how you would establish the matched pairs of students for the purpose of this study.

(3 *marks*)

(i) Why do you think that it may be important to ensure that the same teacher takes both classes?

(2 *marks*)

(j) Non-parametric tests are not generally as powerful as their parametric equivalent. What is meant by the term 'powerful' in this statistical sense?

(2 *marks*)

(k) Considerable time and expense is spent on copying the hand written work of the control class students on to a word processor and producing the printed copies. Why is this an essential feature of the experimental design?

(2 *marks*)

(l) The work of both classes is assessed by an experienced teacher from another school. Explain briefly why this is necessary.

(2 *marks*)

AEB Psychology A level, Paper 2, June 1991, Section A
Answer **all** the parts of the question.

1 A psychotherapist wanted to assess the effectiveness of a technique for treating people suffering from animal phobias.

Research into reaction-time had already shown that phobics took longer to respond to words related to their phobia that to neutral words. In view of this, the psychotherapist reasoned that effective therapy should result in a reduction in the reaction-time to phobia related words.

To test this idea, the psychotherapist selected 10 clients who had phobias about animals whose skin was covered in hair or fur. Reaction times of each client were tested by asking them to read aloud two lists of words. One list (the experimental list) contained both neutral and phobia-related words, for example:

> record, apple, monkey, window, table, candle,
> rainbow, hamster, curtain, rabbit, picture, paper.

This list was extended to 40 words in total. The other list (the control list) consisted of 40 neutral words.

Before therapy began, the 10 clients were given standardized instructions in which they were asked to read aloud the two lists as quickly as possible. The time taken to complete each list was recorded. Half the clients read the experimental list first and then the control list, the other half read the control list first followed by the experimental list.

When the course of psychotherapy was completed, the reaction-times of the 10 clients to the two lists were tested in the same way as before. The psychotherapist was then able to compare reaction-times measured before and after treatment. Since the data met the requirements for a parametric test, it was decided to use a related t-test to analyse the results. The significance level chosen was $p \leq 0.05$.

(a) The psychotherapist was confident enough to use a one-tailed hypothesis for this investigation. What is meant by a one-tailed hypothesis?

(1 mark)

(b) In this study

    (i) name one independent variable.

(1 mark)

    (ii) what is the dependent variable?

(1 mark)

(c) Had the data not fulfilled the criteria for a parametric test, what non-parametric test of differences could be used in this investigation?

(1 mark)

(d) One of the criteria that data need to fulfil before a parametric t-test is employed is that both sets of data to be compared should have 'similar variance'. Suggest one way in which you would check if both sets of data had similar variance.

(1 mark)

(e) Suggest one way in which it can be established whether or not a sample of data is normally distributed.

(1 mark)

(f)   Half the clients read the experimental list first and then the control list, the other half read the control list followed by the experimental list.
What is the reason for this procedure?

(1 mark)

(g)   The control lists used in this investigation may appear to be redundant. However, there are good reasons for their inclusion. Briefly explain one such reason.

(2 marks)

(h)   Comparing clients' reaction-times for the control list and the experimental list, would you expect these reaction-times to be

(i)   the same or different before the course of psychotherapy?

(1 mark)

(ii) the same or different after the course of psychotherapy?

(1 mark)

(i)   The psychotherapist decided to use the $p \leq 0.05$ level of significance for this investigation.

What is meant by the expression $p \leq 0.05$ level of significance?

(1 mark)

(j)   Explain why a 0.05 rather than a 0.01 level of significance was chosen as an appropriate level in this investigation.

(1 mark)

(k)   The psychotherapist ensured that all the words chosen for this study were of two syllables and of similar length. Suggest one reason why this was done in this investigation.

(2 marks)

(l)   In the example from the experimental list you will see that phobia-related words such as rabbit or hamster do not appear at the top of the list. What could be wrong with putting phobia-related words at the top of the list?

(2 marks)

(m) Each client received standardized instructions before their reaction-times were tested.

(i)   What is meant by the term standardized instructions?

(1 mark)

(ii) Briefly explain why standardized instructions were used.

(1 mark)

(n)   It is important that the control lists used before and after the course of psychotherapy show reliability.

(i)   What is meant by reliability in this context?

(2 marks)

(ii) How would you test for reliability in this investigation?

(2 marks)

(o) The measurements employed in this investigation could be challenged as lacking in validity.

What does the term mean in this context?

(*2 marks*).

CHAPTER SUMMARY

Now you have worked through this chapter you should be thoroughly familiar with the requirements of the compulsory methodology and statistics question on the examination paper. You will have seen that each year much the same kind of question is set, and that what it requires from you is a demonstration of the knowledge you will have gained from working through this book, and from carrying out Psychology practicals.

Appendix A

Sample student practical report

An Experiment Into The Effectiveness Of Adjunct Questions On Recall Of Information From Text

By Karen Cook

ABSTRACT

The aim of this experiment was to investigate the effectiveness of inserting adjunct questions in a piece of text on the recall of information contained in the text. An independent samples design was used with 20 subjects, 10 studying a piece of text with adjunct questions and 10 studying the same text but without the adjunct questions. Subjects were then tested for their ability to recall information about the text.

The subjects' scores were analysed using the Mann-Whitney test and a statistically significant difference was found ($P < 0.025$). The null hypothesis was therefore rejected. The conclusion was drawn that subjects recalled significantly more about a piece of text when the text contained adjunct questions.

INTRODUCTION

Studies reviewed by Gates (1917) showed that asking people questions about what they are reading can increase the learning and retention of what they are reading. Since then, many investigations into the effect of questions on learning and retention have been carried out in different forms. More recently Rothkopf (1966) has restimulated the interest in this area of psychological study.

Rothkopf's 1966 study showed that adjunct questions – i.e. questions regarding the text administered at the time of study – have both direct and indirect effects when compared with control groups who simply read the text without the guideline questions. The direct effects are where the adjunct questions make up the criterion test of questions which is administered to both groups when the study time is over. The indirect effects are where the groups who receive the adjunct questions do better on the criterion test than the control group, when the criterion test does not contain any of the adjunct questions. This means that questions administered during the reading of a text have a result on the learning and retention of information that is directly questioned, and also that which is not.

Rothkopf carried out his study on college students who were made to read a 20 page selection from a book on marine biology. Two questions were asked regarding the text either before or after each passage or two or three pages. The questions did not require long drawn out answers, but rather one or two-word answers. His results showed that regardless of the placings, people who received the adjunct questions fared better in criterion tests of repeated and new questions than did the control groups who didn't receive any adjunct questions. However, those questions placed after the relevant part of the text tended to have slightly more favourable indirect results than did the adjunct questions placed before the section of the text to which they were relevant. The direct effect of adjunct questions after sections of text is four times as great as the indirect effect. The significance of this knowledge to the educator is that if questions are asked during learning, on the particular points that are of most importance, then students are more likely to master those points. Hence the whole subject matter will in turn become more learnable and retainable to the student whose knowledge will therefore increase.

So the conditions under which adjunct questions are most likely to yield positive effects are important to educators and their students. Anderson and Biddle have found a number of optimum conditions for the functioning of adjunct questions by studying 35 studies carried out by other psychologists. They found in 16 out of 17 relevant studies that adjunct questions placed after passages resulted in better performance on new criterion tests. Experiments by Frase (1968) and Frase et al. (1970) found better performance, both direct and indirect, on criterion tests when the adjunct questions were placed after each paragraph, as opposed to every five paragraphs. A later study by Boyd (1973) found these results to be positive for direct effects, but irrelevant for indirect effects. From their study of Clark (1940), Raffel (1934), and Van Maitre et al. (1974), Anderson and Biddle conclude that one or two-word answer questions yield strong direct and indirect effects than do longer-answer questions or multiple choice questions. However, some tests have shown that multiple choice answer questions can be equally as effective as short-answer questions with regard to positive direct effects. A possible theory for this not occurring in novel, indirect effects is to do with the methods of recall and storage in memory and with the different processes of the two methods of question answering.

In this practical, the questions for group 2 (who receive adjunct questions) are placed after each paragraph in the text. They are short-answer questions and they require an overt response, i.e. they must be written down ready to be checked by the examiner. This is because studies by Anderson (1967) and Holland and Kamp (1965, 1966) have shown that overt answers as opposed to mental thoughts are better at producing both direct and indirect positive effects. The criterion questions are also asked orally by the examiner because experiments by Rothkopf (1972) show that this gives added incentive to the subject. The subjects know ahead of time that the criterion questions will be asked orally and it is therefore concluded that they will receive motivation to study the text more carefully from this knowledge.

Some of the questions used in this practical require comprehension of the text and are even on a 'higher order' basis. This is in line with studies by Craik and Lockhart (1972) which show that questions requiring comprehension of the text promote deeper processing of this information and therefore more learning and better recall occurs. The 'higher order' questions are in line with results from the studies of Berliner et al. (1973) which showed that questions in this form have added positive results on learning and remembering as well.

All the studies referred to here have been carried out on reading matter and questions. However, the same results have been found regardless of the medium of presentation (for example, text, taped lecture or film). Also, the results apparently apply over a wide range of topics and age groups. Positive effects of adjunct questions are apparent in many experiments covering all these ranges.

Aim
The aim of this experiment is to examine the effect of adjunct questions on the learning of an historical text.

Null hypothesis
Any differences in scores on the criterion test between group 1 (who do not receive adjunct questions) and group 2 (who do receive adjunct questions) is strictly due to chance.

Experimental hypothesis
The subjects who study a piece of text containing adjunct questions will recall more information contained in the text than subjects who study the same text without adjunct questions.

METHOD

Design
An independent subjects design was used in this experiment. This design was chosen because it was considered to be important that subjects in both of the experimental conditions study the same piece of text. This could not be done using a repeated measures design.

Subjects
There were 20 subjects used in this experiment and they were all studying for A levels. Care was taken to ensure that none of the subjects had studied history at either A or GCSE level so that they were unlikely to have any knowledge of the historical topic covered by the text. The subjects were all aged between 17 and 20 years of age and there were 5 males and 5 females in each condition.

Materials
These are shown in the Appendices:-

1 text with adjunct questions (Appendix A)
2 text without the questions (Appendix B)
3 the criterion test questions (Appendix C)

Procedure
10 male and 10 female subjects were randomly assigned to one of the two
experimental conditions. The experiment was administered to each group of
subjects separately. Each group was taken to an empty classroom where it
was quiet enough for them to concentrate. Both groups were then read the
following instructions:

'I will give you a short piece of text concerning a historical topic. You
have 7 minutes to study the text after which you will be given a short
test on the material in the text. Any questions'?

After 7 minutes the researcher collected the pieces of text and gave each
subject the criterion question sheet - see Appendix A.

Subjects were given as much time as they required to answer the questions
on the criterion test sheet. When the subjects had written their answers
the sheets were collected and then marked. One mark was awarded for each
correct answer giving each subject a score out of 20. The results are
shown in Table 1.

*(This table and the graphs and calculations have been omitted)

RESULTS

The scores for the two groups can be seen on page *. All of the marks are
out of a possible twenty, the number of questions on the criterion test.

TREATMENT OF RESULTS

The two frequency histograms on page * show the scores out of 20 for each
of the individuals in groups 1 and 2. The histograms show at a glance that
for these 20 subjects, group 2, who received guideline questions within
the test, produced better results than group 1, who received no guideline
questions.

In order to analyse if these results are significant or due to random
error, the Mann-Whitney test was used. This is because the experiment uses
independent samples design, and shows an ordinal level of data. That is to
say that there are no equal scales of measurement of the subjects' memory,
but it can be ordered from highest to lowest. The decision rule for this
test is that if U or U' (whichever is smaller) is less than or equal to the
critical value of U, the null hypothesis is rejected.

Observe Value	Critical Value	Significance level
U = 2	10	0.01

The decision rule states that the observed value of U must be equal or less than the critical value to be significant. Therefore in this experiment the null hypothesis can be rejected.

DISCUSSION

This study set out to discover whether adjunct questions had an overall direct influence on an individual's ability to comprehend, learn, and subsequently recall information in an historical passage. The idea is that if adjunct questions were found to have a positive influence on performance in this instance, it would be likely that such knowledge could be generalised to learning and education as a whole.

The experimenter based the design of the experiment on previous such studies outlined in Anderson and Biddle's paper 'On Asking People Questions About What They Are Reading'. However, most of the experiments they cited were aimed at a specific aspect of the whole process, some of which have hence been employed in the structure of the experiment. The adjunct questions are placed after paragraphs to which they refer, two or three questions at a time, requiring short-answer questions, and some of them required that the subjects think about what they have just been reading in order to evaluate the answers. By using these techniques, the examiner hopes that the results obtained will be increasingly high statistically and hence show that there are methods of teaching than can greatly improve learning.

A glance at the individual results and mean results shows that group 2, who received the adjunct guideline questions, fared much better than group 1, who had no questions administered until the study time was over. However, since the number of subjects is relatively small, it may have been that these results were arrived at by chance – purely a case of random error. As such the Mann-Whitney test is used to asses whether or not the results are statistically significant. This test is chosen based on the design and method of the experiment as outlined in the treatment of results. The results are found to be significant and hence the experiment is pronounced a success in that it is evidence to support the experimental hypothesis.

However, there are some problems, found in both this and other similar experiments. A major problem is the validity of the criterion test – does it actually measure what it claims to measure? It is possible that a subject who scores only 8/20 on the criterion test may have learned more than other subjects who scored 13/20. Perhaps it was just fortunate for the second subject that the information they recalled was of relevance to the criterion test, whereas the information retained by the first subject was not included in the criterion test. As such there is a need for the subject matter and the criterion test to be standardised in some way. In this instance, the subjects were chosen specifically because they were not GCSE level history students and it was therefore likely that they had not come into contact with the GCSE level text book from which the passage was taken. However, in order to standardise the test it must ideally be given to large numbers of subjects of both high and low achievement abilities which would presumably employ high and low learning and remembering ability. Examples of such candidates could be people who passed academic exams at a high level, or failed them at a low level. The criterion test could then be standardised on an average of the collective results and hence it would be a more sound basis for an experiment aiming to support and eventually prove the theory.

Despite the pitfalls of the experiment in its present form, the results achieved are statistically significant. Further related experiments on the matter may be similar to those carried out by past psychologists referred to by Anderson and Biddle, and seek to concentrate on various individual aspects of the process of adjunct questions and how they affect learning/remembering. By using the same passage, some external order effects common in comparisons of different studies could also be alleviated. Thus it would be possible to examine for oneself the significance of the previous results which outlined optimum levels of operation for use as a comparison to the overall experiment used in this practical.

The relevance of this and similar experiments is that such knowledge can be expanded for use in wider society. Concrete statistical evidence from such reports could serve to revolutionise education. Teaching practices could be revised on the basis of such knowledge and result in future generations gaining even better educational achievements than would otherwise be likely. Hence we see the practical use of psychological experiments to society as a whole.

Conclusion
The analysis of results in this experiment conclude that adjunct questions do improve the learning of an historical test. Hence the null hypothesis which states:

<u>Any differences in scores on the criterion test between group 1 (who do not receive adjunct questions) and group 2 (who do receive adjunct questions) is strictly due to chance</u>

is rejected because the results were found to be significant and hence the experimental hypothesis is accepted as the best possible option:

<u>The adjunct questions given to group 2 will result in better scores on the criterion test than achieved by group 1 without the adjunct questions.</u>

REFERENCES
Anderson and Biddle, <u>The Psychology of Learning and Motivation</u> (Vol. 9).

APPENDIX A

The passage as given to group 1
The Sultan of Turkey had called on his vassal, Mehmet Ali, Viceroy of Egypt, to help him crush the rebellious Greeks. In return for this aid Mehmet Ali had been promised greater independence for his rule in Egypt and an extension of his territory to include Syria Part of his assistance consisted of a naval force, which was at Navarino when the note from the Three Powers was sent to the government of Turkey and the leaders of the Greek rebellion, asking them to cease fighting and agree to the decisions of the major Powers. Canning had sent a British naval squadron commanded by Admiral Codrington to ensure that these peace terms were obeyed.

Mehmet Ali's son, Ibrahim Pasha, commander of his father's forces in Greece, refused to accept the terms laid down by the outside powers, and so on 20th October 1827, Codrington led the navy into the harbour at Navarino, where they sank the Egyptian and Turkish fleets, and so ensured that Greece would become independent.

By this date, Canning had died and it was left to Wellington, as Prime Minister, to apologise to the Turks for this action and so allow Russia to remain as guardian of Christian Greece in the final negotiations leading to Greek independence.

Lane, P (1978) Success in British History: 1760-1914. John Murray.

APPENDIX B

The passage as given to Group 2
The Sultan of Turkey had called on his Vassal, Mehmet Ali, Viceroy of Egypt, to help him crush the rebellious Greeks. In return for this aid Mehmet Ali had been promised greater independence for his rule in Egypt and an extension of his territory to include Syria. Part of his assistance consisted of a naval force, which was at Navarino when the note from the Three Powers was sent to the government of Turkey and the leaders of the Greek rebellion, asking them to cease fighting and agree to the decisions of the major Powers. Canning had sent a British naval squadron commanded by Admiral Codrington to ensure that these peace terms were obeyed.

(a)   Who was Mehmet Ali?
(b)   Where was Mehmet Ali's naval force?
(c)   Who was the note from the Three Powers sent to?
(d)   Who sent out a British naval squadron?
(e)   What was it meant to ensure?

Mehemt Ali's son, Ibrahim Pasha, commander of his father's forces in Greece, refused to accept the terms laid down by the outside powers, and on 20th October 1827, Codrington led the navy into the harbour at Navarino, where they sank the Egyptian and Turkish fleets, and so ensured that Greece would become independent.

(f)   What was Mehmet Ali's son's name?
(g)   What was his position/job?
(h)   What happened in the attack?

By this date, Canning had died and it was left to Wellington, as Prime Minister, to apologise to the Turks for this action and so allow Russia to remain as guardian of Christian Greece in the final negotiations leading to Greek Independence.

(i)   What was Wellington's position?
(j)   Who took charge of Christian Greece until their independence?

Lane, P. (1978)<u>Success in British History: 1760-1914.</u> John Murray.

APPENDIX C

<u>List of questions on the criterion test</u>
1   Who called on Mehmet Ali to help him crush the Greeks?
2   Who was Mehmet Ali?
3   What was Mehmet Ali promised in return for his help? (one of two)
4   Mehmet Ali was also promised that his territory would be expanded to include which country?
5   Where was Mehmet Ali's navel force?
6   Who was the Note from the Three Powers sent to?
7   What did it request?
8   Who sent out a British naval squadron?
9   Who commanded the British naval squadron?
10   What was it meant to ensure?
11   What was Mehmet Ali's son's name?
12   What was his position/job?
13   He refused to accept the outsiders' peace plan and so Codrington entered Navarino on what date?
14   What did they do in the attack?
15   What did this ensure?
16   Who had died by this time?
17   What was Wellington's position?
18   What did he then have to do?
19   Who then took charge of Christian Greece until their independence?
20   Who wrote this passage?

Appendix B

AEB Guidance notes

Notes to be Issued to Candidates on their Reports of Psychological Investigations

A loose-leaf format using A4 size paper is preferred. There should be an index at the front of the report and the pages should be numbered. A clear and orderly presentation will impress. Whenever appropriate, tables, diagrams and graphs should be used and these always should be clearly labelled.

There is no single 'correct' way of writing a report. There are, however, widely accepted standards and conventions which you should follow. A useful model for a report may be obtained from reading a good journal article, for example, The British Journal of Psychology or The Quarterly Journal of Experimental Psychology. Although there may be minor variations in the order and manner of presentation of material, the same sort of information is always presented. It is suggested, therefore, that the following format is adopted with each section clearly labelled:-

> TITLE
> ABSTRACT or SUMMARY
> INTRODUCTION: Aim
> METHOD:
> > Design
> > Subjects
> > Apparatus or Materials
> > Procedure
> RESULTS
> DISCUSSION
> CONCLUSION
> REFERENCES
> APPENDICES

TITLE: Aim for something concise which will allow the reader to know at a glance the nub of your study. A title like 'Attitude Measurement' or 'Reaction Time' is too vague, whereas titles like: 'Attitudes to Nuclear Power Development of a Likert-type Scale for use with Adolescents' or 'Sex Differences in a Two-Choice Reaction Time Task' would be about right.

ABSTRACT: This should be succinct – no more than a single fair-sized paragraph and should state what had been investigated and why; how and upon whom; and with what outcome. Thus, it should contain no more than a sentence or two (at most) on background and aim; a very brief statment of design and sample; an indication of the measures used; and should end with a statement of the principal, normally statistical, conclusions.

INTRODUCTION: This contains the background to your investigation and should, whenever possible, be based on the psychological literature relevant to the topic under investigation. Usually it is sensible to begin in broad terms by delineating the area; then to give brief descriptions of one or two important and relevant studies reported in the literature; then to go on to develop the rationale behind the present investigation; and to conclude with a specific statement of the aim of your investigation – and where appropriate – of the specific hypotheses being tested.

METHOD: In the Introduction you have told your readers in broad detail what your study is about. It is now time to tell them **precisely** what you did. You must give them enough information for them to be able to exactly replicate your study.

The precise form of presentation that you choose may vary a good deal. Choose that form which allows you to convey to the reader simply and concisely what you actually did. The main subsection is the 'Procedure', where you say exactly what you did. However, if your study is complex, you might have to include so many details that your reader would be in danger of getting lost without the help of further headings. Thus, you can make your reader's task easier by using several sub-sections. However, remember that sub-sections are intended primarily to facilitate your reader's understanding of the 'Procedure' section, so don't include them for their own sake. If you think that other sorts of headings or combinations of headings would be useful, do not be afraid to use them. Alternatively, if you think that you can say all that you need to say in the 'Procedure' sub-section, don't include any others. (In practice, it is rare to omit the 'Subjects' sub-sections.)

Below are some hints on what to include in the sub-sections:-

Design: This details the structure of your investigation, whenever it is an experiment. It should contain such information as: the number of groups or conditions; the number of subjects per group and/or trials per condition; the relationship between the groups or conditions; and all details of control (e.g. the order of application of treatments).

It should not include details of procedure. Rather it is a brief depiction of the logical framework of the experiment – and this framework will usually dictate the nature of the principal statistical analysis to be done.

Keep everything as concise as possible.

Subjects: '10 Ss were used' is inadequate and ten life histories depressing. Give such details as are relevant to the particular study you are reporting. Age and sex are usually safe bets, as is an indication of the subjects' naivete and intelligence (e.g. second year psychology students, or non-psychology students). Examples of details which may be relevant to specific studies would be handedness and native language.

Apparatus or materials: Strike a sensible balance, giving details and make of technical apparatus, but not of pencils. With complex arrangements, a schematic diagram may be useful.

Procedure: Give a fairly detailed account of the experimenters' operations and what the subject(s) or group(s) were required to do. Any crucial instructions (for example, those intended to influence the subjects' 'set') should be reported verbatim but avoid the 'and the subject said O.K.' variety. Keep in mind that the function of this whole section on 'METHOD' is to give the reader sufficient detail to be able to replicate the investigation.

RESULTS: A summary table of results (e.g. means and standard deviations of the actual scores obtained) MUST be put in this section. Details (e.g. individual scores) belong in the Appendix. The summary must provide appropriate headings (e.g. Experimental Group; Control Group) and units of measurement must be staged. **All** tables and figures should be clearly labelled.

TREATMENT OF RESULTS: Next say what kind of analysis has been carried out and why. Where appropriate, indicate the outcome in terms of the value of the obtained statistics, degrees of freedom, p, significance level, and whether derived from one or two-tailed tables. Graphs which help interpret the findings can be included, but calculations belong in the Appendix.

DISCUSSION: Describe **in words** your findings and say how they relate to the hypotheses put forward. Use psychological (not statistical) terms. Avoid jargon: e.g.

<u>Write:-</u>   'Subjects who had knowledge of results learned significantly faster than those who did not'.

<u>Don't write:-</u>   'The acquisition functions for Ss in Gp.ii (Exptl.) differed significantly ($p < 0.01$) from those for Ss in Gp.i (Control)'.

Relate the results to the theoretical context, particulary as referred to in your INTRODUCTION. Present tentative explanations for unexpected findings and internal analyses. Where alternative explanations are offered, outline briefly how a further study might help to decide between them.

Next consider the shortcomings of the methodology of your investigation, suggesting appropriate remedies. Try to avoid being morbid or 'nitpicking' about this. For example, unless you have firm grounds for believing that fluctuations in background noise, ambient temperature, or daylight could seriously have affected your subject's response, do not mention it. On the other hand, where there has been a serious omission in design control, e.g. a failure to counterbalance or lack of a control condition, then this must be discussed.

CONCLUSION: This should be a brief summary of the main statistical conclusions expressed in verbal from.

REFERENCES: All references cited in the body of the report should state the name and year, thus:- Watson (1982). They should **all** then be tabulated in alphabetical order in this section, thus:-

Watson, D., (1982) The actor and observer: how are their perceptions of causality different? *Psychological Bulletin*, 92 (3), 682–700

Book references take the following format:-

Seligman, M.F.P., (1975) *Helplessness*, San Francisco: Freeman.

APPENDICES: This is used to present additional information such as raw data, statistical calculations, copies of instruction sheets, questionnaire sheets, etc. Use separate sheets and include in the page numbering.

AEB marking scheme for coursework

MARKING SCHEME FOR COURSEWORK
PAPER THREE – A level Psychology (651)
PAPER TWO – AS level Psychology (998)

Teachers are required to mark separately the reports of five psychological investigations for A level and three for AS level.

Mark Allocations

A	Planning and carrying out an investigation	Total:	8 marks

A1. Planning and implementation (3 marks)
A2. Reporting (5 marks)

B	Results and findings	Total:	5 marks
C	Interpretation and discussion	Total:	7 marks

Each report is marked separately and 20 marks are available for each report. Up to a maximum of 3 bonus marks beyond the 20 marks can be awarded to candidates who show independence in planning and implementing the investigation. No candidate can score more than 100 marks for A level or 60 marks for AS level. This is designed to reward candidates who show independence but allow those who do not to score maximum marks. An example of how the bonus mark system works can be found later in this document.

To achieve a particular mark under any one of the above sections, candidates do not necessarily have to satisfy **all** criteria for that mark. Thus, some compensation may be gained by virtue of excellence with regard to some criteria to offset weaknesses with regard to others. Equally, it is possible for candidates to achieve a mark intermediate between two because they fulfil some criteria for the higher mark and also some of the lower **ALTHOUGH HALF MARKS CANNOT BE AWARDED**. Thus, for example, candidates may be awarded 3 marks because they may fulfil some criteria for 4 marks and fail to reach other criteria at higher than 2. Teachers should look for opportunities to give credit and treat the marking exercise as an additive rather than subtractive operation. The variety of background studies referred to in the report should reflect the extensiveness or paucity of relevant research.

It is the responsibility of teachers to ensure that their candidates follow the ethical guidelines produced by the British Psychological Society covering the conduct of research.

A Planning and carrying out an investigation

NB. Marks under A1 are allocated for design decisions and formulation of hypotheses/aims while those in A2 are for reporting these decisions.

A1 Planning and implementation

3 marks   The methodology adopted was appropriate to the aims of the investigation, and all reasonable attempts were made to design and carry out the investigation competently. Hypotheses and/or aims were clearly and correctly formulated.

2 marks   The methodology adopted was appropriate to the aims of the investigation and a reasonable attempt had been made to design and carry out the investigation competently. Hypotheses and/or aims were adequately formulated.

1 mark   The methodology adopted was either ineffective given the aims of the investigation, or was inadequately implemented. Formulation of hypotheses and/or aims was less than satisfactory although still appropriate to the investigation.

0 marks   The methodology adopted was either inappropriate to the aims of the investigation, or was seriously flawed in its application. Hypotheses, where appropriate, were either incorrect or missing. The candidate did not show awareness of the real aim of the investigation.

A2 Reporting

5 marks   The investigation was appropriately located in the relevant psychological literature. Reporting of the literature was concise and led logically into the aims of the investigation. The aims were expressed clearly and, where appropriate, restated in the form of precise hypotheses. The structure of the investigation was clearly evident. Details of the method were precisely and clearly described so that replication would be possible. Descriptions included where appropriate, design and other strategies to control variables, selection of subjects, materials, procedure and instructions. The reference section followed the conventions of this section.

4 marks   The investigation was appropriately located in the relevant psychological literature. Reporting of the literature showed some misunderstandings or minor omissions but still led logically into the aims. The aims, and where appropriate, hypotheses were correctly stated. The logical structure of the investigation was apparent. Details of method were, with minor omissions, well documented permitting reasonable replication. Descriptions included, where appropriate, design and other strategies to control variables, selection of subjects, materials, procedure and instructions. The reference section demonstrated an awareness of the conventions of this section although there may have been a few omissions.

3 marks   The investigation was supported by some relevant psychological literature though there were important omissions. An attempt was made to link the aims of the investigation to the literature cited. The aims and, where appropriate, hypotheses were stated satisfactorily. The logical structure of the investigation was not always clear. There were some omissions in details of method which would make replication difficult. A fair summary was provided. The reference section demonstrated an awareness of the conventions of this section although there may have been several omissions.

2 marks   The investigation received minimal support from relevant psychological literature. It was difficult to see how the aims of the study arose from the literature cited. The statement of aims and, where appropriate, hypotheses were inadequate. The logical structure of the investigation was rarely clear. There were many minor omissions in detail of method which would make replication very difficult. A poor summary was provided. The reference section demonstrated little awareness of the conventions of this section and there were many omissions.

1 mark   The investigation received virtually no support from relevant psychological literature. The relationship between literature cited and the investigation undertaken was barely discernible. The statement of the aims and, where appropriate, hypotheses were muddled or incoherent. Fundamental omissions in reporting details of the method would make replication of the investigation impossible. There was no summary or reference section.

0 marks   The investigation seemed to exist in a psychological vacuum or was incoherent. No statement of aims or hypotheses were made. Omission or incoherence of the method section made it impossible to know how the investigation was implemented. There was no summary or reference section.

B Results and findings

5 marks   Treatment and presentation of findings were appropriate to the stated aims. Where relevant, a suitable choice of tables, graphs, charts etc. was made to describe and summarise data. A correct choice of statistical test(s) was made and justified. The implementation and interpretation of significance levels was appropriate for the investigation. Presentation of data was precise, accurate and clearly labelled. Where inferential statistics were not appropriate, the findings were logically and clearly presented in ways that were coherent.

4 marks   Treatment and presentation of findings were appropriate to stated aims. Where relevant, a suitable choice of tables, graphs, charts etc. was made to describe and summarise data. A correct choice of statistical test(s) was made and some attempt made to justify this. The implementation and interpretation of significance levels was satisfactory for the investigation. Presentation of data was precise and clearly labelled. Where inferential statistics were not appropriate, the findings were logically presented in clear ways that had some coherence.

3 marks   Treatment and presentation of findings were reasonably appropriate to the stated aims. Where relevant, a fairly satisfactory choice of tables, graphs, charts etc. was made to describe and summarise data. A correct choice of statistical test(s) was made and a limited attempt was made at justifying this. The implementation and interpretation of significance levels was satisfactory for the investigation. Presentation of data was limited in terms of precision and clarity of labelling. Where inferential statistics were not appropriate, the findings were logically presented, in ways that had some coherence.

2 marks   Treatment and presentation of findings were marginally appropriate to the stated aims. Where relevant, the choice of tables, graphs, charts etc., made to summarise data was inadequate. An acceptable choice of statistical test(s) was made even though the justification was incorrect or absent. The implementation and interpretation of significance levels was satisfactory for the investigation. Presentation of data was very limited in terms of precision and clarity of labelling. Where inferential statistics were not appropriate, the findings were presented in ways that had some coherence.

1 mark   It was difficult to see how the treatment and presentation of findings were appropriate to the stated aims. Where a choice of tables, graphs and charts etc. had been made, they were irrelevant or incorrect. An inappropriate choice of statistical test(s) was made and the justification was incorrect or absent. The implementation and interpretation of significance levels was incorrect or inadequate for the investigation. Presentation of data lacked precision and clarity of labelling. Where inferential statistics were not appropriate, the findings were presented in ways that had little coherence.

0 marks   The treatment and presentation of findings were inappropriate or absent. Where they would have been relevant, tables, graphs and charts were incorrect or omitted. An incorrect choice of statistical test(s) was made and the justification was incorrect or absent. The implementation and interpretation of significance levels was incorrect or absent. Presentation of data was inaccurate and muddled. Where inferential statistics were not appropriate, there were no findings or they were presented in ways that were incoherent.

C Interpretation and discussion

7 marks   The investigation was appropriately discussed in the light of relevant background research and/or theory. A coherent attempt was made to explain the outcome of the investigation in terms of the hypotheses and/or aims. The candidate demonstrated an understanding of most of the limitations of the investigation and was able to suggest apt modifications. Where appropriate, reference was made to the methodology and statistical treatment used. The effects which these may have had on the conclusions drawn were discussed pertinently. The implications of the findings were discussed and appropriate suggestions for further research were made.

6 marks   The investigation was appropriately discussed in the light of relevant background research and/or theory. A good attempt was made to explain the outcome of the investigation in terms of the hypotheses and/or aims. The candidate demonstrated an understanding of some of the limitations of the investigation and was able to suggest modifications. Where appropriate, reference was made to the methodology or statistical treatment used. The effects which these may have had on the conclusions drawn were discussed pertinently. Some implications of the findings were discussed and suggestions for further research were made.

5 marks   The investigation was discussed in the light of relevant background research and/or theory. A reasonable attempt was made to explain the outcome of the investigation in terms of hypotheses and/or aims. The candidate demonstrated a degree of understanding of some of the limitations of the investigation and was able to suggest some modifications. Where appropriate, some reference was made to the methodology or statistical treatment used. The effects which these may have had on the conclusions drawn were discussed.

4 marks   An effort was made to discuss the investigation in the light of relevant background research and/or theory. An adequate attempt was made to explain the outcome of the investigation in terms of the hypotheses and/or aims. The candidate showed a partial awareness of the limitations of the investigation and was able to suggest occasional modifications. Where reference was made to the methodology or statistical treatment used, the effects which these may have had on the conclusions drawn were discussed briefly, or with only limited success.

3 marks   A limited effort was made to discuss the investigation in the light of relevant background research and/or theory. A limited attempt was made to explain the outcome of the investigation in terms of the hypotheses and/or aims. The candidate barely mentioned the limitations of the investigation, and proposed weak or inappropriate modifications. Little reference was made to methodology or statistical treatment used and the conclusions drawn were brief or did not follow logically from the discussion.

2 marks   A very limited effort was made to discuss the investigation in the light of relevant background and/or theory. No attempt was made to explain the outcome in terms of the hypotheses and/or aims, or explanations offered were inappropriate. Mention of limitations or modifications was sparse. Only the briefest reference to methodology or statistical treatment was made.

1 mark   A barely discernible effort was made to discuss the investigation in the light of relevant background research and/or theory. No attempt was made to explain the outcome in terms of the hypotheses and/or aims. Mention of limitations or modifications were extremely limited or non-existent. Almost no reference to methodology or statistical treatment was made.

0 marks   There was little or no attempt to discuss the investigation. Inarticulate or irrelevant expression was used, and there was no evidence that the candidate knew the purpose of this section.

Bonus marks for independence

Where the candidate demonstrated some independence in planning and implementing the investigation, bonus marks should be awarded as follows:

PLANNING

a)   The candidate designed the investigation with minimal aid from the teacher.
b)   The candidate was an active member of a small group which designed the investigation with minimal teacher guidance.

IMPLEMENTATION

c)   The candidate conducted the investigation with minimal aid from the teacher.

d)   The candidate conducted the investigation as an active member of a small group working with minimal teacher guidance.

3 marks – a and c

2 marks – EITHER a and d OR b and c OR b and d

1 mark – EITHER a OR b Or c OR d

Teachers should note that these are additional marks to the 20 awarded for each report and marks should **not** be deducted if these criteria are not satisfied. Teachers should refer to the section 'With reference to the syllabus, what is meant by "the work of the candidate"?' in the Further Information for Teachers section of this document for the list of situations where candidates do not work independently but can still score full marks for a report (but not score bonus marks).

Example

Candidate A, an excellent candidate, shows independence in three of the five reports completed and receives a total of 103 marks. This will be recorded as the maximum, mark of 100 on the Coursework Marksheet. Candidate B, a very good candidate, also shows independence in three of the five reports completed. This candidate scores the following marks:

18 (no bonus marks)
18 (no bonus marks)
19 (one bonus mark)
20 (two bonus marks)
<u>21</u> (three bonus marks)

Total   <u>96</u>

This candidate's total mark should be recorded as 96 on the Coursework Marksheet.

Appendix C

THE BRITISH PSYCHOLOGICAL SOCIETY

Ethical principles

The document 'Ethical Principles for Conducting Research with Human Participants' was considerably revised in 1990 and the revised version was published in *The Psychologist* (June 1990) after approval by Council. In 1990 it was agreed that the revised version would be reviewed after a two-year trial period, during which researchers were asked to inform the Chair of the Scientific Affairs Board if they experienced any difficulties with the wording. The review has now been completed. In the light of certain comments, an important addition has been made to Clause 3.3. The amended version of the principles, as approved by Council in October 1992, is published below.

All psychologists engaged in research with human participants are required to abide by these principles which supplement the Society's Code of Conduct. Violation could form a basis of disciplinary action. It is essential that all members of the psychological profession abide by the principles if psychologists are to continue to retain the privilege of testing human participants in their research. Psychologists have legal as well as moral responsibility for those who help them in their studies, and the reputation of the discipline in the long term depends largely on the first-hand experience of those taking part in psychological investigations.

Ethical principles for conducting research with human participants

1 Introduction

1.1 The principles given below are intended to apply to research with human participants. Principles of conduct in professional practice are to be found in the Society's Code of Conduct and in the advisory documents prepared by the Divisions, Sections and Special Groups of the Society.

1.2 Participants in psychological research should have confidence in the investigators. Good psychological research is possible only if there is mutual respect and confidence between investigators and participants. Psychological investigators are potentially interested in all aspects of human behaviour and conscious experience. However, for ethical reasons, some areas of human experience and behaviour may be beyond the reach of experiment, observation or other form of psychological investigation. Ethical guidelines are necessary to clarify the conditions under which psychological research is acceptable.

1.3 The principles given below supplement for researchers with human participants the general ethical principles of members of the Society as stated in the British Psychological Society's Code of Conduct (1985) and subsequent amendments to this Code. Members of the British Psychological Society are expected to abide by both the Code of Conduct and the fuller principles expressed here. Members should also draw the principles to the attention of research colleagues who are not members of the Society. Members should encourage colleagues to adopt them and ensure that they are followed by all researchers whom they supervise (e.g. research assistants, postgraduate, undergraduate, A-Level and GCSE students).

1.4 In recent years, there has been an increase in legal actions by members of the general public against professionals for alleged misconduct. Researchers must recognise the possibility of such legal action if they infringe the rights and dignity of participants in their research.

2 *General*

2.1 In all circumstances, investigators must consider the ethical implications and psychological consequences for the participants in their research. The essential principle is that the investigation should be considered from the standpoint of all participants; foreseeable threats to their psychological well being, health, values or dignity should be eliminated. Investigators should recognise that, in our multi-cultural and multi-ethnic society and where investigations involve individuals of different ages, gender and social background, the investigators may not have sufficient knowledge of the implications of an investigation for the participants. It should be borne in mind that the best judges of whether an investigation will cause offence may be members of the population from which the participants in the research are to be drawn.

3 *Consent*

3.1 Whenever possible, the investigator should inform all participants of the objectives of the investigation. The investigator should inform the participants of all aspects of the research or intervention that might reasonably be expected to influence willingness to participate. The investigator should, normally, explain all other aspects of the research or intervention about which the participants enquire. Failure to make full disclosure prior to obtaining informed consent requires additional safeguards to protect the welfare and dignity of the participants (see Section 4).

3.2 Research with children or with participants who have impairments that will limit understanding and/or communications such that they are unable to give their real consent requires special safeguarding procedures.

3.3 Where possible, the real consent of children and of adults with impairments in understanding or communication should be obtained. In addition, where research involves any person under sixteen years of age, consent should be obtained from parents or from those *in loco parentis*. If the nature of the research precludes consent being obtained from parents or permission being obtained from teachers, before proceeding with the research, the investigator must obtain approval from an Ethics Committee.

3.4 Where real consent cannot be obtained from adults with impairments in understanding or communication, wherever possible the investigator should consult a person well-placed to appreciate the participant's reaction, such as a member of the person's family, and must obtain the disinterested approval of the research from independent advisors.

3.5 When research is being conducted with detained persons, particular care should be taken over informed consent, paying attention to the special circumstances which may affect the person's ability to give free informed consent.

3.6 Investigators should realise that they are often in a position of authority or influence over participants who may be their students, employees or clients. This relationship must not be allowed to pressurise the participants to take part in, or remain in, an investigation.

3.7 The payment of participants must not be uses to induce them to risk harm beyond that which they risk without payment in their normal lifestyle.

3.8 If harm, unusual discomfort, or other negative consequences for the individuals's future life might occur, the investigator must obtain the disinterested approval of independent advisors, inform the participants, and obtain informed, real consent from each of them.

3.9 In longitudinal research, consent may need to be obtained on more than one occasion.

4 *Deception*

4.1 The withholding of information or the misleading of participants is unacceptable if the participants are typically likely to object or show unease once debriefed. Where this is in any doubt, appropriate consultation must precede the investigation. Consultation is best carried out with individuals who share the social and cultural background of the participants in the research, but the advice of ethics committees or experienced and disinterested colleagues may be sufficient.

4.2 Intentional deception of the participants over the purpose and general nature of the investigation should be avoided whenever possible. Participants should never be deliberately mislead without extremely strong scientific or medical justification. Even then there should be strict controls and the disinterested approval of independent advisors.

4.3 It may be impossible to study some psychological processes without withholding information about the true object of the study or deliberately misleading the participants. Before conducting such a study, the investigator has a special responsibility to (a) determine that alternative procedures avoiding concealment or deception are not available; (b) ensure that the participants are provided with sufficient information at the earliest stage; and (c) consult appropriately upon the way that the withholding of information or deliberate deception will be received.

5 *Debriefing*

5.1 In studies where the participants are aware that they have taken part in an investigation, when the data have been collected, the investigator should provide the participants with any necessary information to complete their understanding of the nature of the research. The investigator should discuss with the participants their experience of the research in order to monitor any unforeseen negative effects or misconceptions.

5.2 Debriefing does not provide a justification for unethical aspects of an investigation.

5.3 Some effects which may be produced by an experiment will not be negated by a verbal description following the research. Investigators have a responsibility to ensure that participants receive any necessary debriefing in the form of active intervention before they leave the research setting.

6 *Withdrawal from the Investigation*

6.1 At the onset of the investigation investigators should make plain to participants their right to withdraw from the research at any time, irrespective of whether or not payment or other inducement has been offered. It is recognised that this may be difficult in certain observational or organisational settings, but nevertheless the investigator must attempt to ensure that participants (including children) know of their right to withdraw. When testing children, avoidance of the testing situation may be taken as evidence of failure to consent to the procedure and should be acknowledged.

6.2 In the light of experience of the investigation, or as a result of debriefing, the participant has the right to withdraw retrospectively any consent given, and to require that their own data, including recordings, be destroyed.

7 *Confidentiality*

7.1 Subject to the requirements of legislation, including the Data Protection Act, information obtained about a participant during an investigation is confidential unless otherwise agreed in advance. Investigators who are put under pressure to disclose confidential information should draw this point to the attention of those exerting such pressure. Participants in psychological research have a right to expect that information they provide will be treated confidentially and, if published, will not be identifiable as theirs. In the event that confidentiality and/or anonymity cannot be guaranteed, the participant must be warned of this in advance of agreeing to participate.

8 *Protection of Participants*

8.1 Investigators have a primary responsibility to protect participants from physical and mental harm during the investigation. Normally, the risk of harm must be no greater than in ordinary life, i.e. participants should not be exposed to risks greater than or additional to those encountered in their normal lifestyles. Where the risk of harm is greater than in ordinary life the provisions of 3.8 should apply. Participants must be asked about any factors in the procedure that might create a risk, such as pre-existing medical conditions, and must be advised of any special action they should take to avoid risk.

8.2 Participants should be informed of procedures for contacting the investigator within a reasonable time period following participation should stress, potential harm, or related questions or concern arise despite the precautions required by these Principles. Where research procedures might result in undesirable consequences for participants, the investigator has the responsibility to detect and remove or correct these consequences.

8.3 Where research may involve behaviour or experiences that participants may regard as personal and private the participants must be protected from stress by all appropriate measures, including the assurance that answers to personal questions need not be given. There should be no concealment or deception when seeking information that might encroach on privacy.

8.4 In research involving children, great caution should be exercised when discussing the results with parents, teachers or others *in loco parentis*, since evaluative statements may carry unintended weight.

9 *Observational Research*

9.1 Studies based upon observation must respect the privacy and psychological well-being of the individuals studied. Unless those observed give their consent to being observed, observational research is only acceptable in situations where those observed would expect to be observed by strangers. Additionally, particular account should be taken of local cultural values and of the possibility of intruding upon the privacy of individuals who, even while in a normally public space, may believe they are unobserved.

10 *Giving Advice*

10.1 During research, an investigator may obtain evidence of psychological or physical problems of which a participant is, apparently, unaware. In such a case, the investigator has a responsibility to inform the participant if the investigator believes that by not doing so the participant's future well being may be endangered.

10.2 If, in the normal course of psychological research, or as a result of problems detected as in 10.1, a participant solicits advice concerning educational, personality, behavioural or health issues, caution should be exercised. If the issue is serious and the investigator is not qualified to offer assistance, the appropriate source of professional advice should be recommended. Further details on the giving of advice will be found in the Society's Code of Conduct.

10.3 In some kinds of investigation the giving of advice is appropriate if this forms an intrinsic part of the research and had been agreed in advance.

11 *Colleagues*

11.1 Investigators share responsibility for the ethical treatment of research participants with their collaborators, assistants, students and employees. A psychologist who believes that another psychologist or investigator may be conducting research that is not in accordance with the principles above should encourage that investigator to re-evaluate the research.

Reference

The British Psychological Society (1985). A Code of Conduct for Psychologists. *Bulletin of The British Psychological Society*, **38**, 41–43.

See also proposed revisions to this code in **The Psychologist, 5**, 562–563.

Copies of this article may be obtained from The British Psychological Society, St Andrews House, 48 Princess Road East, Leicester LE1 7DR.

Source: adapted from *The Psychologist*, Vol 6, No. 1 January 1993

Appendix D

Statistical tables

Critical values of Spearman's Rho (r_s)

	Level of significance for a two-tailed test			
	0.10	0.05	0.02	0.01
	Level of significance for a one-tailed test			
	0.05	0.025	0.01	0.005
n=4	1.000			
5	0.900	1.000	1.000	
6	0.829	0.886	0.943	1.000
7	0.714	0.786	0.893	0.929
8	0.643	0.738	0.833	0.881
9	0.600	0.700	0.783	0.833
10	0.564	0.648	0.745	0.794
11	0.536	0.618	0.709	0.755
12	0.503	0.587	0.671	0.727
13	0.484	0.560	0.648	0.703
14	0.464	0.538	0.622	0.675
15	0.443	0.521	0.604	0.654
16	0.429	0.503	0.582	0.635
17	0.414	0.485	0.566	0.615
18	0.401	0.472	0.550	0.600
19	0.391	0.460	0.535	0.584
20	0.380	0.447	0.520	0.570
21	0.370	0.435	0.508	0.556
22	0.361	0.425	0.496	0.544
23	0.353	0.415	0.486	0.532
24	0.344	0.406	0.476	0.521
25	0.337	0.398	0.466	0.511
26	0.331	0.390	0.457	0.501
27	0.324	0.382	0.448	0.491
28	0.317	0.375	0.440	0.483
29	0.312	0.368	0.433	0.475
30	0.306	0.362	0.425	0.467

For $n > 30$, the significance of r_s can be tested by using the formula:

$$t = r_s \sqrt{\frac{n-2}{1-r_s^2}} \quad df = n - 2$$

and checking the value of t.

Calculated r_s must EQUAL or EXCEED the table (critical) value for significance at the level shown.

Critical values of χ^2 (Chi-square)

df	Level of significance for a one-tailed test					
	0.10	0.05	0.025	0.01	0.005	0.0005
	Level of significance for a two-tailed test					
	0.20	0.10	0.05	0.02	0.01	0.001
1	1.64	2.71	3.84	5.41	6.64	10.83
2	3.22	4.60	5.99	7.82	9.21	13.82
3	4.64	6.25	7.82	9.84	11.34	16.27
4	5.99	7.78	9.49	11.67	13.28	18.46
5	7.29	9.24	11.07	13.39	15.09	20.52
6	8.56	10.64	12.59	15.03	16.81	22.46
7	9.80	12.02	14.07	16.62	18.48	24.32
8	10.03	13.36	15.51	18.17	20.09	26.12
9	12.24	14.68	16.92	19.68	21.67	27.88
10	13.44	15.99	18.31	21.16	23.21	29.59
11	14.63	17.28	19.68	22.62	24.72	31.26
12	15.81	18.55	21.03	24.05	26.22	32.91
13	16.98	19.81	22.36	25.47	27.69	34.53
14	18.15	21.06	23.68	26.87	29.14	36.12
15	19.31	22.31	25.00	28.26	30.58	37.70
16	20.46	23.54	26.30	29.63	32.00	39.29
17	21.62	24.77	27.59	31.00	33.41	40.75
18	22.76	25.99	28.87	32.35	34.80	42.31
19	23.90	27.20	30.14	33.69	36.19	43.82
20	25.04	28.41	31.41	35.02	37.57	45.32
21	26.17	29.62	32.67	36.34	38.93	46.80
22	27.30	30.81	33.92	37.66	40.29	48.27
23	28.43	32.01	35.17	38.97	41.64	49.73
24	29.55	33.20	36.42	40.27	42.98	51.18
25	30.68	34.38	37.65	41.57	44.31	52.62
26	31.80	35.56	38.88	42.86	45.64	54.05
27	32.91	36.74	40.11	44.14	46.96	55.48
28	34.03	37.92	41.34	45.42	48.28	56.89
29	35.14	39.09	42.69	49.69	49.59	58.30
30	36.25	40.26	43.77	47.96	50.89	59.70
32	38.47	42.59	46.19	50.49	53.49	62.49
34	40.68	44.90	48.60	53.00	56.06	65.25
36	42.88	47.21	51.00	55.49	58.62	67.99
38	45.08	49.51	53.38	57.97	61.16	70.70
40	47.27	51.81	55.76	60.44	63.69	73.40
44	51.64	56.37	60.48	65.34	68.71	78.75
48	55.99	60.91	65.17	70.20	73.68	84.04
52	60.33	65.42	69.83	75.02	78.62	89.27
56	64.66	69.92	74.47	79.82	83.51	94.46
60	68.97	74.40	79.08	84.58	88.38	99.61

Calculated value of χ^2 must EQUAL or EXCEED the table (critical) value for significance at the level shown.

Taken from Fisher and Yates; *Statistical Tables for Biological, Agricultural and Medical Research*, published by Longman Group UK Ltd., 1974.

Critical values of T in the Wilcoxon signed ranks test

Sample size	Levels of significance			
	One-tailed test			
	0.05	0.025	0.01	0.001
	Two-tailed test			
	0.1	0.05	0.02	0.002
$N = 5$	$T \le 0$			
6	2	0		
7	3	2	0	
8	5	3	1	
9	8	5	3	
10	11	8	5	0
11	13	10	7	1
12	17	13	9	2
13	21	17	12	4
14	25	21	15	6
15	30	25	19	8
16	35	29	23	11
17	41	34	27	14
18	47	40	32	18
19	53	46	37	21
20	60	52	43	26
21	67	58	49	30
22	75	65	55	35
23	83	73	62	40
24	91	81	69	45
25	100	98	76	51
26	110	98	84	58
27	119	107	92	64
28	130	116	101	71
30	151	137	120	86
31	163	147	130	94
32	175	159	140	103
33	187	170	151	112

Calculated T must be EQUAL TO OR LESS THAN the table (critical) value for significance at the level shown.

Critical values of *t*

	Level of significance for a one-tailed test			
	0.05	0.025	0.01	0.005
	Level of significance for a two-tailed test			
Degrees of freedom	0.10	0.05	0.02	0.01
1	6.314	12.706	31.821	63.657
2	2.920	4.303	6.965	9.925
3	2.353	3.182	4.541	5.841
4	2.132	2.776	3.747	4.604
5	2.015	2.571	3.365	4.032
6	1.943	2.447	3.143	3.707
7	1.895	2.365	2.998	3.499
8	1.860	2.306	2.896	3.355
9	1.833	2.262	2.821	3.250
10	1.812	2.228	2.764	3.169
11	1.796	2.201	2.718	3.106
12	1.782	2.179	2.681	3.055
13	1.771	2.160	2.650	3.012
14	1.761	3.145	2.624	2.977
15	1.753	2.131	2.602	2.947
16	1.746	2.120	2.583	2.921
17	1.740	2.110	2.567	2.898
18	1.734	2.101	2.552	2.878
19	1.729	2.093	2.539	2.861
20	1.725	2.086	2.528	2.845
21	1.721	2.080	2.518	2.831
22	1.717	2.074	2.508	2.819
23	1.714	2.069	2.500	2.807
24	1.711	2.064	2.492	2.797
25	1.708	2.060	2.485	2.787
26	1.706	2.056	2.479	2.779
27	1.703	2.052	2.473	2.771
28	1.701	2.048	2.467	2.763
29	1.699	2.045	2.462	2.756
30	1.697	2.042	2.457	2.750
40	1.684	2.021	2.423	2.704
60	1.671	2.000	2.390	2.660
120	1.658	1.980	2.358	2.617
∞	1.645	1.960	2.326	2.576

Calculated *t* must EQUAL or EXCEED the table (critical) value for significance at the level shown.

Taken from Fisher and Yates; *Statistical Tables for Biological, Agricultural and Medical Research*, published by Longman Group UK Ltd, 1974.

Critical values for the Mann-Whitney Test
Critical values of U
One-tailed test at 0.05 (significance) **or** two-tailed test at 0.10

n_2 \ n_1	1	2	3	4	5	6	7	8	9	10	11	12	13	14	15	16	17	18	19	20
1	–	–	–	–	–	–	–	–	–	–	–	–	–	–	–	–	–	–	0	0
2	–	–	–	–	0	0	0	1	1	1	1	2	2	2	3	3	3	4	4	4
3	–	–	0	0	1	2	2	3	3	4	5	5	6	7	7	8	9	9	10	11
4	–	–	0	1	2	3	4	5	6	7	8	9	10	11	12	14	15	16	17	18
5	–	0	1	2	4	5	6	8	9	11	12	13	15	16	18	19	20	22	23	25
6	–	0	2	3	5	7	8	10	12	14	16	17	19	21	23	25	26	28	30	32
7	–	0	2	4	6	8	11	13	15	17	19	21	24	26	28	30	33	35	37	39
8	–	1	3	5	8	10	13	15	18	20	23	26	28	31	33	36	39	41	44	47
9	–	1	3	6	9	12	15	18	21	24	27	30	33	36	39	42	45	48	51	54
10	–	1	4	7	11	14	17	20	24	27	31	34	37	41	44	48	51	55	58	62
11	–	1	5	8	12	16	19	23	27	31	34	38	42	46	50	54	57	61	65	69
12	–	2	5	9	13	17	21	26	30	34	38	42	47	51	55	60	64	68	72	77
13	–	2	8	10	15	19	24	28	33	37	42	47	51	58	61	65	70	75	80	84
14	–	2	7	11	16	21	26	31	36	41	46	51	56	81	66	71	77	82	87	92
15	–	3	7	12	18	23	28	33	38	44	50	55	61	66	72	77	83	88	94	100
16	–	3	8	14	19	25	30	36	42	48	54	60	65	71	77	83	89	95	101	107
17	–	3	9	15	20	26	33	38	45	51	57	64	70	77	83	89	96	102	108	115
18	–	4	9	16	22	28	35	41	48	55	61	68	75	82	88	95	102	109	116	123
19	0	4	10	17	23	30	37	44	51	58	65	72	80	87	94	101	109	116	123	130
20	0	4	11	18	25	32	39	47	54	62	69	77	84	92	100	107	115	123	130	138

(Dashes in the body of the table indicate that no decision is possible)
If U value (from your data) $\le$ critical U value (from table above) then result is significant

Appendix E

Answer notes for past examination questions
(These answers are the sole responsibility of the author and have not been provided or approved by the board.)

1987 A level examination paper 2, section A

a) The major advantage in using a repeated measures design is that it eliminates subject extraneous variables. This can result in it being easier to see if the IV has had an effect on the DV.
Note: this is what I would consider to be the **major** advantage but there are other advantages to the repeated measures design. See Chapter 6, pp. 79–80.

b) Two disadvantages of the repeated measures design are, order effects and the fact that different stimulus material may be needed if each subject does both of the experimental conditions.
Note: for other disadvantages with this design see Chapter 6, pp. 79–80.

c) A null hypothesis for this experiment would be, 'Any difference in the number of anagrams correctly solved between the experimental group (with noise), and the control group (silence), is due to chance'.
Note: the concept of the null hypothesis is explained in Chapter 2, p. 11.

d) The experimental hypothesis should be two tailed because the researcher is predicting that there will be a difference in the number of anagrams correctly solved between the experimental and control groups, but not the direction of the difference.
Note: it says in the second paragraph that some students feel they work more effectively with music, while others find silence a more effective background for study. There is no basis, therefore, upon which to predict that one condition will be more effective than the other, which is what is needed for a one-tailed hypothesis. See Chapter 2, pp. 9–10.

e) An alternative sampling technique which might give a more representative sample of A level students is stratified sampling. With this sampling method the population of A level students could be divided into those studying arts subjects and those studying science subjects. Then a random sample of twenty arts students and twenty science students could be chosen. It might be that music is an aid to studying arts subjects but a distraction for science subjects. Stratified sampling can ensure that there are an equal number of arts and science students in the sample studied. With random sampling equal numbers of arts and science students would not be guaranteed.

Note: there are a number of other methods of sampling that could be used in answer to this question. But you do need to explain what advantage they have over random sampling. See Chapter 5, pp. 61–3.

f) I must admit that I am not exactly sure what the examiners require here. One line of argument could be that forty seems a reasonably large sample of A level students. The larger the sample the more likely it is that the sample will be representative of the population from which it has been drawn. However, as we are not told how many A level students there are at the college it is not really possible to say whether forty is a large sample or not! If there were 200 A level students then forty (nearly a quarter of the population) would be considered a large sample. If there were 2000 A level students however, then forty would not be a large sample.

   Another line of argument could be that an independent samples design with a sample of forty would give twenty subjects each in the experimental and control conditions. From a statistical point of view this gives a reasonable chance of testing the null hypothesis. With small samples it can be very difficult to establish a statistically significant result using the independent samples design because of the potentially large amount of random error arising from subject extraneous variables.

g) Two variables that the experimenter should have taken into account when choosing the anagrams are the frequency of the words i.e., whether they were frequently or infrequently used words, and the letter order used to turn the words into anagrams. Both these factors have been shown by research to influence the time taken to solve anagrams.

h) 'This is an experiment on problem solving. I am going to give you a list of thirty, seven-letter anagrams and your task is to solve as many of the anagrams as you can in fifteen minutes. Please do not remove your headphones while the experiment is in progress. Any questions?'

i) An answer the examiner might be looking for is something like verbal intelligence. This is a variable which could affect the DV (number of anagrams correctly solved) other than the IV (the presence or absence of music). However, I must admit that I disagree with whoever set this question. My understanding of random error is that it may obscure the effect of the IV on the DV but, if the error is random, then it does not confound the experiment. However, some books talk of a confounding variable as anything which affects the DV, other than the IV. In which case random error which does affect the DV could be said to lead to confounding. There is clearly a difference in terminology here and I expect you are are saying, 'well if teachers cannot agree among themselves what hope is there for me'! This would certainly be my reaction. However, my experience of examining at A level is that if a problem like this arises then credit is given to either answer.

j) Demand characteristics are cues which suggest to the subject what the aim of the research is, or what outcome the experimenter expects. They are sometimes also called **expectancy effects**. They may be shown by subjects in this case if they suspected that the music is supposed to affect their performance and if they behave accordingly.

k) The control group needs to wear headphones to prevent the results of the experiment being confounded (properly this time!). This is because there would be more than one systematic difference between the experimental and control groups if all the subjects did not wear headphones. In an experiment the only systematic difference between the two conditions should be the IV. That is the variable the experimenter manipulates; in this experiment it is the presence or absence of music. If a difference in the number of anagrams correctly solved were found between the groups to what should we attribute this? The presence or absence of music; or the presence or absence of headphones. After all wearing headphones may be uncomfortable or distracting which could influence the subjects' ability to concentrate on solving the anagrams.

l) The criteria that should be met before a parametric test is applied are:
  i   The data should be interval or ratio level.
  ii) The data should be drawn from populations which are normally distributed.
  iii) The data should come from populations which have homogeneous (equal) variance. See Chapter 8, pp. 116–17.

m) The unrelated *t* test.
Note: this would be used because a difference is being predicted, you are told a parametric test can be used, the design was independent samples, therefore an unrelated parametric test is needed. See Figure 4.2 in Chapter 4, p. 36.

n) A type 2 error is made when a researcher accepts the null hypothesis when in fact they should have rejected it. They are concluding that the IV did not effect the DV when it did. A significance level of 0.001 (1 in a 1000) is a very stringent level of significance and the more stringent the level of significance the more likely a type 2 error is. See Chapter 2, pp. 12–13.

1988 A level examination paper 2, section A
a) The level of measurement used in the table of rank order in academic subjects is ordinal. See Chapter 4, p. 38.

b) The IQ scores in descending order are:

IQ Scores	Ranks
80	1.0
100	2.0
102	3.0
110	5.0
110	5.0
110	5.0
115	7.0
132	8.0
140	9.5
140	9.5

Note: I have assigned the lowest rank to the smallest score which is what you would do if you were applying the Spearman's Rho test to the data. However, the question does not specify that the lowest rank must be given to the smallest score therefore if you have allocated the ranks the other way round your answer would still be marked correct. Assuming of course, that you have carried out the ranking correctly! See Chapter 4, in which you used Spearman's Rho.

c) The term standard deviation refers to a descriptive statistic which measures the amount of dispersion, spread or variability in a set of scores. It does this by calculating the square root of the average of the deviations from the mean, squared! (I do not think you would be expected to include the last sentence). See Chapter 3, p. 24.

d)

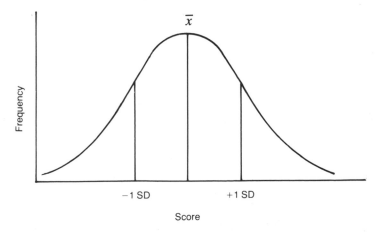

Figure 1

e) The answers are:

 i) 34% (approximately)
Note: if the mean of IQ is 100, and the standard deviation is 15, then an IQ score of 115 is 1 standard deviation above the mean. Study the figure below which shows the normal distribution with the standard deviations marked.

Figure 2

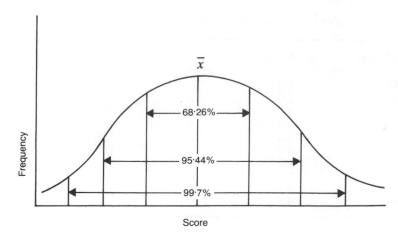

You will also see the percentage of scores which lie between + and – 1, 2 and 3 standard deviations from the mean. If 68.26% of scores lie between + and – 1 standard deviation then a half of this, approximately 34%, will lie between the mean and a 0.1 standard deviation above the mean.

ii) 2.5% (approximately).

Note: an IQ of 130 is 2 standard deviations above the mean – if 1 standard deviation is 15 then 30 is 2 standard deviations. Again, if you consult Figure 2 above you will see that 95.44% of scores lie between + 2 and – 2 standard deviations from the mean. This means that approximately 5% of scores lie outside this i.e. above and below. However we are only interested in the percentage of scores that lie 2 standard deviations above the mean. As the normal distribution is the same shape on either side we can divide the percentage of scores falling beyond + and – 2 standard deviations from the mean (5%) to give us the answer we want. Therefore 5% divided by 2 gives us the answer of 2.5%.

f) To find out if 0.85 is significant at the 0.05 level you need to work out the appropriate critical value. To work out this out you must first know the number of subjects (N) – in this case it is 10. The table shows that the critical value for an N of 10, at the 0.05 level is 0.591. The decision rule, in the case of correlation, is that the observed value (0.85) must be equal to or greater than the critical value (0.591). As this is the case the result of 0.85 is significant at the 0.05 level.

Note: I have discussed the issue of significance at length in your practicals. See Chapter 2, p. 12.

g) The phrase 'the result is significant at the 0.05 level' means that the probability of the results occurring by chance is equal to, or less than 1 in 20. See Chapter 2, p. 12.

h) A 0.01 level of significance might be preferred to a 0.05 level in circumstances where there are important consequences or application which might follow from the research findings. A 0.01 level of significance reduces the possibility of a type 2 error giving greater confidence that researcher has a **real** result. An example of a situation where the 0.01 level of significance might be used is if a drug company was investigating the effectiveness of a new drug and was considering whether to spend a great deal of money in producing it on a large scale. The company would want to feel sure that the drug was effective before investing the money.

i)

i) An interval level scale exits where the measuring instrument has equal units of measurement but does not have a true zero. The measurement of temperature in degrees centigrade is an example of an interval level of measurement.

ii) A nominal level of measurement is where the data consist of counting frequencies for named categories, such as the number of male and female drivers who stop for pedestrians at zebra crossings. See Chapters 4 pp. 37–8 and 5 p. 67.

j) The reliability of IQ tests could be assessed by giving the same group of subjects the test(s) on two separate occasions and correlating the results. This would measure the test/retest reliability of the test(s). IQ tests are often produced in two or more forms and the alternate form reliability of a test can be evaluated by giving the same group of subjects both versions or forms of the test and then correlating the results. See the Practical 1 in Chapter 4.

k)

i) A one-tailed hypothesis states the direction a difference or correlation will take, whereas a two-tailed hypothesis simply predicts that there will be a difference or correlation.

ii) A suitable two-tailed hypothesis would be, 'There will be a correlation between the pupils' rank order in academic subjects and their IQ score'.

l) To select a random sample of thirty children from a school population of 500 you could either:

i) Use the lottery method. Take the names of all 500 children from the registers, write them on pieces of paper and then place them all in a container. Mix them up then pick out thirty names.

ii) Use random number tables. Using the registers number all the children from one to 500. Then use random number tables to pick thirty numbers between one and 500; the children with these numbers are the ones who would be studied.

See Chapter 5, pp. 61–2.

1989 A level examination paper 2, section A

a) Two reasons for carrying out a pilot study are: to check the level of inter-observer reliability; and to check the validity of the categorization system. The topic of validity is discussed in Chapter 4, pp. 30–1.

b) Two reasons why it is necessary for the investigators to have good inter-observer reliability are: because without this the observations of each investigator cannot be meaningfully combined; and without reliability the validity of the study would be called into question.

c) Face validity refers to whether or not the measure being used appears to measure what it is supposed to. In this case, do the categories being used appear to be measures of rough and tumble play. Play chasing accompanied by smiling and laughing lacks face validity because it does not necessarily involve anything **rough**. See discussion of validity in Chapter 4, pp. 30–1.

d) Two reasons for using the Chi-squared test are: the level of data is nominal, and the design is similar to independent samples.
Note: this study is not a true experiment as the researchers are not manipulating an independent variable. However, for the purposes of selecting a statistical test this study is considered to use an independent samples design. This seems reasonable as you are either a boy or a girl, therefore you cannot take part in both conditions! See Chapter 4 Figure 4.2, p. 36.

e) Two reasons why it is useful to choose a school with staggered playtimes are: it enables the researchers to study 5/6 year olds and 9/10 year olds separately; and having fewer children in the playground would enable more accurate observations to be made.

f) With one student observing and another one recording, a continuous record can be kept of behaviour of interest. If each researcher had to do both then they would need to interrupt their observations frequently to do the recording.

g) Reactivity to being observed could be minimized by either having a period of acclimatization or concealing the observers.

With acclimatization the observers would need to be present in the playground for a period of time so that the children got used to their presence. During the period of acclimatization no observations are made.

It might be possible for the researchers to observe the children at play from a classroom so that the children were unaware of being observed.

h) It is preferable to set a minimum level of significance before the main investigation begins because this level may vary depending upon the nature of the hypothesis being tested. Two factors are important in determining an acceptable level of significance. The first is the plausibility of the null hypothesis. If the null hypothesis represents a widely accepted assumption in a particular area of research then there will need to be strong evidence (a stringent level of significance) before it is rejected.

Secondly, the level of significance required to reject the null hypothesis will depend on the consequences of any decisions that might follow from it. Thus, if rejecting the null hypothesis in favour of the research hypothesis is going to lead to a change from an existing drug to a new expensive alternative, then convincing evidence will be required that the new drug is more effective than the existing one.

i) This means that the probability of the results occurring by chance are greater than 1 in twenty. A probability level of 0.05 is usually considered the minimum necessary for statistical significance and therefore if a result does not reach this level the null hypothesis would be accepted. See Chapter 2, p. 11.

j) An appropriate null hypothesis for a) would be: Any difference in the number of girls and boys engaging in rough and tumble play is simply due to chance. See Chapter 2, pp. 11.

k) The three criteria which must be met before a parametric test is applied are:
  1 The data should be interval or ratio level.
  2 The data should be drawn from populations which are normally distributed.
  3 The data should come from populations which have homogeneous (equal) variance. See Chapter 8, pp. 116–17.

l) One way in which the categorization system might mask age and sex differences in rough and tumble play is that it only counts the number of children engaging in such behaviour, not the frequency of the behaviour itself. For example, the same number of boys and girls might engage in rough and tumble play but boys might engage in such play more frequently. The same may be true for age differences.

1990 A level examination paper 2, section A

a) An appropriate null hypothesis would be, 'Any difference in the median score for GCSE English Language coursework between a group of students who use word processors to write their coursework and a group who use paper and pen, is due to chance. See Chapter 2, p. 11.

b) A relevant one-tailed experimental hypothesis would be 'The median score for GCSE English Language coursework will be higher for a group of students who use word processors to write their coursework than a group who use pen and paper to write their coursework'. See Chapter 2, pp. 9–10.

c) A 0.05 level of significance would be appropriate for this hypothesis because it gives a reasonable balance between the possibility of making a type 1 and a type 2 error. See Chapter 2, pp. 12–13.

d) A related t test would be appropriate if the data had fulfilled the criteria for a parametric test because the design involves matched samples and therefore a related parametric test is required. See Chapter 4 Figure 4.2, p. 36.

e) Two criteria the investigator might have taken into account are:

i) The description of the study says that the median coursework score used was calculated for each subject. This implies that the level of data is ordinal.

ii) The design of the experiment is matched samples and therefore a related test would be needed. See Chapter 5, pp. 66–7 and Figure 4.2, in Chapter 4, p. 36.

f) In relation to the study:

i) One advantage of the matched subjects design is that it eliminates the subject extraneous variables that the researcher has matched subjects for.

ii) One disadvantage of the matched subjects design is that subject extraneous variables, other than those the researcher has matched for, are simply left to chance.

Note: there are a number of other advantages and disadvantages of the matched subjects design which could have been used to answer this question. See Chapter 6, p. 81.

g) In this study:

i) The independent variable is the two conditions i.e. whether the subjects used word processors or pen and paper to do their GCSE English Language coursework.

ii) The dependent variable is the subject's median score for coursework over the academic year. See Chapter 2, p. 14.

h) I would match the students for sex and a measure of the students' performance in English Language for the previous academic year. If a measure of performance was not available then the teacher's rating of each student's ability in English Language could be used.

i) It is important that the same teacher takes both classes because otherwise the results of the experiment could be confounded. If differences were found between the experimental and control conditions they might have been caused by one teacher being more effective than the other, not the use of word processors/pen and paper. See Chapter 6, pp. 82–3.

j) Power efficiency in the statistical sense describes a test's ability to reject the null hypothesis correctly. Generally speaking, you are less likely to make a type 2 error when using a parametric test.

Note: the situation is not quite as clear-cut as I have suggested above but for two marks the examiners are not expecting you to debate the issue in great detail.

k) If the handwritten work was not typed then again the experiment might be confounded as there would be another systematic difference between the two conditions other than the IV.

Note: research has found that examiners/teachers tend to award higher marks to neatly typed essays than handwritten ones, even when the content of the essays is identical. (So rush out and buy your word processor now!) See Chapter 2, pp. 13–14.

l) Having a teacher from another school assess the work is

necessary to avoid the possibility of personal bias influencing the marks given for the coursework. A teacher from another school presumably would not know the students whose work he/she was marking and, therefore, would mark it more objectively.

1991 A level examination paper 2, section A

a) A one-tailed hypothesis predicts the direction that a difference or correlation will take. See Chapter 2, pp. 9–10.

b)
 i) One independent variable is the two lists of words, the experimental list with both neutral and phobia-related words and the control list with just neutral words.
 ii) The dependent variable is the subjects' reaction times to the two lists before and after treatment. See Chapter 2, p. 14 and Chapter 6, p. 77.

c) The Wilcoxon test would be suitable. See Figure 4.2 in Chapter 4, p. 36.

d) The assumption that underlies the use of parametric tests is that the data comes from **populations** which have similar variance. You could calculate the variance of both sets of data to see if they were similar but this would not really tell you whether the populations from which the data was drawn had similar variance. Also the assumption of similar variances only applies to the independent *t* test not the related *t* test. See Chapter 8, pp. 14–15.

e) The honest answer to this question is that you cannot really check whether the data comes from a normally distributed sample or not. In fact the idea of a normally distributed sample doesn't make a great deal of sense. The normal distribution is a mathematical model which some variables aproximate given very many scores. A largish sample can be subjected to the Chi-square **goodness of fit test** (which is not on the syllabus). Perhaps what the examiner is looking for is that you draw a frequency histogram or polygon and examine the shape to see if it **looks** normal i.e. bell shaped. See Chapter 8, for a discussion of the assumptions underlying a parametric test, pp. 114–15.

f) This procedure is known as counterbalancing and is an essential control for order effects. Without counterbalancing the experiment would be confounded. See Chapter 6, pp. 79–80.

g) One important reason for the control lists is that the researcher can see if other factors affect the dependent variable – the subjects' reaction times. In theory there should be little or no change in before and after reaction times for the neutral lists. However, if there were changes in these times then the researcher would need to consider the possibility that some factor other than the IV was affecting the results. See Chapter 6, pp. 78–9.

h)
i) You would expect the reaction time for the lists to be different before the course of psychotherapy.
ii) You would expect the reaction time for the lists to be the same after the course of psychotherapy.

i) The expression $p \leq 0.05$ means that the probability of the results occurring by chance are equal to or less than 1 chance in twenty. See Chapter 2, pp. 11–12.

j) A 0.01 level of significance would increase the probability of a type 2 error, accepting the null hypothesis when it should be rejected.

k) It is necessary to have words with the same number of syllables and of similar length as both of these factors could affect the dependent variable; the subjects' reaction times.

l) Puzzling question! One would think that the lists would be constructed by randomly allocating the neutral and phobia-related words to their positions in the lists. Presumably the examiner feels that if phobia-related words were at the beginning then the subjects might experience so much anxiety that they could not continue with the experiment! Any other suggestions?

m)
i) The term **standardized instructions** means that the same set of instructions are read to each subject.
ii) Standardized instructions are used in order that each subject receives identical instructions about how to perform the experiment. If they did not this could be a source of error which could obscure the effect of the IV on the DV or possibly confound the results.

n)
i) Reliability refers to the consistency of a measure. In this experiment reliability means that similar times are found for the neutral lists before and after psychotherapy.
ii) To test for reliability you could correlate the subjects' reaction times for the neutral lists before and after psychotherapy. A strong positive correlation would indicate that the lists were reliable.

o) Validity refers to whether measurements measure what they are claimed or supposed to measure. In this experiment it could be argued that the reading aloud of the word lists is not a valid way of measuring reaction times. See Chapter 4, pp. 30–1.

Appendix F: Essays and examination

Get briefed
The requirements for written assignments vary from subject to subject, course to course, examination board to examination board. If you are asked to complete an essay without being given detailed guidance on how it should be presented, you have every right to complain. This is not something you should be left to guess about.

Understanding the brief
Study the brief carefully. You can solve a lot of problems at this stage. Right from the start try to imagine what the finished product will look like. This may well raise questions of interpretation. Make a list of these and ask for guidance from a tutor. If this is not forthcoming, discuss the problem with someone else. You will often find that simply putting your problem into words makes the problem disappear.

Organizing your time
For large pieces of work, especially those which require research, it is essential to make a plan showing what you are going to do and by when. All kinds of contingencies may cause problems for you: the book you require is on loan to someone else, the person you want to interview is on holiday, some data you require isn't published until after your deadline, etc. The better you plan, the easier you will find it to adjust to changing circumstances.

Organizing your mind
Many people find that the best way for them to organize their mind is to use a spider diagram like the one shown overleaf. Many of the spider's legs will turn out to be irrelevant, but at least you will know which ones are there to be cut off.

  When you have thought around the assignments in this way and as you think further about it, you can start to assemble materials. Look at your lecture notes, activity responses and file cards. Check reading lists. Look at the contents pages and indexes of your textbooks. By the time you have done this you will probably have to draw another spider diagram.

Start drafting
Unless you are a very skilled writer, you simply won't be able to start writing an essay at the beginning to reach a successful conclusion at the end. Before it reaches this point, your work will have to

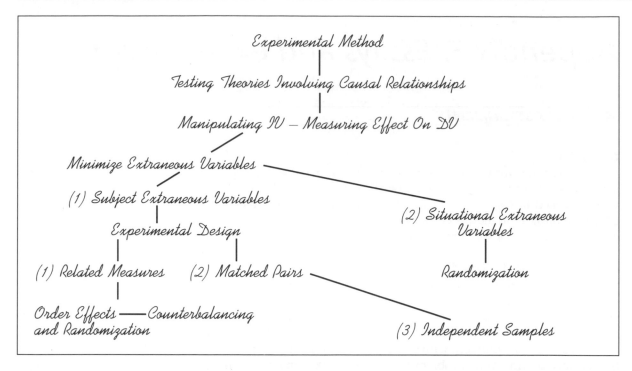

go through several drafts. Either keep your early drafts in note form, or if you write them more fully, be prepared to cut them, and reassemble them in a different order. If you use a word processor this is easy.

If you get stuck

If you get stuck, the first thing to do is to try to make a list of your difficulties. Say to yourself 'I can't do this because . . .' A lot of the confusion surrounding your difficulties will then disappear and the real problems should emerge. If you have any left take the list of difficulties to a tutor or some other source of help. The worse things to do if you get stuck are to stay up night after night getting nowhere, or to give up without seeking advice.

Check before you finalize

When you have a draft, check it against the brief. Be tough with yourself. Will this draft, when written up, really meet the requirements? If it doesn't then make a list of the ways in which it fails. Use the list to redraft and repeat.

Sleep on it

If you possibly can, leave the work alone for a few days. When you come back to it you will see its strengths and weaknesses more clearly.

The final version

This may be the second or third version. It should be clearly written and correctly spelled and punctuated. Leave wide margins on the page for tutor's comments. Make sure you follow any local requirements for length, line-spacing and structure. It may well require a bibliography. Failing any local advice, references quoted in the text should take one of the following forms:

Either '(Maglennon 1993)' or 'as Maglennon says (1993)'. Then at the end list the references in alphabetical order according to author name. For book references the references are: second name, initial or first name, publication date, publisher. For articles: second name, first name or initial, date, title, periodical title, volume, part or part number, page. And where your reference appears in a book edited by someone else: author's second name, initial or first name, date, title, editor's second name, initial or first name, title of book, publisher.

Check the final version and hand it in on time.

REVISION

In an ideal world you would be reviewing your work from the second day of your course. But we don't live in an ideal world and most people leave revision until the last few weeks before the examination. Nevertheless, if you have taken some of the advice offered earlier, you will have been maintaining good, easily retrievable notes and file cards throughout your course and so be off to a flying start when revision time comes.

Work out a revision timetable, with realistic learning objectives at each stage – you will find many of the chapter objectives in this book useful, but you will have to make some up for yourself. Use past papers, but NOT to question spot. Question-spotting is a bad mistake. Use past papers to identify which broad topics and themes the examiner usually asks about and revise them carefully. Analyse past papers for their commands. Make sure you know the differences between 'describe', 'account for', 'analyse', and so on. What you must not do is to revise actual questions and prepare model answers. Model questions rarely come up!

Ask yourself questions and answer them. Try to think like an examiner. As you approach different topics ask yourself, what questions could the examiner ask me about this.

Revise actively

Make notes and summaries all the time. Make notes of notes, summaries of notes and notes of summaries. Annotate your notes with notes from a textbook and then produce a tidy version. Convert notes in continuous text into notes in diagram or table format, or vice versa.

As your revision proceeds, try to reduce the whole course to a series of trigger words and phrases – just enough to jog your memory. Practise writing your answers under the pressure of time. How much can you get down in the time available? Practise writing answers of that length.

▶ Make sure you know how you will be examined. How many exams? How long? What choice of questions? Will there be compulsory questions, essay questions, data-response questions, short answer questions? These all require different skills and different ways of revising.

▶ Establish how much of your syllabus you should revise.

▶ Check the assessment objectives which are printed in the syllabus document produced by your board.

▶ Read the Chief Examiner's report for previous years. Note well what these reports say. Not only does the Chief Examiner have experience of the mistakes of thousands of students, he/she actually decides what is mistaken and what is correct.

▶ Taking an active approach to revision is essential. Passive revision, i.e. sitting reading through notes and textbooks is both boring and ineffective.

▶ Revise with friends, discussing questions and trying to explain things to each other.

Work in regular sessions with breaks every hour, but get used to working for three hours at a time before taking a longer break.

THE EXAMINATION

Think of the examination as an opportunity for you to give a performance, with an audience of one – the examiner. You are displaying your knowledge, understanding and skills to someone who wants to applaud you.

Here are some key points to bear in mind:

► Give yourself time off, especially on the day before the examinations start.

- make sure you know when and where the examination will be held. If it is an unfamiliar place, try to visit it beforehand and check your travel arrangements
- the evening before the exam. Make sure you have all the pens, pencils and other equipment you will need
- arrive in good time, but don't stand around chatting. Go for a walk to loosen up and get the oxygen flowing to the brain

► Examiners want you to do well. They are instructed to mark your work by giving you credit for everything you do properly, not to penalize you for your mistakes. Your marks start at zero and go on up whenever you do something right. The examiner is looking for opportunities to reward positive achievements, so supply plenty of these and make it easy for the examiner to find them. Examination answers are vehicles for you to display your achievement.

- when the exam starts, read through the whole paper (or those parts which relate to your options)
- do NOT start writing immediately, but settle down, get the feel of the paper, check the instructions and find the questions you feel ok about. Take a few minutes to double check that you are following the rubric correctly
- choose your probable questions, but don't firm up your choice at this early stage

► If you suffer badly from nerves, learn to relax through the use of deep breathing techniques. Don't take pills, except under medical supervision. Don't drink alcohol before and exam. It relaxes the wrong part of your brain.

- the marks allocated to each question, or parts of each question are a rough guide to how much you should write on each. If two marks are allocated, make two good points and stop. You won't get more than two marks however many brilliant points you make
- draw up a rough timetable for yourself – 'by 10.35 I should have finished the first question', etc.
- start your first question. Now for the golden rule of exams

ANSWER THE QUESTION SET: DO WHAT THE EXAMINER TELLS YOU TO DO

► The most common reason for candidates failing to get the marks they should is not lack of knowledge or skill, but failure to observe the golden rule. Make sure you do what the examiner asks you to do.

- for all but very short answers, make a plan
- think all the time. Don't just try to remember things, but think about how to apply what you know to the question set
- don't overrun your time on a particular question. It takes much longer to get a few more marks at the end of an answer than at the beginning of another

► Presentation and layout are important, because they should help the examiner to find your good points easily. Use short sentences and paragraphs to make your points clearly and concisely.

- take rests during your exams. Loosen up physically; breathe, stretch, shut your eyes while you are thinking
- leave enough time for checking and polishing your answers. A single additional mark could mean a higher grade.

► GOOD LUCK!

Author index

Subject index